In the
Shadow of Death

In the Shadow of Death

Living Outside the Gates
of Mauthausen

———

Gordon J. Horwitz

THE FREE PRESS
A Division of Macmillan, Inc.
NEW YORK

Collier Macmillan Canada
TORONTO

Maxwell Macmillan International
NEW YORK   OXFORD   SINGAPORE   SYDNEY

The Free Press
A Division of Macmillan, Inc.
866 Third Avenue, New York, N.Y. 10022

Collier Macmillan Canada, Inc.
1200 Eglinton Avenue East
Suite 200
Don Mills, Ontario M3C 3N1

Printed in the United States of America

printing number

1 2 3 4 5 6 7 8 9 10

Library of Congress Cataloging-in-Publication Data

Horwitz, Gordon J.
    In the shadow of death: living outside the gates of Mauthausen/
Gordon J. Horwitz.
        p.   cm.
    Includes bibliographical references and index.
    ISBN 0-02-915040-X
    1. Mauthausen (Mauthausen, Austria: Concentration camp)
2. Mauthausen (Austria)—Moral conditions.   3. World War, 1939–1945—
Prisoners and prisons, German—Moral and ethical aspects.
I. Title.
D805.A8H67   1990
94054'7243'094362—dc20

                                          90–37738
                                          CIP

For my parents

Contents

Acknowledgments

We are citizens of the century that brought Mauthausen into the world. Now long inactive, Mauthausen remains one of the defining institutions of our era. One does not venture lightly into an examination of what happened in and near this place, but it is of inestimable value when doing so to know that committed friends and colleagues are on hand to provide help and encouragement.

Simon Schama, Bernard Wasserstein, Ernest May, and Dennis Klein kindly and enthusiastically supported my original research proposal, and I also wish to thank both the Krupp Foundation and the National Foundation for Jewish Culture for providing funding for my initial year of research in Austria. In Vienna the staff of the Archive of the Mauthausen Museum graciously provided access to their collection of documents on Mauthausen. At the Documentation Archive of the Austrian Resistance, Dr. Herbert Steiner, Dr. Wolfgang Neugebauer, and their dedicated co-workers provided a welcome home for a scholar abroad, cheerfully placing at my disposal their outstanding collection of materials on Austria during the war, and assisting me in arranging interviews. Dr. Siegwald Ganglmair of the Documentation Archive was both friend and guide, leading me toward invaluable documents, discussing my progress, and generously sharing the preliminary results of interviews he and Christian Limbeck-Lilienau conducted with residents who lived near one of Mauthausen's satellite camps in their native province of Upper Austria. Similarly, in Linz, Peter Kammerstätter patiently an-

swered my questions and directed me toward his pioneering investigations into the behavior of the civilian population in and around
Mauthausen in 1945.

At Harvard, Patrice Higonnet encouraged my foray into this theme
and patiently saw my dissertation through to completion. Charles Maier
added needed encouragement, comment, and solid criticism. So too am
I indebted to my former undergraduate advisor at Princeton, Arno Mayer,
who all too long ago suggested I one day tackle what was bound to be an
agonizing theme, and who at a decisive juncture during my revisions
prompted me to rethink my approach. Raul Hilberg also kindly examined
drafts of the manuscript, bringing to the task his invaluable expertise. I
also wish to thank Shulamit Volkov of the Institute for German History
at Tel Aviv University for enabling me to come to Israel for several
months and discuss aspects of my work during an unusually lively seminar
at the Wiener Library, co-chaired by Saul Friedländer, on fascism and
neo-fascism. Joyce Seltzer, Senior Editor at The Free Press, brought to
the project an experienced eye and judicious criticism, and I thank her
for believing in the importance of this project.

The presentation of this book marks the end of a journey. To the
many friends and teachers who accompanied me at least part of the way,
offering learned advice and best wishes, I am much indebted. This book
is better for their assistance. However, as I knew from the start this
journey would have to be, ultimately, a solitary one. Needless to say, it
is I who bear responsibility for any shortcomings in the work.

In the
Shadow of Death

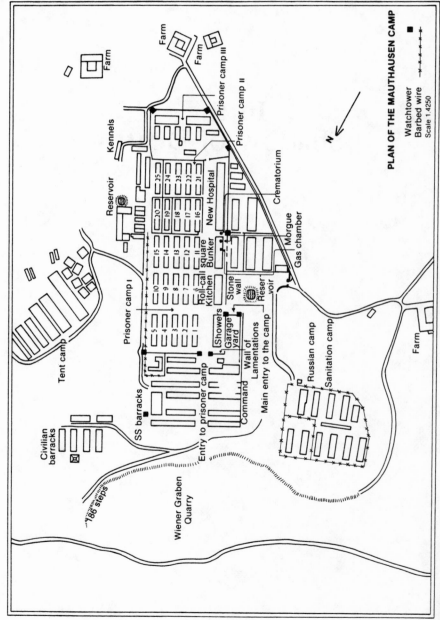

PLAN OF THE MAUTHAUSEN CAMP

Watchtower ■
Barbed wire ✶-✶-✶-✶-✶
Scale 1.4250

Farm

Farm

Prisoner camp III

Prisoner camp II

Kennels

Crematorium

Reservoir

25 24 23 22 21
20 19 18 17 16

New Hospital

Morgue

15 14 13 12 11
10 9 8 7 6

square
Bunker

Gas chamber

Roll-call
Kitchen

Stone
wall

Reser-
voir

Prisoner camp I

5 4 3 2 1

Showers
Garage
yard

Wall of
Lamentations

Russian camp

Main entry to the camp

Sanitation camp

Command

Entry to prisoner camp

SS barracks

Tent camp

Civilian
barracks

Farm

Farm

186 steps

Wiener Graben
Quarry

N

Courtesy Evelyn Le Chêne

Prologue

On 4 May 1945, forces of the 71st Division of the U.S. Third Army entered a pine forest just south of Wels, Austria, and came upon the concentration camp of Gunskirchen, an outpost of the notorious Mauthausen concentration camp. As soldiers neared the camp they found "hundreds of starving, half-crazed inmates lining the roads begging for food and cigarettes. Many of them had been able to get only a few hundred yards from the gate before they keeled over and died. As weak as they were, the chance to be free, the opportunity to escape was so great they could not resist, though it meant staggering only a few yards before death came." The horrifying sight of these stragglers was compounded by "the next indication of the camp's nearness—the smell. . . . It could almost be seen and hung over the camp like a fog of death."[1]

Shortly thereafter, a small detachment of the 571st Signal Company of the 71st Infantry Division pulled into Wels. As they went about their work establishing a command post on the main square, thousands of local citizens who had recently emerged from places of hiding in homes and air raid shelters stepped forward to gaze upon and greet them. A United States Army corporal who witnessed the scene noted how the residents made a point of "assuring" the men "that there were no Nazis among them, only good Austrians who loved Americans and hated Hitler and Company." But then something curious happened:

> About two o'clock in the afternoon, for some reason not apparent to us at the time, the crowd began to melt away . . . back into shuttered homes,

1

down twisting alleyways to storm shelters . . . by twos and groups they left us, in quiet contrast to their noisy, enthusiastic approach. It wasn't long before we discovered why.

　Drifting down the great square, in every conceivable conveyance, on foot, on hands and knees—utilizing every inch of the wide streets—came the former inmates of Gunskirchen Lager near Lambach. With hardly a sound they slowly engulfed the cobble-stoned avenues that led inwards, like an irresistible but languid flood, driving the civilians back to their homes before them.[2]

What had been a near, yet hidden, presence—the inmates of the nearby camp—appeared in the open. They invaded the territory of the living, staking claim to the center of the town. The residents understood who these people were. Rather than confront the survivors of the camp, the townspeople chose to withdraw. They did not want these wretched souls in their midst. They dared not endure the sight of these victims, nor could they bear to be seen by them in return.

In the spring of 1945, everywhere, bystanders to the horror of the concentration camps cautiously slipped from view. To the outside world they have remained invisible ever since. To be sure, once the surviving inmates passed on, the citizens of towns and cities in the vicinity of the camps reestablished themselves and went on with their lives. But they did not step forward to speak of what they had known of the camps, or try to explain their own behavior. Unlike the survivors, many of whom overcame the burden of reliving their suffering in order to inform the world, the bystanders have not shown any marked desire to communicate their own experiences.[3] Undoubtedly, feelings of guilt, embarrassment, fear, and also simple indifference have served to assist in the repression of these matters.

We think of the concentration camp as an isolated realm; the victim enters and is cut off from the light of human solidarity. He is impressed with the knowledge that his life has no meaning, and that he will pass from the face of the earth as if he had never existed. Without the witness of others to acknowledge his life or confirm his death, the victim vanishes and leaves no trace. The darkness envelops a life, and it is as if that life never were.[4]

Those who experienced the camps as inmates knew of that deadly isolation. But they were actually aware that while they suffered and their family members and comrades died, other persons lived peacefully nearby. For the inmate, this world of life lay just beyond the camp, near, yet inaccessible. The inmates looked to the outside world, knowing instinctively that their isolation was made complete because they had been abandoned and forgotten. Inmates who lived to tell of their experiences found vivid the memory of fleeting contact with the universe of the living. In the words of a survivor of the Mauthausen branch camp of Ebensee, who arrived there at age 16, following four years in Auschwitz:

> I try to repress much, but one thing lodges especially in my memory, very deep in memory. These were the marches, the daily marches upon which we shifted from the camp to work in the tunnels, and especially late in the afternoons, tired, utterly exhausted, dehumanized, on the way from work in the tunnels into the camp. On the left side, on the right side these white houses. It was so frightfully cold. I tried to dream of all that lay behind these walls. And I tried to think, perhaps a mother and children live in this house, but always I was awakened by the shouts of the SS: "Move on! Move on!" But again and again, every day when I left the camp, I tried to have these momentary dreams. That has remained so alive in my memory.[5]

The final departure, the last journey by rail or the trek through a town or village, beyond which lay the concentration camp, was a common image in the testimony of those survivors who arrived in Mauthausen. They remembered the people of the town watching them from a distance. They retained impressions of the local residents whom they saw stealing glances at them from the windows of their apartments. Startled as mice in the night, onlookers darted away in nervous response to the beams radiating from the flashlights of the guards. Former inmates who marched through the town retrace images of indifference: a man seen seating himself at the dinner table, a pair of lovers near the Danube. Others cannot forget acts of hostility. One survivor has written of fat men in Tyrolean costume swearing at thirst-ridden inmates and chasing them from a fountain in the center of the town.[6]

The existence of these bystanders posed a dilemma that inmates who miraculously emerged alive from the camps struggled to resolve, but could not. As Elie Wiesel, a survivor of Auschwitz, has written,

> This, was the thing I had wanted to understand ever since the war. Nothing else. How a human being can remain indifferent. The executioners I understood; also the victims, though with more difficulty. For the others, all the others, those who were neither for nor against, those who sprawled in passive patience, those who told themselves, "The storm will blow over and everything will be normal again," those who thought themselves above the battle, those who were permanently and merely spectators—all were closed to me, incomprehensible.[7]

Inmates who were acutely sensitive to the presence of others just beyond
the confines of the camps later asked of the bystanders: What did you
see? If you knew, why then did you fail to respond?

The passage of time heightens our awareness that during the era
of the Third Reich crimes of unprecedented nature and magnitude occurred while the outside world remained silent. In recent years historians have returned to this issue. They have demonstrated that, even
as they happened, these crimes involved widespread complicity and
were known in the major capitals of the world. Their studies leave
little doubt as to the thoughtless and sometimes deliberate sins of omission of Allied leaders, the religious hierarchy, the press, and the read-
ing public in the face of mounting evidence of unprecedented violence
against innocent civilians in wartime Europe.[8] Still, these institutions
and organizations were at a great remove from the killing centers. Every camp, however, had civilian communities in the immediate vicinity, yet to date remarkably few persons have returned to the sites of
destruction to attempt the delicate task of examining the camps within
this context.[9]

While confirming the widespread dissemination of rumors of mass
shootings witnessed by soldiers serving in the East, historians have been
unable to gauge the extent of public awareness of the existence or of the
inner workings of the concentration and extermination camps. Ian Kershaw has noted: "Documentary evidence can hardly provide an adequate
answer to the question: 'how much did the Germans know?,' and given
the generally prevailing silence and difficulties of interpretation only
tentative suggestions can be made."[10] Despairingly, he writes, "the extent of knowledge will never be known."[11]

One may sense that much more was known than available evidence
indicates. As Walter Laqueur has pointed out, the historian is faced with
a potentially vast yet inaccessible body of information. "For the news was
transmitted through dozens of channels and came from thousands of
individuals, very often by word of mouth," he has written. "Even when
there was at one time a written record, it frequently did not survive."
One might search for correspondence, "but only a fraction still exists.
For every one which we know there may have been ten or more which
were lost. For each kept in a public collection, there may be many in
private hands."[12]

Rare indeed is the surviving document of an extraordinary bystander who dared acknowledge having received word of the atrocities
being committed against the Jews. On 4 February 1944 one Berlin woman
confided to her diary her inability to accept the truth of this horror:

'They are forced to dig their own graves,' people whisper. 'Their clothing, shoes, shirts are taken from them. They are sent naked to their death.' The horror is so incredible that the imagination refuses to accept its reality. Something fails to click. Some conclusion is simply not drawn. Between knowledge in theory and practical application to individual cases . . . there is an unbridgeable gulf. . . . We don't permit our power of imagination to connect the two, even remotely. . . . Is it cowardice that lets us think this way? Maybe! But then such cowardice belongs to the primeval instincts of man. If we could visualize death, life as it exists would be impossible. One can imagine torture, horror, and suffering as little as death. . . . Such indifference alone makes continued existence possible. Realizations such as these are bitter, shameful and bitter.[13]

Dread has acted as an additional barrier to our analytical penetration of the subject. Much like eyewitnesses to the horror, scholars too may at first draw back in disbelief. As Louis de Jong, the eminent Dutch historian has noted: "The whole thing went so much beyond the powers of the human imagination that, as I myself once put it: 'Our mind, once having grasped the facts, immediately spews them out as something utterly alien and unnaturally loathsome?' "[14]

Those who did not experience the concentration camps were surely at a disadvantage in their efforts to imagine what they were like. The inmate found himself confronted with a reality beyond the common comprehension of the outsider. A profound truth lies in the famous aphorism of David Rousset: "normal men do not know that all things are possible." The inmates were "separated from the others by an experience impossible to transmit."[15] And yet many survivors, aware of the urgency to communicate their experiences, sensed that they alone could speak, and were they to fail to do so the memory of countless sufferings would one day perish with them. Writing about Mauthausen as early as 1954, Michel de Bouard, a surviving inmate of the camp, stated: "When there are no more survivors of deportation, then perhaps future archivists will obtain access to certain papers that today are still hidden; but they will lack the principal source, by which I mean the living memory of the witnesses."[16] Forty-five years after the spring of their liberation, the survivors have largely vanished from our midst.

The hour is late. Over time, death claims the lives of the perpetrators and the bystanders as well. The events surrounding the concentration camps pass from living memory into historical consciousness. Even then, "the era of researchers with personal experience of the period who could work with a sense of 'feel' for the documents is coming to an end."[17] Still, one senses that existing documents have not been examined with an eye focused on the behavior of persons who lived adjacent to the camps. In the many years since the war rarely did anyone dare ask them to speak of that time, now distant, when the camps existed in their communities. The labor of succeeding generations cannot be confined to memorialization and remembrance of the victims, vital as these are, but must entail the assimilation of evidence that will enhance our still limited understanding of the dynamic of destruction. An essential aspect of that dynamic was the behavior of the bystanders. For too long they were overlooked. Lest we permit them to slip once more unseen down some alleyway, to be shuttered forever from view, we must seek them out. That the time to return to the centers of killing in order to explore one of the most hidden and least understood issues overshadowing the era has nearly, but not altogether, passed, gives urgency to this effort.

Chapter 1

Mauthausen and the Concentration Camp System

In the spring of 1945 the concentration camps of the Third Reich were open to view. Confronted with the evidence of inhumanity on so vast a scale, outsiders could barely acknowledge them as part of the known world. The readiest metaphor was that of hell. The survivors, viewed in the after-image of army signal corps photos and film, were compared to living skeletons. Death was written across the faces and in the eyes, sunken in dark, hollow sockets.

The enormity and horror of the concentration camp led us to conceive of it as a separate universe. Yet this universe of torment and killing was never completely sealed from the ordinary world beyond its perimeter.[1] It cast a shadow across the surrounding landscape, enveloping the gardens and rooftops of the neighboring towns. Blending with ash spewed from the chimneys of the crematoria, it rode the wind and invaded the homes of nearby residents.

Nowhere was the shadow so dark, so near the world beyond the stone wall, the barbed wire and wooden gates of the camps, than in the towns that bordered them. Citizens living in the vicinity were daily witness to mounting atrocities, and aware of human destruction in and around their communities, were confronted with terrible choices.

One such community resided in Mauthausen, a town that lay in the heart of Austria. Its involvement with the concentration camps began in 1938, the year of the *Anschluss* uniting Austria with Germany. Concentration camps were already an established element in the National Socialist system of terror. At that time four existed in the Third Reich: Dachau, located near Munich, founded in 1933; Sachsenhausen, near Berlin, established in 1936; Buchenwald, outside Weimar, founded in 1937; and Lichtenberg, near Hof, a camp for women, established in 1933. Authority over the camps lay in the hands of the SS, the notorious security force under the direction of Heinrich Himmler. Until 1937, the camps largely contained political prisoners—primarily (though not exclusively) communists, Social Democrats, and trade union leaders that the Gestapo, or Secret State Police, arbitrarily seized under the provisions of a "protective custody" decree issued in February 1933. During this period the camp population reflected the regime's original focus on eliminating political opposition. In June 1936 Adolf Hitler named Himmler to the post of Chief of the German police, paving the way for new seizures. Acting under authority of a new "preventive arrest" regulation issued in December 1937, the Kripo, or Criminal Police, also under Himmler's command, apprehended and sent to the camps additional categories of prisoners. The camp population now came to include criminals and a spectrum of alleged misfits labeled "asocials"—those suspected of vagrancy, or with poor work histories, or accused of begging, drunkenness, or sexual offenses—they included gypsies and Jehovah's Witnesses as well. Those Jews who were sent to the camps had also been singled out on the basis of their political background, criminal histories, or presumed "asocial" behavior. In 1938, however, thousands more were arrested, most of them in association with the Kristallnacht pogrom in November of that year during which the Nazis burned synagogues and destroyed Jewish property throughout the country. As a result of the assault, some 36,000 Jews were sent to the camps of Dachau, Sachsenhausen, and Buchenwald.[2] During this ordeal, about a thousand were killed, "including 244 at Buchenwald alone." Most of the Jews who survived the first months of their confinement were released from the camps after agreeing to leave the country immediately.[3]

The addition of new groups of inmates came at a moment when the regime was at pains to extract, from Germany's increasingly tight labor market, the manpower it needed for state economic projects. Prominent among these was the renovation of selected cities throughout the Reich. In January 1937 Hitler appointed the architect, Albert Speer, to the post of General Building Inspector for the Reich Capital, charged with additional responsibilities for carrying out the projected construction of new buildings and monuments for such favored cities as Berlin, Weimar, Nuremberg, Munich, and Linz. At this juncture, Himmler launched an SS-owned and operated commercial enterprise of crucial significance for the further development of the concentration camp system. This enterprise was the German Earth and Stone Works Corporation (DEST), established in April 1938 to acquire stone quarries and brick works capable of supplying, at a profit to the SS, construction materials for the Reich building program. Inmates drawn from the expanding camp population formed a ready pool of slave labor for these operations. Among the new corporation's acquisitions in its first year of operation were stone quarries in Flossenbürg, located near Weiden in the Upper Palatinate, and Mauthausen, near Linz, in Upper Austria. Accompanying the SS acquisition of these quarries, new concentration camps were established at both these sites, followed by the establishment of additional camps beside granite quarries in Gross-Rosen in the Striegau district of Silesia in 1939, and Natzweiler, near Rothau in Alsace by 1942.[4]

The beginning of the war marked a further expansion of the population of the concentration camps which grew from some 7,000 inmates in early 1937 to nearly 25,000 when war broke out in September 1939.[5] Successive military campaigns against Poland (1939), Denmark, Norway, France, and the Benelux countries (1940), and the Soviet Union, beginning in June 1941, were accompanied by the arrest and deportation to the camps of tens of thousands of additional prisoners. Those from the West were usually arrested in connection with resistance activities. In Poland, in an effort to decapitate potential opposition following their invasion, the Nazis targeted members of the intelligentsia for immediate execution or shipment to the camps. But on the whole, in keeping with the Nazi ideological concept of the Slavs as an inferior race, the SS were less selective in the East than in the West, rounding up prisoners wholesale for shipment to the camps. Within a year of the invasion of Poland some 20,000 Poles were sent to camps inside Germany.[6] At this time the camps functioned largely as centers for holding and killing political prisoners and foreign enemies of the Third Reich. "The years 1940 and 1941—when National Socialism spread across Europe by means of brute force and set out to put into practice its concepts of racial domination—constituted, at least for the non-Jewish prisoners, the most terrible years in the history of the concentration camps."[7]

The SS intended Mauthausen to be the harshest of the concentration camps. In January 1941 Reinhard Heydrich, Chief of the Security Police and Security Service, devised a classificatory scheme in which he divided the existing camps into three categories of ascending severity. Mauthausen alone was placed in a separate class for prisoners deserving the harshest treatment.[8] Inmates sent to Mauthausen were deemed incapable of being rehabilitated and hence not qualified for eventual release. In practical terms, the issuance of an order to Mauthausen represented a life term or death sentence for the inmates. They were sent there never to return.[9] Comparison of camp mortality rates bears out that, following proclamation of the decree, the inmate population in Mauthausen died at a rate higher than those in the other camps. It is estimated that in 1941, for example, 7,058 inmates out of a total of 15,900, or 58 percent of the camp population, died at Mauthausen and its subsidiary camp, Gusen. This contrasts with a mortality rate of 36 percent in Dachau, which registered 2,700 deaths among its 7,500 inmates; 19 percent in Buchenwald (1,522 dead among 7,730 inmates); and 16 percent in Sachsenhausen, where 1,816 of a total of 11,111 inmates perished that same year.[10]

While Mauthausen was a leading center of killing among the concentration camps, surpassing it and all others in the magnitude of human destruction were six killing facilities that began operating on occupied Polish territory in late 1941 and 1942. Four of them—death centers exclusively—bear the names Chelmno, Belzec, Sobibor, and Treblinka. These were death camps in the fullest sense of the term where the victims, the Jews, were either killed in mobile vans as at Chelmno, or immediately upon arrival by rail processed for death in stationary gas chambers. To this category belong as well the camps at Auschwitz-Birkenau and Lublin (Majdanek) which, in addition to being stations for immediate destruction by gas, served as concentration camps supplying slave labor for German industries.

By the spring of 1942 the continuing war effort made critical demands on the German labor force. Responding to pressures from the Armaments Ministry under the direction of Albert Speer, the SS agreed to provide German defense industries with slave labor drawn from the inmate population. This involved siting armament works at or near existing concentration camps and a network of satellite outposts radiating outward from the main camps. That same spring, a shift in emphasis toward conscious efforts to exploit labor more effectively was signalled by administrative changes: a single new agency, the Economic and Administrative Main Office (WVHA), was created within the SS to oversee the concentration camps and coordinate the economic exploitation of the inmate labor force.

Under the guidance of Oswald Pohl, head of the Economic and Administrative Main Office, the SS directed efforts to carry out a more "rational" exploitation of inmate labor in the interest of raising productivity. While the new policy did succeed in reducing mortality in the camps, the economic performance of the inmate slaves, who remained mistreated, badly nourished, and ill-clothed, continued to be substandard. Simultaneously, however, the camps continued to fill their original ideological role as a place for the torture and physical elimination of political opponents and racial enemies of the Third Reich. The inmates were routinely worked to death, their places immediately filled from a seemingly inexhaustible supply of expendable labor.[11]

From the fall of 1944 to the spring of 1945, conditions inside the camps deteriorated sharply. Supplies assigned to the camps dwindled, and as camps closest to the front were dissolved in the face of approaching enemy forces, the Nazis forced inmates on relentless and deadly evacuation marches toward camps in the interior.

The six death camps of Chelmno, Belzec, Sobibor, Treblinka, Lublin (Majdanek), and Auschwitz-Birkenau had done their work quickly. In all, these six camps alone accounted for the destruction of some 2,700,000 of an estimated 5,100,000 Jews killed in the Final Solution.[12] In mid-1944 only one, Auschwitz-Birkenau, remained in operation. On 17 January 1945, with the sounds of the advancing Red Army audible in the distance, a final roll call, accounting for 66,020 inmates still in the Auschwitz-Birkenau complex, took place. The following day, January 18, Auschwitz-Birkenau was abandoned in the face of the approaching Soviet forces. With the exception of a remnant of those too ill to march, tens of thousands of Auschwitz survivors were forced to trek, in the dead of winter, toward still existing concentration camps in the interior of the Reich. Between January and May 1945, in dozens of death marches, the SS brutally shunted prisoners from one camp to the next.

> The dehumanized murderers did not see the prisoners as human beings at all. The idea that these creatures should be allowed to be liberated was absolutely preposterous. They were enemies of the Reich, and it was incumbent on every good Nazi to see to it that they remained under Reich control. They belonged in a camp, and if the camp to which they were assigned was full, they would be marched to another one so long as someone of higher rank issued an order stating to which they should be sent. . . .
> From the descriptions of survivors, it appears that transport command-

ers had but the vaguest idea of what to do with the prisoners beyond a general order to kill all the stragglers . . . it is here that the general concensus of the Nazi regime in relation to its real or imagined opponents came into its own. The SS lieutenant or NCO in charge knew by training and experience that these were enemies, and that the fewer who remained the better. . . . He took them over at a certain point as less than humans, and when he left them they were either corpses buried in the ground or walking skeletons—he had fulfilled the intentions of his superiors and had done a distasteful job thoroughly and conscientiously . . . the marches were intended to continue the mass murder in the concentration camp by other means. [13]

The death marches took a devastating toll. Above and beyond the millions of Jews already killed, well in excess of 700,000 inmates of all categories were still in the concentration camp system in January 1945. Of these, from one-third to one-half, or from a quarter million to 350,000 or more, died in the following weeks and months along the routes of march, in the overcrowded, disease-ravaged camps of the interior, and, still suffering from the effects of their mistreatment, in camps and hospitals in the wake of the liberation. No less than one-half were Jews. [14]

The history of Mauthausen closely parallels the overall development of the Nazi concentration camp system. One may note the four principal phases in the camp's history. [15]

Phase I: This stage lasted roughly from 8 August 1938—the date of arrival of the first 300 inmates, Austrian and German criminals, from Dachau—until the late summer of 1939. Between 8 August and 31 December 1938, 780 more inmates arrived from Dachau and Sachsenhausen. Until May 1939, the camp population consisted largely of criminals, with additional small numbers of "asocial" inmates. The first political inmates, an unspecified number of communists and socialists from the Sudetenland, arrived on 8 May 1939. Further transports from Czechoslovakia arrived on 10 May and 15 June, followed by an unquantified shipment from Dachau on 27 September. On 29 September an additional 1,600 German and Austrian inmates—594 political internees, 144 Jehovah's Witnesses, 571 asocials, 53 homosexuals, 11 emigrants, and 227 criminals—were shipped to Mauthausen from Dachau. By this date the camp held 2,995 inmates, the largest categories consisting of 958 criminals, 1,087 gypsies primarily from the eastern Austrian province of Burgenland, and 739 German political prisoners. [16]

During this period the inmates began "working in the quarry . . . leveling the area, laying an approach road and constructing buildings in

the camp." These first buildings became the core of the protective custody camp, comprising the first 20 barracks of Camp I (*Lager I*). The
units were arrayed in rows of 5, with the lead barracks, numbers 1, 6, 11,
and 16, facing onto a central roll call area where the inmates assembled
to be counted. Blocks 16 through 19 served until the spring of 1944 as a
quarantine area for incoming inmates who were held there for the first
2–3 weeks following their arrival. In 1941 and 1942 Soviet prisoners
were held here for 7 months. In addition, barrack number 20, separated
from the others by a stone wall and barbed wire, was used as an isolation
block for Soviet prisoners of war.

While building the camp was hard, the inmates involved in that
work were afforded relatively good provisioning—including clothing,
bedclothes, and adequate food rations—in comparison to inmates admitted during later periods. Compared to the following periods, at this
time "the mortality rate was still low." Thirty-six inmates are recorded as
having died in 1938, and 445 in 1939, with 149 deaths occurring from
January through September, and 296 from October through December.[17]

Phase II: Between the outbreak of war in the late summer of 1939
and June 1943, Mauthausen underwent both a rapid expansion and a
diversification of its inmate population, emerging as a full-blown center
for the torture and murder of political and racial minorities. This period
was characterized by the influx of inmates from territories occupied by
the advancing German armies. Inmates streamed in from Poland as well
as Czechoslovakia, the Soviet Union, the Netherlands, Belgium, Luxemburg, and France.

In 1940, 11,000 additional inmates arrived in Mauthausen. On 9
March the first contingent of 448 Poles arrived among a transport of
1,000 inmates sent from Buchenwald. By April they began arriving
steadily in groups from Sachsenhausen and Dachau, as well as directly
from Poland, reaching a total of 8,000 by year's end. On August 8, 1940,
came 392 Spaniards, refugees of the Spanish Civil War who had been
interned in France; a total of 7,800 arrived in Mauthausen by 1942.
Their ranks included the first children sent to the camp. In this phase of
the camp's history the Spaniards, along with the Poles, were subject to
brutal mistreatment and suffered their greatest casualties. By the time of
the liberation only 1,600 of the Spaniards had succeeded in surviving the
ordeal.[18]

Until early 1944, Jews who came to Mauthausen commonly had
been arrested by the Gestapo, charged with political offenses, and sent
there to be killed. Mauthausen's first Jewish inmate, however, was a
Viennese-born man arrested as a homosexual, who was enrolled at Mau-

thausen in September 1939 and was recorded as having died in March 1940. During 1940 an additional 90 Jews arrived, of whom all but about 10 were listed as dead by year's end. From 1941 through 1943 some 2,600 more Jews arrived, 1,350 of them from Holland, the remainder from Czechoslovakia, Austria, Poland, and Romania. With the exception of little more than 30 Jews transferred from Mauthausen to Auschwitz in October 1942, all but a handful were recorded as having died in Mauthausen the year of their arrival.[19]

All inmates were distinguished by category through colored triangles sewn to their outfits, standard issue being fatigues that were vertically striped blue, white, and gray. Criminal inmates wore green triangles; political inmates, red; "asocials," black; Jehovah's Witnesses, purple; homosexuals, pink; and Jews, yellow, routinely combined with another "to form the Star of David."[20]

During this period provisions declined as crowding intensified and supplies of food diminished. In congested conditions, typhus and dysentery swept the camp.[21] In accordance with the guidelines establishing Mauthausen as a camp for the most reprobate of all inmates, the SS carried out a process of deliberate extermination. The result was a steady and brutal slaughter of the inmates. In 1942 the camp recorded a death toll of 14,293. The bloodletting continued unabated into the new year. From January through April 1943, 5,147 more perished. The dead were valued according to their weight in gold: in 1942 alone the camp forwarded to Berlin eleven and one-half pounds of dental gold torn from the mouths of its victims.[22]

So much killing required a means of disposal, hence cremation facilities were installed inside the camp. For the first year and a half of its existence the camp had to rely on a nearby municipal facility in Steyr, 15 miles south of Mauthausen. Mauthausen victims were cremated in Steyr beginning on 5 September 1938, and the practice continued until, on 5 May 1940, the first of 3 ovens manufactured by the Erfurt firm of J. A. Topf and Sons were made operational inside the camp. After this date the Steyr facility served only in limited instances as a disposal site for inmates killed in the outlying camps of the Mauthausen network, three of which—Gusen, beginning on 29 January 1941; Ebensee (4 August 1944); and Melk (November 1944)—received their own cremation facilities. Between September 1938 and May 1945 the bodies of 1,863 inmates were burned in Steyr. Figures on the number of corpses processed in the Mauthausen crematoria are incomplete, but from 1940 to 1942 at least 9,441 bodies were burned. The numbers rose to 27,556 by 29 April

1945. In Gusen, from 29 January 1941 to 2 May 1945, some 30,000 bodies went through the ovens; no fewer than 8,192 were processed in the Ebensee camp crematorium, and 4,068 in the crematorium at Melk.[23]

During this period work continued on the protective custody camp, the compound where the inmates were housed. The inmates erected the twin towers flanking the main portal, a stone wall along the south perimeter of the camp, garages with a courtyard, the commandant's building, SS barracks, and a barbed wire fence along the rear perimeter. In 1941 the compound grew to include Camp II (*Lager II*), containing barracks 21 through 24. These barracks served for a time as workshops, and in the spring of 1944 took over as quarantine blocks to house the new inmates. Also added was Camp III (*Lager III*) comprising 6 additional inmate barracks constructed in the spring of 1944. On 1 October 1941, work began on the so-called "Russian compound," also designated as the camp hospital (*Krankenlager* or *Sanitätslager*). It lay below the camp walls near the approach road. Originally designed to hold Soviet war prisoners, by 1943 it had come to house the sick. It contained 10 barracks for inmates, a wash house that doubled as a mortuary, and an inmate kitchen, and was surrounded by electrified barbed wire.[24]

From the protective custody compound inmate labor battalions set out to work in the quarries and workshops around which the camp's outer cordon was established. Like a sea under the tidal sway of the moon, the camp population swelled to an outer perimeter by day, and contracted into its inner compound by night. At dawn, as the gate to the inner compound opened, the inmates marched outward to the quarries and workshops. Guards took up their posts around the work sites, some mounting the "storks," make-shift wooden towers arranged 88 to 164 yards apart. With the approach of nightfall, the outer cordon was drawn in: the inmates who survived the day filed back to the camp, bearing for disposal in the crematorium their flotsam of dead. The guards withdrew from the storks, and once again the ring tightened about the small, inner cordon of the protective custody camp. Defining the limits of the nocturnal perimeter were the walls and wire of the compound, including the granite wall, 8 feet high, 462 yards around, and topped with barbed wire charged with 380 volts of electricity.[25] Guard towers stood around the perimeter at intervals of 88 yards.[26] On the north side of the camp enclosure the stone wall was incomplete. Here stood a fence of more high-tension barbed wire, upon which, as upon the wire atop the stone wall, hung shaded lights and red emergency lamps. To comply with air raid regulations, the lamps radiated a minimum of light. At 547 yards'

distance their beams diffused and faded into the darkness of the landscape; beyond a height of 109 yards they disappeared into the sky and
were lost in the shroud of night.[27]

In addition to the quarry, which was 260 to 330 feet deep and
seven-tenths of a mile long, the prisoner complex eventually comprised
an area of some 67,200 square yards (approximately 14 acres).[28] Beyond
this core lay a vast preserve nearly three times as large, or some 180,000
square yards in area (37 acres), comprising a surrounding zone of "workshops, kennels, depots, an agricultural estate, an SS playing field, a
riding school, as well as housing for the SS-Führer, SS-Unterführer, and
SS guard troops."[29] Together they defined the bounds of a demonic
Atlantis, a "city of 95 barracks, tents, and stone buildings."[30] All within
its inner precincts was designed to convince the inmate that there was no
escape and no connection with the outside world he had left behind.

The wall and wire marked the outer limit of the "death-world"[31] of
the camp; the quarry floor or the execution bunker comprised its nadir.
Characteristically, death in Mauthausen was a matter of descent, of
falling into a pit or dark enclosure. While the victims fell into the
canyon, the executioners commanded the heights. The direction of dominance was inward—toward the center—and downward—toward the
abyss. The camp's architecture, both natural and man-made, expressed a
thermodynamics of destruction: to force a man to merge into a mass, to
carry oppressive weights, to force him to drop like a rock or a sack of
potatoes; to become heavy as a corpse.

By the middle of 1943 the Mauthausen quarry was filled with an
average of 1,500 to 3,500 men per day, including as many as 400 at a
time assigned to the murderous *Strafkommando*, or punishment detail.[32]
Inmates in this detail had to carry 66- to 132-pound stones on their
shoulders, often marching double-time, again and again, subject to the
shouting, whipping, shoving, and gunfire of "The SS men [who] in their
skull-buckled uniforms, crouched on the side of the stairs like gar[g]oyles
on the eaves of a cathedral."[33] To relieve the boredom of a hot afternoon
in "late June 1942" some 25 Jews were chased up the 186 steps by the
guards. At the summit, the SS men merrily jabbed the Jews in their hind
ends with rifle butts until they dropped over the edge. In the midst of the
sport, the SS men were heard to shout: "Attention! Parachutists!"[34]
while the victims, dead weight, hurtled precipitously to their deaths.
Those who miraculously survived the ordeal were drowned in a pool of
stagnant water at the bottom of the canyon.

The downward spiral of the quarry led to ever deeper and narrower
spaces and, ultimately, to a man-made, subterranean cavern. Off the

roll-call square in the center of the protective custody camp a staircase led to the bunker, an underground complex of confinement cells, execution devices, a medical experimentation room, mortuary, crematorium, and gas chamber. Construction of this basement labyrinth began in October 1941. In the dark corridors and rooms inmates under sentence of death—"special treatment" was the euphemism—were hung after climbing onto an automatically operated, collapsible stool. Others were lined up and shot from behind. Deceived into believing they were to be measured or photographed (a device draped with a black cloth made to resemble a camera stood nearby) the inmates pressed against a wall into which holes had been bored. Through these openings an SS man, armed with a sub-caliber gun, fired into the victim's neck. After each execution, from behind the door of the adjoining mortuary an inmate swiftly emerged to wipe up the traces of the killing and drag away the body; he then closed the door just before the next victim arrived. In this manner the inmates could be killed individually at a rate of 2 per minute, or up to 30 per hour.[35]

One of the frequently used methods of killing inmates was to force them beyond the wire, where the guards then shot them. Officially their deaths were marked in the register as "shot while trying to escape." In all, in Mauthausen more than 2,500 inmates were recorded as having died for such a transgression.[36] These "escapes" were little more than an excuse for murder.[37] One ruse the SS used was to hand inmates tin containers and order them to pick fruit beyond the cordon. In 1941 and 1942 such "raspberry picker details" were frequently assembled as a means of eliminating those who were in an ill or weakened condition.

Inmates were also drowned *en masse* in shower rooms. The method was perfected in Gusen. "Especially in the period from October 1941 to January 1942," inmates were selected at roll call and sent to the baths. Crammed into the shower area 30 to 50 at a time, held in check by guards armed with whips and clubs, they were forced to endure a relentless stream of cold water. With the drains already sealed or clogged as bodies fell, guards shoved them under the rising water. Death by drowning or "acute circulatory collapse" was the inevitable result. Any survivors of the ordeal invariably succumbed within days to "pneumonia or illnesses related to the cold."[38]

The first gassing of Mauthausen inmates took place at a nearby castle, Hartheim, located just west of Linz. Originally a center for the physical destruction of the mentally ill, in 1941–42 and again in 1944 Hartheim functioned as a site for the killing of inmates as well.[39] Gassing operations in the main camp complex began just as the first cycle of gassing of inmates in Castle Hartheim was coming to an end. In the first week of March 1942, over 150 Soviet prisoners of war were herded into a sealed isolation barrack in Gusen and killed after hydrogen cyanide crystals were thrown in. In late April 1942 Mauthausen's own gas chamber, situated in the bunker, underwent a trial run: a batch of rats was exterminated; only days later, on 9 May more than 200 Soviet prisoners of war were gassed.[40] In the Mauthausen chamber inmates were pressed into a space 19 square yards in area and nearly 8 feet in height;[41] in an adjacent room, deadly gas pellets were inserted into a filling apparatus, and heated with a hot brick; the warmth speeded the conversion of the pellets into lethal gas that then streamed into the chamber. In this way, as many as 65 to 70 persons could be killed at once.[42] The killing operation lasted approximately "10 to 20 minutes." An SS physician, monitoring the procedure from one of the spy holes situated on the two doors, then signaled for the automatic ventilation of the chamber to begin. For the processing of a load of 30 persons, for example, from initial examination of the victims to their removal the process lasted anywhere from 90 minutes to two and one-half hours. Operating from 9 May 1942 until 28 or 29 April 1945, the Mauthausen chamber took an estimated 4,000 lives.[43]

Beginning in the middle of 1942 and extending for at least another year, a gas van coursed the 3 mile route between Mauthausen and Gusen. Thirty victims at a time were herded into the back of a sealed truck. During the journey the victims were asphyxiated with carbon monoxide gas. By the time the vehicle arrived in Gusen, the corpses were unloaded for disposal in the crematorium. Completing the cycle, an additional 30 victims from Gusen were crammed inside, killed in like manner, and emptied at Mauthausen. They too were dumped and burned. An estimated 900 to 2,800 inmates were killed in this way.[44]

Throughout 1942 and well into the first half of 1943 Mauthausen remained almost exclusively a center in which inmates worked solely for firms owned and operated by the SS. At the principal branch camp established at Gusen, only 3 miles to the west, inmates were also set to work in rock quarries. In this phase the inmates remained concentrated in the Mauthausen/Gusen core complex. In 1942 only 8 per cent of the inmates had been diverted to armaments work. On 14 March 1942 roughly a thousand inmates were spared to labor in the Steyr-Daimler-Puch armaments works in Steyr; 20 inmates were sent to Linz to construct a new camp, Linz I, in December 1942, and 400 others were transferred to Linz in March 1943 to work in a metal processing plant established by the SS-controlled German Earth and Stone Works and the Stone and Earth Company, an offshoot of the Hermann-Göring-Works.[45]

Phase III: The SS did not lightly yield its exclusive claim to destroy at will or exploit for its own enterprises the inmates within its sphere of dominance. In spite of the call for intensified use of inmates in war industries, it was not until the middle of 1943, under outside pressure, that Mauthausen ceded a portion of its callously abused inmate population to contribute to the war effort. In all, at a time "when some 6,000 inmates were set to work in the rock quarries and some 4,000 in the workshops of Mauthausen and Gusen the SS leadership hindered, if not sabotaged the transfer of inmates to firms which did not belong to SS firms."[46] The escalating spiral of killing in Mauthausen continued well into 1943.

By the spring of 1943, however, mounting labor shortages led to increasing demands for a more "rational" use of the inmate population in Mauthausen. Austria, as yet out of reach of Allied bombers, in mid-1943 remained a vital and protected zone attractive as a site for the transfer of war industries. Under the prodding of Albert Speer, Mauthausen grew to take on major tasks for the increasingly desperate German war effort. Following his inspection of Mauthausen in March 1943, Speer, exasperated, noted in a memo of 5 April to Himmler that in the face of existing labor shortages the SS was still taking "more than generous" advantage of its pool of captive labor to meet its own requirements, and strongly recommended a "more sensible" use of inmates in the armaments program.[47]

Beginning in June 1943 Mauthausen expanded outward from its principal core in Mauthausen-Gusen, until it eventually comprised a vast network of some 49 satellite camps extending across the length and breadth of prewar Austrian territory. The size of the camp population skyrocketed from approximately 14,800 in Mauthausen and Gusen in March 1943 to nearly 26,000 by December of that year, reaching a peak of 84,500 inmates in all camps of the Mauthausen network by March 1945.[48] Yet, well over half of these, or approximately 45,000, were still concentrated in the two original camps. Moreover, whereas 80 to 95 percent of the inmates assigned to the new satellite camps were involved in labor for war industries, only some 10 percent at Mauthausen-Gusen were involved in such work. Until the camp's final days, the remainder worked for the SS-owned German Earth and Stone Works.[49]

Inmates assigned to the Mauthausen branch camps worked for war industries in major Austrian industrial centers such as Linz, Steyr, St. Valentin, Wiener Neustadt, and Vienna; as well as in locations such as

Ebensee, Melk, and Redl-Zipf, where inmates had to dig underground factories for German armaments industries; and at a host of additional sites focusing mainly on construction of air raid bunkers, power plants, roadways, as well as rubble clearance and agricultural projects. Among the satellites were 3 large camps, with from 5,000 to 17,000 inmates; 8 camps of intermediate size, whose populations were in excess of 1,000; and some three dozen small outposts, generally of short duration, containing anywhere from 5 to 1,000 inmates.[50]

Above all, it was the decision to develop a fleet of rockets capable of reaching England that contributed to Mauthausen's expansion. Plans for the creation of such missiles may be traced to Hitler's decision of 12 December 1942, to support Speer's order for the creation of a special commission for development of a rocket, code-named *Aggregat-4* (A-4), also known as the V-2, for *Vergeltungswaffe*, or weapon of retaliation. The expansion of the A-4 program to include concentration camp labor was the driving force behind the widening of the camp complex centered in Mauthausen. In the fall of 1943 inmates were set to work constructing underground tunnels and testing sites for the preparation of the new weapon. They would carve labyrinths out of the sides of mountains. In the summer of 1943 contracts for the widened activities of the A-4 program were granted to a number of Austrian firms, including the Heinkel-Werke in Tyrolia, manufacturer of turbo pumps, and the Rax-Werke in Wiener Neustadt, located south of Vienna. Subcontracts were also awarded to the firms of Hofherr & Schrantz of Vienna-Floridsdorf and the newly created Steinverwertungs A. G., located in Redl-Zipf.

The loss of German command of the skies to the Allies and increasingly Allied assault on both civilian and military targets in Germany necessitated moving much of this labor to underground facilities. In 1943, over 200,000 tons of bombs fell on the country. There were devastating attacks on major German cities, including Cologne (30 November 1942); Hamburg (early August 1943); and Berlin (commencing in August 1943). For Austria, the last zone in Germany to fall within range of Anglo-American aircraft, was looked to as the "air raid shelter of the Reich." As such she was a desirable site for the relocation of harried armament works.[51] Yet Austria afforded only short-lived security, becoming threatened in the summer of 1943 as Allied aircraft began launching attacks on Austrian territory, first from bases in North Africa, and then from Italy. Assaults on Mauthausen's own province of Upper Austria began in February 1944.[52] "By the middle of the year 1944 the Americans were the absolute rulers of the skies over Austria."[53]

Masses of additional Jewish prisoners arrived in Mauthausen in the spring of 1944. The first wave came in transports from Auschwitz in May and June. Among them were some 8,000 Hungarian Jews, and they were followed in August by 4,600 Polish Jews from Plaszow. Thousands of these Jewish inmates were shipped on to Mauthausen's satellite camps, where they were set to work on the construction of underground tunnels to be used as workshops for the armaments industry, or in weapon and aircraft assembly facilities already in operation. Upon arrival in Mauthausen, however, they remained subject to selection in which those unfit for work were removed for execution. Those transferred to the branch camps were routinely singled out for the worst assignments and punishments. "Men who reached Mauthausen in perfectly fit condition became wrecks within a month or two and were barely able to drag themselves from one place to another. Many prisoners died each day at work."[54]

Phase IV: The final phase of the camp's existence lasted from the fall of 1944 until the liberation in May 1945. The period was marked by a general breakdown of the camp routine and a steep rise in mortality. Bodies could no longer be fully accommodated in the existing ovens inside the camp and were emptied into mass graves on two sites, one lying north of the camp in Marbach bei der Linde where 9,860 corpses were interred, the other at the town's World War I prisoner of war cemetery which filled with 2,000 bodies. Additional inmates were buried near towns along the route where inmates were shot during evacuation marches in April 1945.[55] The period was characterized by numerous acts of murder and brutality repeatedly acted out within sight of, and often with the active complicity of, wide sections of the civilian population.

Jews again reached Mauthausen in large numbers in the winter of 1944–45. With the dissolution of the Auschwitz complex in the face of the approaching Soviet forces, many of the surviving Jewish inmates were sent to Mauthausen and its branch camps. From 25 January 1945 onward, some 9,000 Auschwitz inmates, "the majority of them Jews," arrived in Mauthausen. It is reported that as many 1,500 bodies from these Auschwitz tranports were unloaded dead at the Mauthausen railway station, and some 500 new arrivals died in the camp courtyard after having been forced to stand long hours in the cold while awaiting registration. Those Jews who survived were put to work in the tunnels.[56] In February more than 6,500 inmates from Gross-Rosen and Sachsenhausen also reached Mauthausen. On 3 March approximately 2,700 additional Gross-Rosen survivors arrived in the Mauthausen satellite camp at Ebensee by way of the main camp. Of these, however, only 2,048 were still alive to be registered on March 7. On 9 March came 1,799 women from

Ravensbrück. Additional inmates, some 142 from Sachsenhausen and 216 from Dora-Nordhausen, reached Mauthausen on 12 and 15 April respectively. Yet others were transferred to Mauthausen from Gestapo prisons in Slovakia and Austria.

At this time Hungarian Jews constituted the final and heaviest wave of Jewish inmates to reach Mauthausen. Thousands who, since the fall of 1944, had been set to work on the construction of defensive fortifications along the Austro-Hungarian border, as well as thousands more, including families, who had been sent to work in factories in Vienna, were forcibly marched toward Mauthausen beginning in the winter and spring of 1945. Their agonizing trek, directed by SS guards and civilian militia, followed two main routes. One led westward through Vienna along the north bank of the Danube; the other wound west from the Hungarian border toward Graz, then north through the mountains of Styria.[57] Because the camp had become so crowded, an additional compound consisting of 14 tents was established outside the main camp to accommodate the influx. Crammed together in groups of 3,000–4,000 per tent, forced to live on muddy ground under the worst of sanitary conditions, the Jews inside and outside these tents were prey to typhus and dysentery, as well as outright execution. Thousands died here and at Gunskirchen, located some 35 miles to the southwest, as well as along the route of march between the two camps. In all, "the total number of Jews who died in Mauthausen is 38,906; one-third of the victims in the entire Mauthausen complex of camps, which, at a modest estimate, totalled 119,000."[58]

If today one seeks to locate the physical traces of the camps, he will find them in the midst of hundreds of unremarkable towns and villages across the center of the European continent. It is beside these host towns and villages of the concentration camp system, little communities with gardens and thoroughfares, trim houses and railway stations, that we find the vestiges.

Between 1938 and 1945 the citizens of Mauthausen lived adjacent to one of the most notorious concentration camps in the history of the Third Reich. Did they not see, not hear, not speak of what was going on so near? Like good neighbors, did they choose not to interfere? Did they in some way contribute to the crimes? The questions are directed not only to the townspeople, but to all humanity for whom the events of this era remain an unending "chain of enigmas/hung on the neck of night."[59]

Chapter 2

In the Shadow of
the Camp

Mauthausen sits amid lovely rolling hills whose fields cover the Austrian landscape like the bedspread of a giant. The town nuzzles peacefully along the north bank of the Danube, whose swift current is quickened by the nearby confluence of the Enns, a major alpine waterway. Mauthausen is a stroller's paradise. Marked hiking routes provide shaded paths to nearby churches and castles. Beautified resting spots afford pleasing views of the Alps and of the Bohemian forest. Mauthausen lies just 14 miles downriver from Linz, the provincial capital of the province of Upper Austria; 90 miles due east the spire of St. Stephen's Cathedral, the landmark of Vienna, rises to meet the sky. To the north and beyond lie the forests of the *Mühlviertel*, home to deer and rabbits, pheasant and grouse, pigeons and owls, running buck and wild boar: a hunter's haven. Of all the area's treasures, however, those most significant to our story are the great, yawning pits of granite.

Mauthausen is synonymous with its rock quarries. The town was long esteemed as a principal supplier of granite construction material for the streets, bridges, and monuments of Vienna, Budapest, and host of lesser cities in Central Europe. It was the presence of the hard and durable stones that drew the attention of Heinrich Himmler who, in March 1938, was embarking on a bold expansion of his SS-operated

23

economic empire. Accessible by river and by rail, the modest town of Mauthausen proved an ideal setting for the establishment of what was to become one of the most notorious camps in the history of the Third Reich.

Under the best of conditions, stone quarrying is dangerous, even violent work. Granite is hard and requires enormous effort to loosen and break apart. The rock is stubborn and must be blown clear by means of explosives. Much difficult labor is involved in blasting, hammering, picking, and hauling blocks of stone. One needs a rugged constitution for outdoor activity, keen eyes with which to work the rock, and healthy feet to remain standing long hours. During the labor, stone dust may rain down upon the work site, and strong lungs are required to withstand it. In working the rock, fingers have a way of being overlooked; hands are bloodied in handling sharp edges; bones may snap or a body flatten in a fall from great heights.[1]

When undisturbed by the explosions and the hammering that characterize active stone operations, the quarries were quiet refuges, hidden and isolated, to which people often retreated. "Children like it here," one author noted in 1938, relating the adventures of a family visit to one quarry, "few people enter, most do not know the way in. It's as if one were inside a fortress, hidden and protected." Yet even amid the calm, the landscape suggested terror. The youngsters enjoyed scaling the steep cliffs. There the trees seemed to totter along the upper rim, their exposed roots seemingly ill-equipped to prevent them from falling into the canyon. The peril of heights set the tone for the children's playful cries for help. Seen from above, the people in the pit below took on an insect-like appearance. The boys returned from the top and related that from such a distant perspective their father resembled a fly or a beetle.[2]

Throwing stones at one another was said to have been a favorite sport among youngsters growing up in the region, and it was taken for granted as a "harmless" part of boyhood. One chronicler noted that, at the turn of the century, Adolf Hitler and his young friends chose an abandoned quarry near Linz, the Mayerbruch quarry, to stage mock battles of the Boer war. As the younger boys gathered stones for ammunition, Hitler, leader of the band of stone-hurling Boers of Leonding, commanded attacks against the youth of nearby Untergaumberg who were invariably cast in the despised role of the British forces.[3]

One of Mauthausen's leading businessmen was Anton Poschacher, owner of the Poschacher stone works. He was also an enthusiastic supporter of the Nazi party, whose local Mauthausen chapter, or *Ortsgruppe*, claimed 130 members in 1938.[4] Expecting a long-awaited renewal of economic activity in the building sector, Herr Poschacher warmly welcomed the party's attainment of power in Austria. The end of the First World War had brought hard times to the Poschacher stone works. In 1920 tensions erupted in a bitter labor dispute, with violence directed against him and his chief engineer. New contracts and funds were difficult to come by, wages fell, and jobs were few. In his view, the industry was in its death throes. He complained of long hours lost in fruitless efforts to secure new contracts. He recalled frustrating meetings with government agencies. Adding to his worries, he noted, was the modern architects' preference for concrete over granite.

Better times, however, might be on the way. His travels to Hitler's Germany revealed that builders there still esteemed the quality of natural stone construction materials. In 1936, on the occasion of the Olympiad, he spoke with colleagues in Germany, and characterized his visit as "a true revelation." "Everywhere industry was in full swing, money was being invested and one even complained of a labor shortage! I could hardly believe my eyes and ears, and I returned home certain in the knowledge one need only hang on and then we too shall enjoy an upswing. And so came the winter of 1937–38, and in March the Anschluss with the great German fatherland." Confidently he took on new workers and stocked up reserves of steel and coal, for "I knew that before long there would be plenty of work, and so there was." His labor force grew to 700, plus 80 apprentices. New contracts came in from the city of Vienna, his oldest customer, which placed orders on a scale unsurpassed since 1914. Important contracts were also forthcoming from Germany. The Reich government engaged his firm for prestigious undertakings such as erecting Nazi party buildings in Nuremberg, and constructing autobahn bridges as well as the new Danube bridge in Linz. Herr Poschacher considered it "a happy omen" that, after years of struggle, the one-hundredth anniversary of the firm's founding in 1839 took place at a moment of such great promise.[5]

In 1938 Hitler had grandiose plans for his hometown of Linz. In addition to the new bridge across the Danube, he planned a town hall, an art museum, a monument to commemorate the Anschluss, another to honor the memory of Anton Bruckner, a stadium overlooking the city, a home to which he hoped to retire one day, as well as a Nazi party headquarters with a tower and crypt to house his mortal remains.[6]

The new building program presented an opportunity for the SS both to enhance its influence in an area central to Hitler's concerns and to promote its financial independence as well. The construction business was to be an important source of revenue for Heinrich Himmler's organization. Moreover, a concentration camp devoted to the extraction of granite was ideally suited to the exploitation of the growing pool of slave labor anticipated for the war to come. In the stone-cast buildings of Linz Hitler envisioned a lasting monument to his power. So, too, Himmler's Mauthausen was to be of stone; like a fortress it was to be built to endure.

All that was needed to destroy a man was implicit in the stones. Himmler and his lieutenants instinctively saw in the quarry a natural embodiment of the terror and punishment they were to perfect in the concentration camp. They read into the steep 300-foot cliffs, the heavy rocks, the explosions needed to pry loose vast slabs and boulders a natural setting of terror. The concentration camp was born of the quarry. In-mates lifted the edifice stone by stone, arduously climbing to the rim of the canyon to assemble the camp in a field above the pit. Beginning in 1938, for seven years the quarries of Concentration Camp Mauthausen would yield up hundreds of thousands of stones for streets and monu-ments and buildings—stones that were all blasted free of the quarry walls, hammered loose, and heaved upon the shoulders of inmates weakened by meager rations, long hours, and inhuman treatment from their overseers.

Stone manifests additional qualities: opaqueness, strength, silence, and terror. Stone obstructs vision.[7] When dislodged from the sides of a cliff, stacked and cemented into a wall, stone encloses. Whatever lies within its boundary will be invisible to those viewing it from the outside. Nevertheless, the quarry walls do not form a perfect circle. On one side the Mauthausen quarry opens, and borders a roadway. The stone perim-eter of the camp, hauled from the stone pit above which it stands, is completed with wire. The camp is built with gates for passage in and out. No dome save the dark of night covers the quarry and the camp. Just as the dust of explosions in the quarry may scatter with the four winds, so too will the ash spewing from the chimneys of the camp carry the refuse of a man from the ovens below, upward and over the walls, raining down on field and forest.

The Concentration Camp Mauthausen did not spring from a wilder-ness. The area was inhabited. Less than three miles away lay the center of a town. From the beginning the camp confronted civilian authority and touched the lives of the citizenry. In carving a place for itself, the camp asserted its dominance and enforced compliance. Its first tasks were bound up with achieving title to the land; gaining superiority over ex-isting public authorities and placing itself above the law; securing the material and logistical assistance of local contractors, suppliers, and la-borers; and winning the compliance of the local population. This was not accomplished without a measure of tension. Neither the mayor, the district governor, the police, nor the state's attorney willingly abided overt disruption of public order. In the face of the camp's superior power, however, their challenges proved ineffectual and the camp easily brushed them aside. Emboldened in their strength, camp personnel ran roughshod over the rights and sensitivities of the town residents. In their off-duty hours, SS men behaved boorishly. Drunkenness, petty thievery, desecration of religious symbols, and brawling became a source of concern to the local population.

On the other hand, the camp offered material benefits to the townspeople. It revived the stone industry and provided jobs for civilian workers and supervisors in the SS-owned and operated quarries. The camp passed out contracts to shippers, suppliers, and craftsmen. Townspeople were able to compensate for wartime shortages through lucrative exchanges of scarce agricultural commodities for rare items seized from the prisoners.

Beyond overcoming the objections of local authorities, the camp sought the complicity of residents living in the immediate vicinity. True, after the first prisoners arrived in August 1938, the camp attempted to keep people from showing undue curiosity. Gaping at the inmates was prohibited. However, the SS was unable to prevent citizens from noticing the mistreatment of prisoners marched through the town from the railway station or to work sites in the area. Inevitably, residents were witness to beatings and shootings. Accumulating evidence of brutality set in motion a series of discussions within the population. The question was less what was happening in and around the camp than how they should interpret what they saw.

It may be argued that in the physical space of Mauthausen there existed two distinct worlds: that of the camp, embodied in the fearful SS organization and the inmates upon whom they worked their will, and that of the town and its residents. Yet the boundaries separating these worlds were never impermeable. The requisites of daily life, and the life of the camp itself, demanded personal as well as commercial bonds that necessitated contact between the two spheres.

Prized for its granite quarries, conveniently accessible to Linz by rail and by water, Mauthausen was thrust into the midst of the Nazi concentration camp system. Not its isolation but its centrality drew the attention of the SS. In 1938 Mauthausen was what it had been for nearly a millennium: a site of convergence, an unavoidable center for those traveling north and south, east and west. It owed its existence to the waterway, and derives its name from the *Mauthause*, or toll house, es-

tablished there to enforce levies upon passing ships. Mauthausen's cus-
toms officers are said to have been exceptionally strict in the fulfillment
of their duties. In 1189 they unwisely dared to tax crusaders traveling the
Danube under the banner of Frederick Barbarossa. The angered crusaders
set the town afire. This was not the only occasion when Mauthausen
was, as one chronicle noted, "witness to bloody events."[8]

In World War I the Austro-Hungarian Empire erected a major
prisoner-of-war camp in Mauthausen. The camp, opened in 1914, held
as many as 15,000 prisoners, mainly Serbian, housed in barracks crowded
with up to 400 persons each. Conditions inside deteriorated rapidly to
such an extent that some 11,000 of the men died, the result of "poor
medical care, epidemics and too little nourishment."[9]

As the seat of one of three district courts in the county of Perg,
Mauthausen was the administrative and commercial center of a network
of 11 towns whose combined resident population in 1934 totaled
14,361.[10] In a county that remained heavily agricultural, Mauthausen
was an important trade center with a strong base in small manufacturing,
trade, and transportation.[11] Of 1,813 persons living and working in
Mauthausen in 1934, 117 were engaged in agriculture and forestry, 861
in industry and handicrafts, 300 in trade and transport, 12 in credit and
insurance; 73 were government employees, 83 free professionals, and 18
were domestic servants. There were 336 without an occupation, while
the profession of 13 persons went unrecorded.[12]

Like all towns and cities in the province, Mauthausen was largely
Catholic: 1,772 of the town's 1,813 residents were Catholic.[13] There
were no Jews living in Mauthausen. However, of the only 11 Jews residing in the county, 9 lived in the neighboring town of Schwertberg,
about four miles to the north. Most of the 966 Jews who lived in the
province of Upper Austria in 1934 were clustered in the cities of Linz
(671) and Steyr (78), and the county of Gmunden (116).[14]

Far from being a secret enterprise, the Mauthausen concentration
camp was a publicized undertaking from its inception in 1938. On 30
March of that year, the *Times* of London reported that "Gauleiter Eigruber, of Upper Austria, speaking at Gmunden yesterday, announced that
for its achievements in the National-Socialist cause his province was to
have the special distinction of having within its bounds a concentration
camp for the traitors of all Austria. This, according to the *Völkische
Beobachter* aroused such enthusiasm in his audience that the Gauleiter
could not continue his speech for some time."[15]

For the broad populace, Mauthausen was intended as a deliberate
warning to all who might oppose the regime, or whom the regime might

designate as a threat; therefore its existence was purposely made known. In a practical sense, it would have been impossible to keep such an enterprise entirely out of public view. Land had to be leased and purchased; local authorities called upon to cooperate and to help in maintaining order; civilians were needed to assist in the construction of quarters, in operating the rock quarries, and in providing supplies. In fact, if during the war one wished to reach the camp, one could simply pick up the telephone and dial 145: the Concentration Camp Mauthausen was in the public telephone directory.[16]

In March 1938, directly following the *Anschluss*, Reichsführer-SS Heinrich Himmler and Oswald Pohl, chief of the administrative office of the SS-Hauptamt, came to tour the granite quarries near Mauthausen and Gusen with an eye toward selection of these sites for their expanding empire. A further inspection took place at the end of May; the participants included Pohl, SS-Gruppenführer Theodore Eicke (former commandant of Dachau and then inspector of concentration camps), and Herbert Karl, a building engineer employed in the SS building division.[17]

The site of the principal camp was atop a hill. Judging by the composition of the soil and the difficulties encountered in supplying the work site, the location seemed ill-chosen. "That camp over there was built in a potato and oat field. That is, muck, muck and then again muck, especially when it rained," noted Phillip M., a former SS-Hauptscharführer and camp weapons master.[18] An inmate who was among the first arrivals recalled that during the construction, water (primarily reserved for the SS) had to be carted up to the camp "three times a day" from the town of Mauthausen.[19]

The SS were interested in two principal quarries in Mauthausen area: the Vienna Ditch quarry chosen as the main site for the Mauthausen camp, and the Bettelberg quarry located in Gusen. These quarries were the property of the city of Vienna. On 7 April 1938, the magistrate director of the city of Vienna wrote to Vienna's mayor stating that on that day representatives of the Reichsführung-SS in Munich and the Landesmuseum Linz had called upon him and reported "that in Mauthausen a state concentration camp for 3,000 to 5,000 people is to be erected." Furthermore, they requested the city of Vienna's immediate "fundamental consent" to their proposal that the Vienna Ditch and Bettelberg stone quarries "be placed at the disposal of the Reich leadership of the SS." The director recommended approval of this request, providing that in the bargain the city of Vienna would be able to secure its needs for stone materials.

The matter was settled in a meeting held on 5 May with the mayor

of Vienna and "two gentlemen from the SS in Munich." "Therein the
lease of the Bettelberg-Marbach quarry as well as an agricultural operation, at first for a period of ten years at an annual rent of RM 5,000.00
[$2,000.00] with participation in the turnover and delivery of stone
material, was provided for." By 16 May, negotiations for the lease of the
Vienna Ditch and Marbach quarries was also completed. Eventually, the
latter two were purchased by the SS construction firm, the German Earth
and Stone Works. The Bettelberg quarry, however, remained in the
city's hands.[20]

The SS was also obliged to purchase land from private individuals
owning property near the new camp. For one farmer, this sale became
the first in a series of mildly advantageous, if sometimes disturbing encounters with the camp. "The grain was still very green when I had to
cede land and when the first inmates came. First temporary barracks were
put up, and then began the first extension of the camp," he recalled in
1965. "My farm lay in the immediate vicinity of what was then the SS
housing estate. . . . I too had to cede portions of my fields to the SS
camp administration, and am of the opinion that the SS did not pay
badly for them."[21]

This farmer, living nearby, could not help observe some of the
happenings associated with the camp. "At the beginning there were only
a couple of hundred inmates here and already things went very badly for
the inmates. I myself saw countless times how inmates were mistreated.
I also saw how inmates were shot." Yet this did not stand in the way of
his dealing with the camp's officers, including the commandant: "All the
SS officers, and also Ziereis, bought milk at my place. I had a good
understanding with Ziereis; if I needed something and turned to Ziereis,
he always met my request. For example, I once needed painters to paint
my house, and he placed two painters with two SS guards at my disposal.
The two inmates were academic painters, and as room painters proved a
failure. I fed all four well."[22]

Local officials soon learned of plans to build the camp in their area.
According to the *Landrat*, or district governor, neither he nor the mayor
of the town of Mauthausen wanted to see the camp built nearby. *Landrat*
Dr. Gustav Brachmann stated that he and the mayor, Gattinger, wrote
a letter to Himmler in which they argued against the construction of a
concentration camp in Mauthausen. "We sought to renounce the establishment of a concentration camp in the market community Mauthausen.
As grounds we credibly conveyed that the establishment in Mauthausen
would hinder the economic construction of the town." The *Landrat* then
on his own wrote yet another note: "after sending the letter I drove to my

office, and then composed a communication to Himmler, wherein I also took issue against the establishment of the concentration camp. But I argued with political views, and in fact I conveyed that in Mauthausen and its vicinity there lived preponderantly former Marxists and clericals who would exploit the establishment of a concentration camp as welcome cause for inciting against the NSDAP. For this reason one might find another location for it." Neither of the letters apparently made the slightest impression on the Reichsführer. Brachmann continued, "I received no answer to my communication. Gattinger, as I understand, received an answer from Himmler. The reply was full of insults and reprimands."[23]

When, following the arrival of the first prisoners in August 1938, their presence in the area became known, the SS took pains to keep the population at a distance. The main difficulty was the presence of a number of persons who regularly whiled away their time about a river ferry launch where inmates were assembling on their way to work. On 18 January 1939, the disgruntled commandant, SS-Sturmbannführer Albert Sauer, sent a message to the district governor complaining of the irresponsible failure of the local police to break up these assemblies of civilians:

> since about 10 days ago inmates from the Concentration Camp Mauthausen are being brought to a distant building site (Ebelsberg near Linz). Daily in the morning at 7 o'clock and in the afternoon at 4 o'clock the inmates have to use the ferry launch in Mauthausen. Every day, especially in the afternoons, 30–40 persons gather in Mauthausen at the ferry launch as curious onlookers. The police headquarters in Mauthausen, which would be duty-bound to disperse such assemblies, does not consider it necessary to intervene, although the situation there was known. . . . Should the Mauthausen police prove incapable of preventing [these gatherings], the camp will do so with SS sentries. Notice will be taken that during any kind of incidents (escape attempts by the inmates) firearms will have to be resorted to without any further consideration. Should civilians be wounded in the process, the Mauthausen police headquarters has to bear the responsibility for it.[24]

For their part, the police were irritated and insulted by the commandant's statement that they were lax in the performance of their duties. Acknowledging that on 18 January the local police station was contacted by the Concentration Camp Mauthausen concerning the matter of these civilian assemblages, the station leader, Fleischmann, insisted that his men responded properly. Police assistance did arrive on the scene. There they indeed found a number of civilians, and duly warned them that "gatherings for the purpose of watching the prisoners are forbidden." Nevertheless, the police were of the opinion that those persons whom they discovered were mostly people who ordinarily passed the time near the river. The police were simply not as alarmed as the SS, who presumed the people were deliberately assembling to watch the inmates and the SS guards. Fleischmann pointed out that the area was a popular spot where "all day" one might find individuals "who particularly enjoy lingering there. Frequently there are also children who when not in school play in the vicinity of the launch."[25]

The commandant nonetheless was justly concerned that civilians might see the rough way guards treated inmates who were being transported to work across the river. On one occasion in 1938 or early 1939 it came to light that SS men had thrown inmates into the Danube during a ferry crossing, prompting the district governor to charge the commandant with "disturbance of the peace." He noted as well that "this behavior stirred sensation and anger among the civilian population."[26]

From the viewpoint of the local officials it was the camp personnel and not the onlookers who were the real threat to public order. The SS quickly developed a deserved reputation in town for ruffianly conduct. Often it was the citizens themselves who were made the object of their misdeeds. In a local restaurant late one night in November 1939, for example, a brawl ensued after an SS man insulted a town resident. Drunken SS men swung their fists, hurled chairs at the customers and tore their clothing; beer glasses shattered and one resident had "his head shoved through the window of the guest room door by an SS man." That the new camp commandant, Franz Ziereis, was also a participant in the fight and failed to maintain order added to popular ill will.[27]

SS men also desecrated religious shrines. They liked to fire their guns at crucifixes on tavern room walls. On one occasion they even lifted a statue of the Virgin Mary from a pillar and defecated into the opening.[28] In a discussion with SS Gruppenführer Ernst Kaltenbrunner on 19 December 1939, the local police commander pointed out that SS men had been involved in numerous "transgressions" including outdoor shooting incidents in which "the personal safety of civilians was endangered"; they had also been involved in "poachings, damage to the property of others, brawls, [and] serious cases of drunkenness" resulting in complaints from the townspeople.[29] In spite of such complaints, the SS behaved as they pleased. By their conduct they demonstrated that they were above the law.

The SS were no less effective in overriding the efforts of the state prosecutor attempting to investigate a mounting series of deaths inside the camp. On 12 January 1939, the state prosecutor's office in Linz was informed of a case involving the gunshot wounding of an inmate, Karl May.[30] As a result of the shooting, May had been in the camp hospital since 27 August 1938 with an injury to the lung. Learning of this, "the office of the state's attorney addressed the camp commandant's office and requested the transmission of the charge and the investigation materials as well as notification of why no charge was filed. Thereupon the camp commandant answered that no charge has been filed because . . . only in cases of death through suicide, accident, breaking of resistance, and hindering escape must the state prosecutor's office be notified."[31]

Upon authorization by the upper provincial court in Vienna, the Linz office managed to interview the wounded inmate. From him they learned only that he had been "suddenly awakened by a strong blow to the back," without having heard either the shot or known by whom or from which direction it had been fired. It was determined, too, that someone next to him had also been hit in the head by a shot. They were able to learn from the attending physician that the wound revealed "the impression of a normal gunshot wound penetrating right through." Additional investigation was hampered in part by the reluctance of the wounded inmate to talk. "According to the oral communication of the head of the Office of the State Prosecutor in Linz, Karl May seems to shrink from making further declarations." As a result, the prosecutor was left in doubt concerning the essential facts: "How it came to this wounding, who fired, and what the cause of the shot was, that is all still completely unsettled."[32]

The prosecutor also saw little chance that the commandant of Mauthausen would assist his investigation. "It is to be assumed that in the future the camp commandant will refuse every explanation and report of the result of his own inquiry." Herein lay a conflict of spheres of authority calling for clarification: "Since the camp commandant, indeed in his capacity as head of a state prison camp is to be interpreted as a public authority, the question remains open how this proceeding is to be brought into accord with regulations of criminal procedure paragraph 84, according to which all punishable acts are to be reported immediately to the state's attorney."[33]

In a similar case, the prosecutor's office learned that on 19 January 1939 inmate Karl Maresch was shot, allegedly while trying to escape. The shooting was determined to have taken place at about 10:15 A.M. The attorney had written testimony of the camp physician who "immediately determined that surgical treatment was necessary." Nevertheless, it was not until around 2:25 P.M. that he was called in to perform surgery on the patient, who by then "already lay dying. Some minutes later he passed away." The attorney's office noted with suspicion this delay in a case requiring urgent treatment.[34]

In a third instance coming to the attention of the state's attorney, again on 19 January 1939 a 65-year-old inmate, Emil Seidel, was known to have been found hanged to death in a building hut at the camp. A court commission was able to determine "that the feet of the body stood on the floor." Such cases, it was already known, were hardly a rarity. "It therefore concerns one of the frequently occurring cases of suicide in the concentration camp Mauthausen," noted a report. Despite this determination, the court commission met with opposition from camp officials when it attempted to have its own chosen physician on hand for the inquiry. "The Mauthausen lower court informed the state's attorney it wanted to call in medical councilor Dr. Niederberger, the established court physician of the inferior court Mauthausen." In fact, Dr. Niederberger appeared at the concentration camp in the company of the judicial functionary carrying out the investigation, but the camp commandant refused permission for the court-appointed doctor to attend.[35]

In support of the camp commandant's position, "an SS major afterwards presented the court authorities a directive according to which SS camp physicians are equal in rank to public health officials; because of which also in cases of unnatural death the consultation of civil health officials is to be refrained from." The state's attorney in Vienna viewed this form of appeal to special directives as a likely attempt to evade a civil proceeding and underscored the necessity of establishing a correspondence between camp directives and regulations covering activities of the justice authorities. This had also to apply, it was argued, to cases in which weapons were used. It had to be determined whether camp officials could be required "to make a statement to the justice officials concerning whether the use of weapons is justified in an individual instance or not." Until such time as this matter is cleared up, the attorney determined, the justice officials simply could not proceed. "As long as these questions are not all regulated, investigations by justice officials are completely without purpose."[36] Though the prosecutor clearly had attempted to carry out his duty to examine cases of harm to individuals, camp officials repeatedly proved capable of blocking outside inquiries into their misconduct.

*   *   *

As time passed, the civil population in Mauthausen was increasingly exposed to the sight of mistreatment, brutalization, and murder of the inmates. Not only did the brutality spill over into the town whenever the prisoners arrived at the railway station, which lay 2.5 miles from the camp, but also the sight of death inside the camp was often unavoidable for those unfortunate enough to live within view of the rock quarries. The sight of repeated horrors caused a severe strain on the nerves of nearby residents. Eleanore Gusenbauer, a farmer, became so disturbed by what she could not help see that she was prompted to file a complaint in 1941:

> In the Concentration Camp Mauthausen at the work site in Vienna Ditch inmates are being shot repeatedly; those badly struck live for yet some time, and so remain lying next to the dead for hours and even half a day long.
>
> My property lies upon an elevation next to the Vienna Ditch, and one is often an unwilling witness to such outrages.
>
> I am anyway sickly and such a sight makes such a demand on my nerves that in the long run I cannot bear this.
>
> I request that it be arranged that such inhuman deeds be discontinued, or else be done where one does not see it.[37]

The police commander of the Mauthausen gendarmerie pointed out to the *Landrat* that the horrible scenes Frau Gusenbauer described were not isolated instances: "Similar things occurred some time ago in the Concentration Camp Gusen where likewise in the vicinity of a woman, inmates [who had been] shot and who did not die immediately were given the death blow by the guards with the placement of shoes upon their throats or with kicks to the head. Furthermore, according to declarations of civilians, the inmates working at the settlement construction in Ufer, community Mauthausen, are likewise being inhumanly mistreated through intense beatings, etc."[38]

Careless though the guards were in keeping such incidents of cruelty from public view, in the camp area itself the SS posted warnings to back its demand for town residents to ignore what they otherwise could not help but notice. Citizens learned that if awareness of what was happening in and around the camp was unavoidable, one might still look away. Although cognizant of the terror in the camp, they learned to walk a narrow line between unavoidable awareness and prudent disregard.

None were more acquainted with that narrow line than the residents of Mauthausen. For them even daily chores might involve contact with the camp and its representatives. One of the roads they used passed behind the Vienna Ditch rock quarry where inmates were set to work and routinely tortured to death. Here the inmates labored up to eleven hours per day, shouldering heavy blocks of stone. Frequently, the guards forced them to run while bearing these weights. Along a set of transportable rails, some twenty-six men at a time maneuvered wagons laden with stones. The wagons were unstable, and often derailed, crushing those who failed to get out of the way. The men were also repeatedly made to carry the stones up a steep staircase of 186 steps where they were commonly beaten, shot, or shoved into the canyon below.[39] Townspeople living beyond the quarry had to walk along the road to get to town to do their shopping. To pass to the other side one had to wait at one of two crossing gates for a guard to admit him. The gates lay at opposite ends along the perimeter enclosing the stone quarry. The section of road between these crossing gates served as a kind of no-man's land. One gate lay close to a stone-crushing device, and the other lay roughly parallel to the staircase. The road did not pass directly through the quarry itself, but ran adjacent to it, intersecting a wider area where inmates were at work, and opened onto the quarry on one side. Once a civilian was admitted, a guard accompanied him through the zone from one barrier to the other. Lest anyone dare show interest or curiosity, a sign warned persons to keep moving on pain of their lives: "Beware! Anyone Setting Foot in the Camp Area will be Shot Without Warning." [*Achtung! Lagerbereich Betreten wird ohne Anruf Scharf geschossen*].[40]

ᴦAccording to one woman from Mauthausen, "everyone was afraid." It was best to look straight ahead and cross the zone as quickly as possible. "It was an unpleasant feeling when one had to go through. That is, they didn't do anything to the people there who often times went through, but once I went through. I didn't feel well there. I had to go with a man who, brr . . . ," she stated, finishing with a laconic expression that likely indicated a chill down her spine. Yet she maintained that one really did not see anything. Only the uncomfortable feeling was present: "There one sees nothing. On the street one saw nothing. That is, that which was really evil, that was in there."[41]

A pedestrian, traversing this path with eyes directed forward, sensed danger. For the length of the path one was inside the camp zone, one's angle of vision regulated by an unequivocal threat. From the view of the masters of the camp this passage was a useful reminder to the citizenry. Once on the opposite side, individuals were free to continue on their way; but the nervous encounter left a fearsome reminder: guns that pointed at the inmates might just as easily be trained on the curious outsider. A person who made the journey learned a valuable lesson in how to behave in the vicinity of the camp. He learned to control his movements, to stop and start on command, to keep his neck stiff, to fix his gaze straight ahead, and pass to the opposite side as quickly as possible. Above all, the resident learned to be thankful he was only momentarily in transit, and not a permanent inhabitant of the camp. He learned that at those points where the worlds of camp and town intersected a strict line against displaying undue interest was drawn. As long as one respected the barrier between camp and town, one could go about one's business unmolested.

Those who worked for the camp had a more extended opportunity to learn of the brutalities committed there. The camp employed civilians inside the quarry, where they were sure to view or participate in the handling of the prisoners. In January 1939, at a time when 375 inmates were assigned to the Vienna Ditch, 171 civilian employees worked in the quarry for the SS-owned German Earth and Stone Works corporation; by December, the number of civilians increased to 210, as compared to 1,066 inmates.[42] Civilians in the rock quarries worked near the inmates and gained first-hand knowledge of their mistreatment. They knew that their positions depended on their remaining silent concerning conditions inside the quarries.

During off-duty hours the civilian laborers retreated to taverns and restaurants where they came in contact with other civilians. Sometimes, their tongues loosened by drink and the flow of conversation, they spoke about what they had seen or heard of the events in the nearby camp. Such discussions could and did lead to the arrest and imprisonment of anyone whose statements revealed criticism of the goings-on in the camps or expressed pity for the inmates.

One such instance involved a recently fired, 56-year-old skilled stone worker, Johann Steinmüller. Before 1934 Steinmüller had been politically active as a prominent local Socialist politician. From 1920 to 1927 he served as the mayor of Langenstein, a community of 1,239 persons[43] some 2.5 miles to the west of Mauthausen. During the failed February 1934 socialist uprising against the Austrian Christian-Socialist regime of Chancellor Engelbert Dolfuss he had been imprisoned for 14 days. He had been a practicing stone mason since 1901. Between 18 March and 27 May 1939 he had worked for the German Earth and Stone Works in the Mauthausen camp as a civilian stone worker responsible for training a group of 10 inmates in the breaking of small paving stones. The Gestapo reported that Steinmüller was fired "because despite repeated warnings he conducted private conversations with inmates and was guilty of other underhand dealings."[44]

Steinmüller displayed the kind of familiarity with and pity for inmates in his charge that was contrary to the behavior expected of overseers. He had been reprimanded by the SS guards for occasionally using the informal "du" in exclaiming "what kind of idiocy are you up to again" when an inmate performed a task incorrectly. As he told the Gestapo in Linz following his arrest for having spoken out about the death of an inmate, "I was dismissed as a civilian laborer because I was too good to the inmates, and wanted to stand up for them. During stone-breaking an inmate sank backward and asked for water. I went to an SS Untersturmführer, whose name I do not know, and requested that I be given water for the inmate." This display of mercy, however, was hardly welcomed by the SS. "It was pointed out to me that I was an impossible person, that you just don't do that, [ask] that water be given out for the inmates, etc. I cannot remember exactly everything that was said to me, and I went immediately back to my workplace. An hour later I was immediately dismissed."[45]

Shortly thereafter, "at the end of May," Steinmüller was seated in the guest room of the Rosenleitner tavern in Mauthausen drinking a glass of cider and a beer. He was alleged to have been sober, however, when he began speaking out about conditions in the concentration camp. Seated at his table was a sawmill owner from Mauthausen; later they were joined by two men, one from the railway directorate and another whom Steinmüller did not identify by profession. Also on hand were a waitress and an unskilled worker. The latter two officially maintained that in the course of conversation Steinmüller had spoken of an incident in which inmates had been shot to death.

Steinmüller was quoted as having said, "It's no longer pretty the way things are going among us in Gusen. Recently they shot some inmates one of whom did not die immediately. They left this one lying for a time, whereupon one of the SS guards took pity and gave him a mercy shot. Naturally, [he did it] with a machine pistol; they are totally incapable of shooting with any other weapon. On this account the populace in Gusen is stirred up."[46]

The waitress who was listening seemed particularly surprised to hear about the reaction of the citizens in neighboring Gusen. "He meant that the populace in Gusen was in an uproar because of this incident," she stated. "I was appalled, namely about that which I heard from Steinmüller, and therefore asked: 'is it then happening like this?' Whereupon he replied, 'yes, yes, the populace in Gusen is in an uproar because of it.' " The waitress seemed more dismayed that people were openly upset about the incident than about the shooting itself. She did not think the inmates were worth the concern. "I then said," reported the waitress, "yes, the inmates of the concentration camp Mauthausen are all hardened criminals with whom one should have no pity, whereupon he replied, 'those are no hardened criminals, they are indeed all 'politicals.' "[47] On the basis of these statements Steinmüller was transported to the concentration camp at Buchenwald, and on 21 March 1940 sentenced to imprisonment for eight months.[48]

News of the killings was spreading. People were not ignorant of what was going on; rather they were groping to interpret what they saw and heard. The quarry worker, who obviously deplored the behavior of the guards, felt that he spoke for many in expressing disapproval of the shooting. The waitress, on the other hand, spoke for those citizens who had no difficulty accepting the killing of an inmate because they agreed with the rulers of the camp that the inmates were outcasts undeserving of mercy. From the stone worker's remark it is impossible to know how extensive was the popular "uproar" over this incident. Added to the complaints the police were receiving with regard to similar occurrences, however, it is plain that there was a measure of concern over the killings. What is equally clear, nonetheless, is that there remained persons, like the waitress, who were willing to testify against Steinmüller because he expressed displeasure with the treatment accorded the inmates and in so doing represented in their eyes a threat to the peace. Thus, persons who dared to defy officially sanctioned opinion risked arrest and censure. Most were cautious enough to keep their thoughts to themselves.

Yet another category of civilians who early on gained some knowledge of the horrors taking place inside the camp were relatives of deceased inmates offered the right to visit the camp and view the bodies of their loved ones. This privilege was granted in 1939–40 to relatives of German and Austrian prisoners. Family members who arrived to view the dead were led to a room set up as a primitive chapel to which the corpse to be shown was brought from a heap in a nearby storage room. The body, placed inside a wooden coffin, was barely identifiable in a room whose darkness was pierced solely by candle light: "only the contours of the face were somewhat visible in shadow. Because of the 'danger of epidemic' it was strictly forbidden to approach the corpse."[49]

Otto Wahl, a political inmate assigned to a labor detail that had a temporary workshop near the corpse chamber, witnessed the scenes that took place after the arrival of the relatives. "The whole thing was arranged like this: the room was small and dark," he noted. "The dead man lay raised in a primitive coffin, clothed in white paper so that only the head was visible; at some distance two candles were lit." Sometimes SS men were on hand to offer their condolences to the bereaved. "Even today," he continued, "I hear sounding in my ears how once Schulz, another time Stütz (both SS officers) made soothing speeches for family members somewhat analogous to this: we all liked your son (or husband) very much, he was a diligent worker and would have been released in the coming days. Unfortunately, he was very ill and all our efforts, yes even our expert doctors could no longer keep him alive. Such or similar was constantly the litany with which the family members were deceived."[50]

Sometimes, however, the charade broke down. Carelessly, camp authorities did not always insure that the corpse on display matched the identity of the man the relatives came to view. To be sure, the dead were duly registered, but afterwards on many of the deceased the identification tags, usually tied to a toe, were missing. The result was an unfortunate mix-up, resulting in horror for the bereaved. "I once experienced how a woman howled wildly, and while sobbing declared that the dead man was not her husband," Wahl recorded. "But even in this case the SS-Führer were not hard pressed for a lie, and were able to calm this woman. When the family members then departed and were out of hearing or viewing distance, these disgusting creatures broke out in resounding, derisive laughter. For them the matter was resolved. The dead man was again thrown onto the heap."[51]

From time to time the camp policy of expressly keeping people at a distance was undercut by brutalities carelessly conducted within view of the population. The SS brooked no interference with their activities on the part of the citizens or government officials. Expressions of disapproval on the part of civilians or the probing attention of the courts were rudely dismissed. Knowledge of what was going on made its way far beyond the walls of the camp. It mattered little what people thought as long as the camp gained their silence. Acquiescence insured that operations would continue without interference. Besides, there were many who approved of their actions, and many who discovered that the camp offered a host of new opportunities.

From the beginning, Concentration Camp Mauthausen depended on local merchants for supplies and services. As early as May 1938, 4 carpenters, 2 each from Ried and Mauthausen, filled orders for the construction of inmate beds for the camp. By the summer of 1940 as many as 1,500 beds had been delivered.[52] In addition, the local transport firm Hartl made daily deliveries of groceries and bread.[53] On 9 October 1941 the camp purchased 1,023 kilograms of calcium chloride disinfectant from the firm of Alois Kapler of Linz. An additional 1,025 kilograms was delivered by this same firm a week later. That same month the Linz firm of Bechberger also delivered 1,000 glasses and 5,000 mess bowls. In late 1941 other purchases included 250 carloads of potatoes for Gusen and 150 for Mauthausen.[54] The concentration camp routinely purchased goods from the local agricultural cooperative in Mauthausen.[55] Moreover, SS personnel and their wives patronized local merchants.[56] When it needed to, the camp called upon the services of local exterminators based in Linz and Vienna to carry out disinfections in Mauthausen and its satellite operations. The Linz disinfectant firm of A. Slupetzky acted as a supplier of the deadly chemical, Zyklon-B, used against inmates in the Mauthausen gas chamber.[57] By purchasing needed resources from businesses in the surrounding community, the camp established itself as an important customer. As suppliers, local merchants were integrated into the camp economy.

The concentration camp also contributed labor for public works projects beneficial to the town and its residents. Inmates were used to carry out ditch and canal work in the town. They also labored for the privately owned Poschacher quarry firm in Mauthausen. Jängi Wolter, an inmate who arrived in Mauthausen on 10 April 1943, recalled having served in a number of labor details outside the camp. With a hundred others he laid a rail line from Gusen to Mauthausen. He also participated in a detail that unloaded foodstuffs from ships on the Danube, and served in another that dredged sand from the river. In addition, he was assigned to work for a farmer living nearby. As a reward for the farmer's wife having given birth to her thirteenth child (Hitler served as the godfather), the SS decided to carry out some construction work for him. Wolter especially recalled "that the farmer's wild boys treated us roughly." Conditions were somewhat better when he and other inmates dug a well for another resident. "The gardener was a friendly person" and "the food good."[58]

Establishment of the concentration camp brought business to local artisans and tradesmen which they welcomed and pursued. The camp needed their skills. They and their employees were assigned to fulfill various tasks inside the camp, and in turn both they and their clients could draw upon the pool of inmate labor for private projects in the community. As one builder noted, "when the camp was started in 1938 all the small construction works formed a big concern" through which jobs were offered. "Each one of us received some sort of contract." The owner of a construction firm established in Mauthausen in 1932, Ernst Kirschbichler employed 25–30 men, including carpenters and foremen.

In 1938 his firm worked on the construction of a compressor room in the Wiener Graben quarry. On 7 September 1939, at the age of 36, Kirschbichler joined the SS, eventually attaining the rank of technical sergeant. "They told me there was no need for me to go to the front but that I could return home, which I did. Then I had to enter Mauthausen," where he immediately took up duties in the camp construction office and served as a site supervisor on sanitation, drainage, and clearing projects.[59]

In spite of his position as an SS member assigned to the camp, he was able to continue as head of his private construction firm in Mauthausen. This enabled him to conduct business in the community, as well as personal projects, for which he and his clients requested and obtained inmate labor. Clients bore the cost of this labor, paying 3 marks per day directly to the camp administration for the use of each prisoner. The inmates were set to work on farms constructing buildings, ditches, and silos. Two foremen with the firm, one employed from July 1938 until March 1942, and the other from 1941 until 1945, estimated that it used "an average of 20 to 50 inmates per day" from Mauthausen on such projects.[60] In one instance the inmates were hired to build a private villa for the owner of the firm. Estate owners noted that Kirschbichler suggested they ask the camp to provide inmates for such work. They claimed that he argued that in this way the men would have a chance to escape the harsh treatment of the camp. In postwar testimony clients who knew enough to avoid unsettling questions concerning the convenience of employing cheap concentration camp labor liked to point out that they provided them food or Christmas supplements of alcohol, meat, and bread. Similarly, other residents who claim to have come across the men while they were eating insisted they were served hearty meals and that the firm's owner fetched them such treats as "sandwiches with sausage." A cap manufacturer testified that on 12 November 1943 he entered the building office to pay a bill and found 3 inmates dining "on a white covered table . . . I noticed that the prisoners had previously had another dish, as used plates were on the table. Upon my asking how they liked it, one of the three prisoners said that it had tasted like at [his] mother's."[61]

Self-serving as some of these onlooker recollections were, undoubtedly inmates working for this man's firm were well treated. Indeed, in its assessment of the evidence brought to bear on this SS sergeant and contractor, the War Crimes Review Board upheld the view that he had "on all occasions actively assisted inmates, especially those assigned to his details," and in stating this lent weight to the testimonies of "seven former inmates who knew the accused and some of whom worked on his details [who] have testified for him, all to the effect that he did every-thing possible to ease the lot of the inmates."[62]

However, the fact remains that the builder acceded to the employ-ment of teams of inmates, just as his clients were directly enmeshed in the routine of the camp to the extent that they requested, received, and paid for slave labor for improvements on their own properties. Moreover, the firm's owner, while never shown to have caused any prisoner harm, continued to do business with the camp, and established recreational and business contacts for the camp commandant, inviting him on hunts, introducing him to game tenants and building suppliers.[63] In this way, a local businessman served and helped the camp and its commanding officer, extended and increased business contacts through the camp, and benefited both his firm and his person materially through the use of inmate labor.

More direct was the involvement of the Director of City Enterprises[64] in Steyr. It was to the public crematorium in Steyr, located just south of Mauthausen, that the bodies of almost 2,000 inmates who died in the Mauthausen concentration camp were sent for disposal both prior to and after the installation of the camp's own crematoria in the spring of 1940.[65] The director successfully fought off unwanted compe-tition from the Linz crematorium, which also vied for the extra business. He formed close contacts with both Mauthausen commandant Zieries and members of the guard troop, "with whom he arranged drinking bouts and [whom he] furnished with wine, cigarettes, food packets, and mon-etary donations," all of which explained away after the war the remark, "I was a businessman!"[66]

Property confiscated from the inmates represented another source of profit for townsfolk living in the proximity of the camp. Such property provided a rich base of goods for exchange both within and outside the concentration camp. There was a brisk trade in such items as gold and silver watches, ladies' coats, soap, suits, manicure sets and the like. The SS used personal effects taken from the victims to aid in the acquisition of such valued items as cigarettes, bread, sausage, bacon, butter, or Schnaps. This entailed dealings with local farmers. Men in charge of outside work details, selected for their position on the basis of their "organizing" skills, acted as conduits. In this way goods confiscated from the inmates made its way into the hands of the townspeople. So great was this flow of property to the outside, that one inmate, who for several years worked as a prisoner in the camp Political Department, concluded that "by far the larger part of these things taken from the inmates wan-dered into the hands of the SS, and from them into the population."[67]

Just how active this trade was can be seen from the fact that "of twelve of the inmates employed in the Political Department, daily, or more correctly said, every hour during working time at least three were busy in the camp organizing something for one or another SS man."[68] Gold removed from the mouths of Jewish inmates was likely to make its way into circulation among the local residents. "If a Jew had gold teeth he survived the work hardly a day," noted Josef Herzler, a former inmate. "Where possible, these inmates were immediately beaten, robbed of their gold teeth, and the gold was probably bartered away with the farmers for highly valuable groceries."[69] Through such trade, outsiders profited from concentration camp contraband.

In spite of this commerce and the camp's proximity, residents who wished to do so found reasons to consider themselves decent and caring. Town officials mobilized them to do good in small ways, such as in the collection of clothing for the winter charity, the construction of toys for orphans at Christmas, the gathering of the harvest in the autumn, and the sweeping of snow from the town square in winter. Nature also provided opportunities to show concern for helpless creatures. Townspeople were prompted to construct little bird houses in summer, so that come winter the sparrows would remain, displaying for the citizenry their delightful play of wings and precious way of fighting one another at the feed trough.[70]

For some residents the war brought its small rewards, new hopes, and light diversions. In the shadow of the camp there was not only fear and silence, but love, care, music, and laughter. For those who sought diversion from oppressive thoughts, Nazi cultural organizations offered entertainment. In the town of Mauthausen during the war one could listen to piano recitals, go to the cinema, or hear a local comedian instigate "salvos of laughter," as the paper reported.[71] Often the SS band from the camp played at local party functions, but there were also visits from outside artists from Linz and Vienna—opera singers and ballet dancers—and lecturers arriving with pictures of exotic locales.[72] At such events townspeople gathered along with personnel serving the camp.

There was yet another bond uniting local citizens to the camp in a highly personal way. For some residents, the ties that joined them to the camp were those of love, or what could pass for it at such a time and in such a place. Not surprisingly, in wartime the well-dressed youths in their black uniforms attracted their share of local women. Although in Weimar the young women reportedly shunned the men from the Deathhead units from Buchenwald (prompting them to borrow other uniforms when they went into town to court the ladies) many of those in the region around

Mauthausen did not.[73] Indeed, some of these encounters between local women and SS men led to betrothal. In the autumn of 1943, for example, an SS man and a domestic servant, both residing in Mauthausen, exchanged marital vows.[74] That same year came the announcement that three SS sergeants had successively fathered two girls, Ursula and Anne-marie, and a boy, Wolfgang.[75]

This is not to say that the SS were known for their gentle courtships. Johann Kohout, police post commandant in Schwertberg, a popular town with the SS, just 5 miles down the road, noted the wild behavior of SS men from Mauthausen during their off-duty hours. They came to this neighboring community to relax following their activities in camp. In Schwertberg too, the young SS men found the ingredients necessary to satisfy their recreational lusts. Alcohol and women existed in sufficient measure to provide for their enjoyment.

> These SS were well represented in Schwertberg, since they came from the nearby Concentration Camp Mauthausen, and these people passed their time free from duty with drinking, womanizing and the roaring of their hit songs drunk with victory. These so-called camp SS needed a narcotic in order to remain strong. In the camp the blood and odor of corpses disturbed them. For this reason, they went to the neighboring locale where unfortunately there were women and girls who, especially in the period of "belt-tightening," waited for their gifts.[76]

The SS also gained access to private quarters in local residences where they were able to carry on intimate parties: "In Schwertberg and unfortunately also in farm houses there were hidden rooms where with wine, Schnaps, and pancakes one could find recovery from the exertions of the day with the female sex. But the 'brotherhood' could handle a lot; there were some among them with 20 liters of wine."[77] If these parties continued until very late and the time approached when they had to go back to work in the camp, they simply found a bicycle "and seated themselves by twos or even threes and rode to the camp, and threw it there in the vicinity in the road ditches. But there were various offensive acts. Intervention was impossible. This power no gendarme possessed. He would have drawn the animosity of all the superior authorities."[78]

While some local women did in fact go out with camp guards and participate in their parties, evidence also indicates that when women learned of the brutalities in which the SS were engaged these relationships were damaged. An incident which took place inside the camp during the final stage of the war illustrates that civilian women who came in contact with SS brutalization of the inmates sometimes courageously resisted the advances of even the officers. In order to free SS men for front line duty during 1943 and 1944 twelve civilian women from the area were enlisted into the camp and employed as secretaries. The women were assigned to the political department, where inmates were also routinely tortured. The SS men in the office naturally took advantage of the presence of the ladies to vie for their attention and favors. Gerhard Kanthack, an inmate clerk working in the office, noted that "from the moment of arrival of the women the SS members occupied themselves with courting" them.[79]

One of the women proved especially attractive, and became a coveted object pursued by several of the men in the bureau. "From the first day on began a downright competition for the favor of this girl. Obersturmführer Schulz tried it first with invitations to wine, coffee and cakes and the like, but obviously got nowhere. It went the same with all the previously mentioned SS members of the political department in so far as they equally competed for this girl; and with the many others from other departments who in the afternoons and mainly in the evenings after the conclusion of duty came to the political department solely and only because of this girl."[80]

In the face of her awareness of the tortures taking place there, however, she steadfastly refused their advances. "Right at the beginning when the women had arrived, an inmate whose screams of pain echoed through all the rooms was tortured as usual. The other women were pale, to some extent left the rooms, or otherwise gave expression to their agitation. The woman mentioned was utterly seized with a very strong fit of crying. When on top of this one of the SS men wanted to calm and console her, she hit him with her hand in the middle of the face."[81]

One local resident who felt compelled to record her memories of this time was Frau Anna Strasser, born in 1921, a lifelong resident of St. Valentin, a town just south of Mauthausen. Beginning on 15 April 1939, for the next 3 years she worked daily as bookkeeper at an agricultural cooperative beside the railway station in Mauthausen. From 15 April 1942 until September 1944, she also worked in the accounting bureau of the Nibelungenwerk, an armaments firm in St. Valentin that used inmates from the concentration camp. Frau Strasser's story resembles other accounts by women who witnessed the appearance of concentration camps in their home areas, and who as bystanders eventually confronted their horror.[82]

Anna Strasser came from a family that had been touched often by death. Her father's first wife died of tuberculosis. His second wife, Anna's mother, bore him 12 children, of whom she was the last. Before her birth in 1921, five of her siblings had died. Three other brothers were to die later, one at age 16 in 1927 of blood poisoning; another, an insurance agent, at age 38 in 1940; the third, a teacher, died at the same age of his wounds during his return from the Russian campaign. In February 1938 her father, Johann Strasser, an insurance representative, shop owner, and Christian-Socialist councilman in St. Valentin, was laid to rest.[83]

As an insurance representative during the Depression, Johann Strasser had a sympathetic eye for the impoverished citizenry whom he met on his travels. He and his colleagues worked the region between Enns and St. Pölten. Anna recalled him saying, "Mother, I cannot look on while these people work for such small wages, and then die. I will help, so that these people also have a more beautiful old age, and go into a home, where one cares for them."[84] It was this concern for the needy that he communicated to his youngest daughter, who also recalled from her childhood, that at Christmas time she and her schoolmates pooled the change they received for their allowance, and sacrificed their own sweets to purchase small gifts—biscuits, cough drops, and hand cloths—to distribute to the residents of the homes for the aged.[85]

Herr Strasser also exposed his family to persons of other political and religious backgrounds. "Our friends came from all political camps," Frau Strasser maintained. Her father had some Jewish acquaintances gained through his business dealings. She remembered a Herr Frinberg from Vienna who dealt in confectionary and cloth. He bought the largest wreath for Herr Strasser's funeral in February 1938. She also recalled a Jew, Herr Seidler, who had an undergarment factory in Vienna.[86]

In the shop where the family sold such items as pullovers, stockings, gloves, and the like, Anna Strasser learned the sales trade. She later studied for a year in Linz, where she was attending a trade course when the Nazis occupied Austria in March 1938. "I saw the enthusiasm of the people for Hitler, but also the sadness on the faces of my friends and their parents."[87]

In the winter of 1939, Anna Strasser was looking for work. She answered a newspaper advertisement offering a position in the *Lagerhausgenossenschaft,* an agricultural cooperative in the neighboring town of Mauthausen. She was accepted, and began work on 15 April 1939. Every day she rode the train, a short ride (about 10 minutes today) to Mauthausen. The cooperative bureau where she was employed lay "about 300 steps distant from the railway station."[88]

At the time of her arrival in Mauthausen she had already heard of the existence of the concentration camps. From the German soldiers who had occupied Austria the year before she had also heard of atrocities committed in such camps. Once in Mauthausen, she watched and listened, hoping to observe what she could of this curious facility. Almost immediately she began seeing evidence of the brutality and terror: "I kept eyes and ears open. Within the very first days of assuming my functions in Mauthausen I saw how one forced the prisoners out of the wagons at the railway station, and how then these unfortunate persons accompanied by the SS guard troop were driven into the camp. With the lightning-swift victories [of the German military] came an increase in these transports. In part, these persons were brought in passenger trains, and in part in cattle wagons." She noted how next to the station a ramp to facilitate the unloading of new arrivals was built by the inmates "under supervision of the SS."[89]

The Mauthausen agricultural cooperative not only bought and sold products to the local farmers, but also acted as a distributor of produce to the concentration camp. "Our cooperative had to supply the camp cabbage, potatoes, corn and beets, which we bought up from the farmers. The accounting was carried out by way of our office." In the course of her duties, Frau Strasser came into frequent contact with SS men from the camp who came in to pay the camp's bills. Whatever the guards were told about keeping silent concerning what went on in the camp, some obviously could not resist the temptation to speak of it. While going over the accounts, she noted, SS personnel casually spoke to her and her colleague of slaying the inmates. "One bragged: 'Today I killed another 2 inmates.' 'How did you do that?', I asked him. 'I chased both of them into a pit of liquid manure, threw a crate over them, and stood on top of it until they drowned.' "[90]

Sometimes SS men boasted of their own exploits, but only in a general way. In trying to impress the women, perhaps they also sought approval for their deeds. In any event, they spoke freely enough so that the townspeople heard from their own mouths details of their brutality. Among the boastful SS men, Frau Strasser in particular recalled one sergeant who attempted to win her favor by claiming to have participated in the attempted Nazi overthrow of the Austrian government in 1934. This young SS man cut an imposing, indeed frightening figure. He left a strong impression on her:

> For throughout perhaps half a year every third day this SS sergeant stood in a wide stance with his hands at his back, and a mocking look, on the street I had to cross in order to come to the restaurant where I took my

midday meal. I suffered deathly fear. After half a year he finally disappeared. He was probably transferred.[91]

There were other SS men who spoke, not with pride, but with anxiety about what they had experienced in the camp. Frau Strasser remembered one "very young" SS man who had come to the office to pay the camp bill. His distressed look caused her to ask him what was the matter. He told her of having witnessed an execution inside the camp. Frau Strasser wrote that she then told him to "place yourself in the service of God. In your position you have enough opportunity to help these unfortunate persons. He gave us his hand and left us with a sad look. We never saw him again. We often prayed for him."[92]

Frau Strasser noted that once, while dining in the nearby railway station restaurant, frequented by "railway employees, workers from the rock quarry, and SS people," an attractive SS man sat down at her table. She could not resist asking him, "how it is possible that persons are held in prisons and concentration camps without due process. He gave me no answer, but diverted the conversation in another direction." Yet her words left their effect upon him, for as she "took [her] walk after lunch," the young man came after her. " 'Do not be alarmed because I am following you. I would like to tell you that you should be more careful with your statements concerning the state of law and so forth. Such statements could also bring you to a place from which there is perhaps no return. I mean you well.' "[93]

Frau Strasser took her midday walks along the platform the inmates had constructed for the camp at the railway station. As she strolled she discreetly dropped various items such as bread, salt, sugar, thread, needles and buttons to be picked up by the inmates.

By this time, Anna Strasser had seen and heard enough to know some of the worst things occurring in Mauthausen. She had witnessed the arrivals of victims at the station, and she had heard the words of individual SS men who had worked in the camp. She knew, quite simply, that all this was a violation of the most basic standards of law and humane treatment. She had already begun in a small way, secretly, to make useful items available to the inmates. She was cautious about revealing to others what she had learned. "With the exception of my dear colleague Annemarie[94] I could speak with no one about these experiences. For nights I did not sleep."[95]

In the fall of 1940 her superior at the agricultural cooperative, Franz Winklehner, was arrested. This episode brought her face to face with the brutality of life and death in the concentration camps. Herr Winklehner, whose work-place was directly opposite the loading ramp at the railway station, occasionally threw bread and cigarettes to the passing inmates. "One day he was observed by an SS man. Herr Winklehner went home to eat lunch. He lived with his family in the same house where we had our office. When he sat down to lunch, there was a knock at the door. Two men took him with them and brought him to the Gestapo in Linz. There he was held five days, and following that was brought to Dachau."[96]

Herr Winklehner's wife first received word of his condition on 26 February 1941. That morning a letter arrived saying that he expected to be freed during an amnesty on Hitler's birthday. Later that same day, however, a telegram arrived bearing crushing news: "Herr Winklehner dead. Body to be viewed within 24 hours. An emotional scene followed. When I knocked on the door, she opened and looked at me, in a questioning and at the same time knowing way. I did not say a word. She took the picture of her husband from the wall, looked at it for a long time and went around with it like a mad person. It looked as if she had lost her reason. I took her in my arms, caressed her, and said: Cry, Frau Winklehner! She threw herself on the bed and screamed and screamed, until finally the tears came."[97]

Together with a friend from St. Valentin, a man named Kern, she and Frau Winklehner drove to Dachau to see the body. Her account of viewing the body of Herr Winklehner resembles similar macabre and equally disturbing encounters experienced by relatives who came to Mauthausen:

> The next morning at six o'clock we were at the camp gate and begged admittance. Our identification was taken, then we were locked in a waiting room. From there we saw the inmates fall in for morning roll call. Later we saw how they marched out to work. We had to wait four hours. We went across the roll call plaza to a tiny house. The door was opened. On a pedestal stood a coffin; Herr Winklehner, embedded in sawdust and with his mouth open, lay inside. Frau Winklehner wanted to caress him. 'Hands off!' screamed the SS man. Herr Kern asked what he died of. 'Disturbances of the circulation—visit ended,' came the short and concise reply.[98]

In 1942 Anna Strasser was ordered to work in the accounting bureau of the Nibelungenwerk in St. Valentin where Panzers were produced by the Steyr corporation, using inmate labor. Here she felt at ease with her new boss, a "jovial" man as she described him, and with her colleagues. Yet she found the physical design of the accounting department office as well as the working hours a source of discomfort. The work schedule was rigorous, often without let-up even on weekends. "Once we worked 13 complete Saturdays and Sundays. These glass offices were unbearably hot in the summer. One absolutely lost one's wits."[99]

Still, it was not the heat and long hours alone that caused her discomfort. From the windows on one side of her office she "saw that the inmates were beaten to death. I simply could no longer endure this great burden. So one day I broke down. I cried and cried. For many weeks I was registered sick."[100]

She explained to the doctor that, in her weakened condition, her nerves suffered. He allowed her to undertake a reduced work schedule, dividing her working day between her family's shop and the factory bureau.[101]

Even at home, in the center of the town of St. Valentin, the misery of the captives was inescapably evident. Frau Strasser remembers that Windberg, a small camp for Hungarian Jews, lay beyond the cemetery. The inmates passed by her family shop on their way to work. "Every day these poor persons were driven by our shop. They had to build bunkers on the sports ground that lay behind our garden. A terrible burden for these persons, because for the most part they were not accustomed to such labor." A doctor among them was able to take advantage of their passing through the town to pass her notes requesting various medicines. She in turn approached a physician in St. Valentin for prescriptions for these items. Her approach was not without some risk, for this physician was a party member. "I told him quite clearly what I needed the prescriptions for. He wrote the prescriptions to my name."[102]

With these signed prescriptions she traveled to various pharmacies in the surrounding cities and towns of Enns, St. Valentin, Haag, Linz, Steyr, and Mauthausen. She did receive a suspicious look from one Mauthausen pharmacist, but like the others he too filled the prescription.[103] At night she crept across an open field beyond the cemetery and hid the medicines in an agreed location. "Sometimes I was frightened to death when the dogs began to bark. But I was always lucky."[104]

By 1941 the camp had undergone enormous expansion, progressing a long way toward overshadowing the town beside which it had developed. The camp had acquired land, and marked out its zone of control in and above as well as beyond the quarry. Its portal towers, main barracks, walls, and perimeter were complete. By 25 May 1940 a branch camp had been established in nearby Gusen. On 31 December the combined complex officially held some 8,200 inmates; during that same year 3,846 inmates died.[105] The camp's activities in sensitive areas were visible to the citizenry. The inmates were exposed to public view at the ferry launch, at work sites, and at the railway station. Those who complained or showed sympathy for the prisoners were subject to arrest. The SS ruled numerous spaces both public and private: taverns and farm houses offered shelter for the release of their aggressions and desires. Initial tensions between the camp and local officials were resolved in the camp's favor. Other difficulties dissolved into a form of accommodation: whatever strains had existed between the district governor and the commandant had been reduced sufficiently for the governor to be invited to lavish, annual year-end parties held in SS quarters inside the camp.[106] Local businesses and individuals had forged commercial bonds with the camp. No fence could have made the camp entirely autonomous from its neighbors. From the beginning the camp enclosure was incomplete and penetrable. The camp and the town were enmeshed in such numerous ways that the killings in and around the camp were never a secret to the population.

In May and June 1941 some 659 Dutch Jews arrived in Mauthausen on three transports.[107] The largest shipment consisted of 348 Dutch Jews who had been seized in the wake of demonstrations and a general strike in Amsterdam in February 1941. They arrived from Buchenwald on June 17, and on the following morning "50 of the newly arrived Jews were chased from the bathhouse naked and driven into the electrified fence." Most of the remainder perished in the Vienna Ditch.

> The second day after their arrival, the Jews where [sic] shunted into the quarry. There were [186] steps leading down to the bottom of the pit, but they were not permitted to use these. They had to slide down the lose stones at the side, and even here many died or were severely injured. The survivors then had to shoulder hods, and two prisoners were compelled to load each Jew with an excessively heavy rock. The Jews then had to run up the [186] steps. In some instances the rocks immediately rolled downhill, crushing the feet of those that came behind. Every Jew who lost his rock in this fashion was brutally beaten and the rock was hoisted to his shoulders again. Many of the Jews were driven to despair the very first day and committed suicide by jumping into the pit. On the third day the SS opened the so-called "death-gate" and with a fearful barrage of blows drove the Jews across the guard line, the guards on the watchtowers

shooting them down in heaps with their machine guns. The next day the Jews no longer jumped into the pit individually. They joined hands and one man would pull nine or twelve of his comrades over the lip with him into a gruesome death. The barracks was "cleared" of Jews, not in six but in barely three weeks. Every one of the [348] prisoners perished by suicide or by shooting, beating, and other forms of torture.[108]

Still others had their skulls smashed in by the guards. "I could never have imagined a scene so terrible," noted one observer. "The pick handles beat on the heads, the bones of which, in cracking, resounded like drums. Brains spurted out, blood flowed. The Jews, distracted with horror, worked with all their strength, thinking their zeal would save them from the blows . . . It was useless."[109]

While all this was going on, others were witness: "the civilian employees at the Mauthausen quarry requested that these suicides by jumping be stopped, since the fragments of flesh and brains clinging to the rocks afforded too gruesome a sight. The quarry was thereupon hosed down and prisoners were posted to prevent men from jumping. The survivors were simply clubbed across the guard line to their death. When new batches of Jewish prisoners arrived, the SS had its fun by dubbing them 'parachute troops.' "[110]

Seeing the Jews in the quarry was one thing; interpreting their fate was another. Forty-two years later, an SS man who saw them enter the camp preferred to believe the Jews leapt to their deaths because they were unable to handle the demands of difficult labor. "One fine day they jumped into the quarry down there near the *Todestiege*. They weren't pushed down. That they were pushed is a fairy tale," he insisted. "They grabbed one another by the hands. It's perfectly clear: [they] hadn't done hard work in [their] whole lives. They had to carry stones from the quarry to the camp. A couple of times they managed it, but then they became desperate. They knew they would never return home. They seized one another by the hand—five, six or ten of them. The first one leapt and pulled the others with him over the wall of the cliff."[111] *Landrat* Brachmann was also in the camp during the arrival of the Jews from Holland. "A short while afterward," he asked commandant Ziereis "how the Dutch Jews have adapted to the work process." Apparently having nothing to hide, the commandant casually remarked, "Ah, hardly a one is still alive."[112]

Townspeople must have sensed the fate awaiting these new arrivals. One Mauthausen resident spoke of having seen a group of Dutch Jews walking with their belongings from the railway station to the camp. She says she implored them to drop their belongings and spare themselves the burden that, as she knew, would be taken from them when they reached the camp. "The Dutch Jews, they were beautifully dressed, with suitcases. And I had just gone to pick up the milk," she recalled, noticing one of them struggling with his luggage. "And I said how far it still is to the camp. . . . I said, 'let it drop, they will take everything away from you anyway.' " But an SS man saw her, and shouted a common threat: "What's the matter there! What's the matter there! You can come right along!" Her voice dropping to a whisper, she explained that despite her plea, the Jews were unable to let go of their baggage. "No. They weren't able to. Couldn't do a thing."[113]

More often, people who observed what was happening did so guardedly, silently. Passing through the town, an inmate saw a woman who watched them make the sign of the cross. "Does she take us for demons?", he asked himself, but then, near a convent he noticed a nun who repeated the gesture: "her look was full of pity."[114] Secure within their apartments, from behind curtains drawn back to afford a glimpse, townspeople peered at columns arriving at night. Seeing the quarry for the first time "illuminated to ghastly effect in the pale moonlight," one inmate "sensed that on this site tragedies of unimaginable nature should play themselves out."[115]

The quarry had claimed new victims. Many more would follow. This cavity had been and would remain the center of destruction in Mauthausen. But not all of Mauthausen's victims would perish in the quarry. The camp was growing, and new methods of extermination were being devised to accommodate an expanding inmate population. In the process ever more civilians would be called upon to lend a hand. Many would not only be observers, but direct participants in the killing.

Chapter 3

The Castle

In August 1941, the first group of inmates from Mauthausen was shipped 18.6 miles to the west to a castle known as Hartheim. Until then death for the inmates of Mauthausen occurred mostly in the open air: chased and driven to despair, they dropped into the quarry, or charged the electrified wire. A burst of gunfire from the tower fatally ripped into members of work details. Applying raw muscle to the task, overseers wielded pick-handles and shattered the skulls of many victims. In Hartheim a new technique brought the killing indoors: a gas chamber was situated on the ground floor. Inside the chamber was a vaulted ceiling of concrete and walls smoothed with tile. Gasket-lined steel doors closed off victims from the outside. Space was narrowed to a minimum; corners were squared. Death, invisible and gaseous, poured through a pipe from above.

In the chamber victims did not plummet through the air to their deaths. Instead, the air was stolen from them. Carbon monoxide filled their lungs. The lethal compound invaded the blood stream, fused with life-sustaining hemoglobin, and blocked the flow of oxygen. Asphyxia resulted. The process worked invisibly. While the gas circulated not a hand was laid upon the victims.

Only after the gassing was completed and the chamber had been cleaned of the lethal fumes, did a team of crematory attendants, operating in two-man shifts, enter and grope among the victims. They pried the corpses loose, and dragged them along water-splashed red tiles into an adjacent mortuary, where they stacked them in preparation for burning. In this ghoulish workshop they wrenched open the mouths of the dead and ripped the gold from their teeth. Then, shoved into the waiting oven, the victims were stripped of their earthly forms and reduced to soot. After the fires cooled, left-over parts were ground in an electric mill.

The crematory assistants were few in number. They endured the sight and touch and smell of human destruction, but they did not work unassisted. In order for the victims to reach the chamber and the oven, a staff of many dozens were pressed into service. This cadre of assistants, drawn in large part from the surrounding population, attended to the myriad tasks of supporting the killing apparatus. They busied themselves in selecting the victims; moving them to the killing center; collecting their clothes, inspecting their teeth for gold; and photographing them to record the parting images of their lives. While most of the assistants did not touch, nor even see the victims at the moment of their death, the staff worked and ate and slept in the same building in which the gas chamber was housed. Their conscientious fulfillment of assigned tasks insured the delivery of the victims into the chamber.

The talents needed to accomplish the tasks were unexceptional. Doctors, nurses, plumbers, bus drivers, office workers, and switchboard operators formed the backbone of the operation. The pool of available talent was large, and readily available in the vicinity of the killing center. At the appointed time, many hands were at the ready, the engines of buses were running; the carbon monoxide containers full, and the gas was waiting to flow.

As pure and undetectable as was the lethal gas, the human body could not be destroyed without leaving a telltale trace. As the bodies burned the odor of burning flesh filled the castle and wafted over the surrounding community. Efforts were made to seal the evidence. Staff members were sworn to silence. Residents living nearby secured their windows at night to prevent the seepage into their homes of the odor of burning. Yet, though lips were sealed, doors and windows shut tight, the traces of murder filled the air.

One reaches Castle Hartheim via the local commuter railway traveling westward from Linz. Stopping first in Leonding, Adolf Hitler's boyhood home, for the next thirty minutes the train makes its way through the rural landscape of Upper Austria. Disembarking at the station in Alkoven, the traveler best approaches the castle on foot along a country road bordered by broad fields. For a time the castle, so visible from a distance as an enormous presence, is blocked from view by a cluster of efficient houses and lanes. At the end of the road the castle reemerges suddenly. Its yellow walls, worn and crumbling, reveal neglect. Directly in their shadow stands a small, modern supermarket.

Today Castle Hartheim provides residential quarters for young families and pensioners. On the inside, the castle reveals a magnificent but decaying Renaissance arcade. In one corner of the arcade a heavy, black door opens onto a wide room with a vaulted ceiling. On the walls are memorial plaques, flowers and enamel portraits of persons who vanished here. This room adjoins another, rather smaller empty chamber whose fixtures reveal its earlier function as a human gas chamber.

Were it not for what lies beyond the black door, one would find it hard to imagine that this noble structure was, for a time, a site of mass murder. Yet, it was here that the technique of assembly line massacre employed in the death camps of Poland and Silesia was perfected. Between 1940 and 1945, some 30,000 human beings—mentally ill, crippled, sick, as well as many in normal health—were brought to Castle Hartheim from homes throughout Greater Germany and the concentration camps of Mauthausen, Gusen, and Dachau, and murdered.[1]

In the autumn of 1939 plans were put in operation to carry out the killing of the infirm and mentally ill under care in hospitals and nursing homes in Germany. Under the pretext of "euthanasia," or "mercy death," persons who were retarded, mentally handicapped, epileptic, or who suffered from a range of serious mental and physical illnesses, were systematically selected for death. The killing project was organized inside the Führer Chancellery in Berlin and given the code name "T4," a designation derived from the operation's headquarters at Tiergartenstrasse 4 in Berlin-Charlottenburg. Under the guidance of Philip Bouhler, director of the Führer Chancellery, his deputy, Viktor Brack, and Hitler's personal physician, Dr. Karl Brandt, a medical commission, a transportation firm, and a financial organization were established to carry out the selection and removal of patients from hospitals and institutes to six killing centers inside the Reich. One of the six was Castle Hartheim, which had to be renovated for the job. Determination of the right of thousands of patients to live or die was left to the medical commission, and it selected patients for killing on the basis of questionnaires sent to the various institutions where the patients were being treated. Those chosen were ordered moved to the killing installations in buses and trains. In an effort to disguise the trail leading to the killing centers, patients awaiting death were often removed temporarily to other hospitals before shipment to their deaths.[2]

Castle Hartheim's renovation, including the installation of a gas chamber, was completed by the middle of May 1940, and that spring for the first time the gassing of patients took place there.[3] The killing of patients under the T4 program continued at Hartheim until August ✳ 1941, at which time the so-called euthanasia killings were officially halted following mounting protests from the public and from leaders of the church.[4] By then, the euthanasia program had resulted in the deaths of more than 70,000 persons, including an estimated 18,000 at Hartheim alone.[5] However, this official halt to euthanasia operations did not signal the end to killings in the castle; rather a new set of victims was selected.[6]

By the summer of 1941 Heinrich Himmler had set in motion plans to use the euthanasia centers also for the killing of sick and weakened concentration camp inmates. Accordingly, the T4 organization sent its representatives into the camps to assist in the selection of victims. After Hartheim's director, Dr. Rudolf Lonauer, and the Mauthausen camp commandant, Franz Ziereis, had met and made the necessary arrangements, beginning in August 1941 inmates from the concentration camps of Mauthausen and Gusen were driven to Hartheim where they were gassed and cremated. At first, inmates from Mauthausen were chosen by the camp physicians in conjunction with Dr. Lonauer and his colleague from Hartheim, Dr. Georg Renno, and commandant Ziereis. In the winter of 1941–42 a medical commission from the euthanasia organization carried out these selections, after which the selections were again conducted by camp doctors.[7] Transports from Mauthausen and its sister camp at Gusen occurred in two phases, the first lasting from August 1941 until February 1942, and the second from April to December 1944. During these two periods at least 4,608 inmates from the two camps were killed in Hartheim.[8]

Prior to 1898 Castle Hartheim had served as a home for handicapped youngsters. The institution was maintained under the caring supervision of nuns from the order of Merciful Sisters.[9] When the Nazi authorities comfiscated the castle in 1939, the 200 children, 20 sisters, and additional staff living there were removed in advance of the arrival of workers who came to remodel the structure for the creation of a death center. Frau Aloisia Ehrengruber, an employee who was able to stay behind, witnessed the castle's transformation. She recalled that after the Nazis took power several officials made repeated visits and "very precisely inspected the premises." She remembered too that "the lads came to Niedernhart [today the Wagner-Jauregg hospital], the girls to Baumgartenberg; later a portion resettled in Engelszell with the sisters."[10]

The move was to be temporary. In May or June of 1940, when Hartheim began operating as a killing center, the children were brought

back to the castle to die.[11] One of the town residents who saw the
children's tragic return was Karl S. Born in 1921, growing up in a house
just outside the castle entrance, Herr S. knew many of the youngsters
from the home. To them his was a familiar and welcome face. Every
Sunday he appeared at the castle to participate as an altar boy in a mass
held inside its chapel. Looking back, he remembers how after he rang a
bell one of the nurses would come to let him in. Some of the children
would see him coming and joyously greet his arrival: "Oh yes, S., S. is
here!," he heard them say. For Karl S., too, these visits were always
special occasions. After mass they would serve coffee from a big pot and
either cake sprinkled with almonds or bread covered with honey and
butter, a rare treat he well appreciated because his own family was obliged
to sell what butter they had.[12]

At harvest time some of the stronger youths were lent out as laborers, helping with the threshing of the wheat. "They weren't all, let's
say, completely insane," S. said. "It was quite variable, as it is today in
the home for the handicapped: there are some who are just not there,
and others who can still work." He remembers as well that up on the
third story of the castle the patients had a workshop. Every year at
Christmas time they displayed their creations. "What they accomplished
at that time was unique."[13]

Living so close to the castle, S. was ideally placed to witness not
only the unfortunate return of the youngsters, but a number of suspicious
events. Writing in 1969 in a letter to the chairman of a euthanasia trial,
S. noted:

> the house of my parents was one of the few houses in Hartheim from which
> one could observe several occurrences. After Castle Hartheim was cleared
> of its inhabitants (around 180 to 200 patients) in the year 1939, myste-
> rious renovations began which, to an outsider, however, one could hardly
> divine, since no indigenous labor was used for it, and the approaches to
> the castle were hermetically sealed. Following completion of the renova-
> tion work, we saw the first transports come and we could even recognize
> some of the earlier residents who showed joy at returning to their former
> home. We could observe this so well because the barn from which we
> made our observations lay directly opposite the big entry gate before which
> the buses had to wait until upon the ringing of a bell the door was opened
> and the vehicle could drive into the courtyard.[14]

Both S. and his sister, Maria, watched the buses as they approached.
The hog barn in which they observed these goings on provided a well
situated, secure lookout. "From the window to the bus it was perhaps *at*

the most 33 feet to the bus, and to the gate another 33 feet," Herr S. declared. "And by the back window there, there one could always look. That was a bit hidden. Practically speaking, no one could see *us*. Besides, we didn't show ourselves openly."[15] His sister, Maria, also remembered watching the buses from a crack in the barn door. She saw victims looking out the windows, on occasion brushing back the curtains. She recognized the handicapped by their facial expressions, and stated that sometimes there were large suitcases on top of the vehicles.[16] Another resident whose farm lay just over 650 yards from the castle similarly recalled a bus rider who pulled back the curtain to wave.[17]

Even more suspiciously, the arrival of the buses at the castle was routinely followed by an unmistakable discharge of loathsome fumes into the atmosphere. "At the beginning, transports (mostly two to three buses) often came as frequently as twice daily, and it never lasted long before enormous black clouds of smoke streamed out of a certain chimney and spread a penetrating stench," Herr S. wrote. "This stench was so disgusting that sometimes when we returned home from work in the fields we couldn't hold down a single bite."[18]

Karl S. and his sister were by no means alone in viewing the buses, arriving full and leaving the castle empty, or in sensing the telltale smoke. Additional residents, as well as foreign laborers working on a nearby farm, testified to having seen the passing buses bearing their living cargo to the castle and remembered the awful smoke.[19]

Also recalling the unbearable smoke was sister Felicitas, a former employee of the home who learned of the burnings from relatives:

> My brother Michael, who at the time was at home, came to me very quickly and confidentially informed me that in the castle the former patients were burned. The frightful facts which the people of the vicinity had to experience at first hand, and the terrible stench of the burning gases, robbed them of speech.[20] The people suffered dreadfully from the stench. My own father collapsed unconscious several times, since in the night he had forgotten to seal up the windows completely tight.[21]

Josef Jungwirth, who throughout the war worked a farm some 440 yards distant from the castle, said as well that "in bad weather there was such an unpleasant odor throughout the area that one couldn't open the windows at all. Now and then thick plumes of smoke hovered above the castle."[22]

It was not just the smoke and the stench that drew the attention of bystanders. At times human remains littered parts of the vicinity. In the words of sister Felicitas, "when there was intense activity, it smoked day and night. Tufts of hair flew through the chimney onto the street. The remains of bones were stored on the east side of the castle and in ton trucks driven first to the Danube, later also to the Traun."[23] Karl S. reported that some persons hid themselves in the woods, emerging after the trucks departed to examine the remains left at the dumping site: "The so-called 'ash wagon,' a closed delivery van, drove almost daily in the direction of the Danube into which the ashes and other cremation residue were thrown. There were people who secretly hid themselves in the Auwald next to the Danube and saw this macabre activity. Then, when the vehicle had left, they took a look and found remains of bone that were recognized incontestably as human bones."[24] When such pieces of unground bone fell from trucks taking the ashes to the river, residents are said to have collected these remains and built "little piles" of them along the roadside to signal to the murderers their awareness of the crime.[25] A Polish laborer working on one of the nearby farms also remembered how late in the war he was summoned to help collect and disperse the remains: "In 1944, on the instruction of the farmer, I had to cart away with the vehicle ashes which lay in a heap and bestrew the paths behind the farm buildings. . . . There was quite a large quantity of these ashes, [requiring] a whole vehicle, with which we otherwise drove the manure."[26]

Evidence of the horrors occurring in Castle Hartheim began accumulating so fast that only two weeks after the burnings began the castle authorities had to call the local citizenry to an explanatory assembly in the "Trauner" tavern. The immediate cause was the spread of an accurate "rumor" concerning the cremation facilities by a mason named Sterrer who had worked in the castle. The mason had made known what others suspected: people were being killed in the castle. The meeting, to which all the local citizens had been "invited," was conducted by a uniformed man who was the castle's notorious director, SS captain Christian Wirth.[27]

Wirth represented the residents with an official explanation of what he hoped they would believe was the cause of the smoke. He told them that the burnings were the result of the disposal of assorted ecclesiastical items. "At the time he maintained that in the castle shoes and images of saints were burned," stated a woman farmer, Maria Meindl.[28] Two other farmers who, like Frau Meindl, worked the land near the castle, also recalled the speaker insisting that all that was burned were "vestments" and "belongings."[29] Karl S., however, remembered the speaker offering yet another explanation for the mysterious, dark vapor rising from the castle: "Referring to the strong smoke and the stench, the speaker had the following version ready: in Castle Hartheim a device had been installed in which old oil and oil by-products underwent a special treatment through distillation and chemical treatment in order to gain a water-clear, oily fluid from it which was of greatest importance for the U-boats."[30]

On pain of severe punishment the residents were warned to halt all rumors contradicting the official explanations. "At the conclusion of this explanatory speech," Herr S. reported, "the threat was made that everyone who further spread these absurd rumors of burning persons would have to reckon with the death penalty or, at the least, with being sent to a concentration camp." Wirth stressed that this applied to anyone who might spread such a rumor, "near or far."[31] His threat to banish them to a concentration camp echoed in the memory of Frau Meindl: "He would send to Mauthausen those who said a word about it."[32]

The killing operation in Castle Hartheim was a uniform procedure requiring a labor force of skilled and semi-skilled persons, approximately 70 in all, to carry out specialized, compartmentalized tasks.[33] In addition to physicians who directed the operation, mechanics were needed to remodel the castle, to install the fittings and fixtures necessary for construction of the gas chamber, and to prepare storage areas and ovens for the disposal of victims. Mechanics were also employed to keep the physical plant in smooth operation. Bus drivers drove and maintained the vehicles used to transport victims from pick-up points at the main railway station in Linz and from mental homes throughout Austria. A team of secretaries staffed a bureau whose task it was fill out correspondence with the euthanasia program's central offices in Berlin, with cemetery officials to arrange for disposal of the remains, and with next-of-kin to inform them of the death of loved ones. Nurses assisted on transports, helping patients onto the buses. On arrival at Hartheim they unloaded the patients and guided them into the castle where they undressed them for inspection by the doctors. A police officer, as superintendent in charge of castle security, oversaw the medical certificates, identity papers, and personal effects of the victims. A photographer photographed and catalogued victims. The photos were then sent by courier to Berlin. Porters were also required to man the castle entries and work the switchboard. Finally, those whose tasks seemed most odious of all were the crematory attendants, known as the "burners," who lifted and disposed of the corpses, sifted the ashes, and poured them into urns.

At the top of the staff hierarchy stood the doctors. According to those who knew him as a colleague and physician, Dr. Georg Renno was a responsible professional, conscientious in the performance of his duties, who displayed warm concern and gentleness toward his trusting patients. "Herr Dr. Renno was always a friendly, humane doctor," remarked one woman who had worked with him during the 1930s in a psychiatric clinic in Leipzig-Dösen. The wife of a patient whom Dr. Renno treated for melancholia described Dr. Renno as a man of worthy character whom one would never dream capable of assisting in the killing of thousands of fellow human beings: "I always experienced him only as a friendly, quiet, and well-balanced person to whom domesticity, family, and profession, as well as his flute playing and music in general, mattered above all. I never heard from his mouth a derogatory word about the mentally ill."[34]

In 1940, at the age of 33, Dr. Renno was recruited for the euthanasia program. In principle, Renno had no objection to so-called mercy killing. "At the time I viewed euthanasia as a blessing for the patients," he noted decades later. "The notion that a state could pass a law that was illegal was beyond my conception, particularly since people of station and name accepted the euthanasia program." He saw his role as one of seeing to it that the program was carried out under the strictest possible controls. "In other respects I believed that the cooperation of a doctor was necessary for the orderly execution of the *procedure* [and] for the avoidance of mistakes."[35]

Dr. Renno had joined the Nazi party in 1930; he became a member of the SS a year later and played the flute in an SS band. Apart from his party affiliations, he did not show much interest in politics. Yet his party membership and acceptance of so-called mercy killing undoubtedly brought him to the attention of the directors of the killing project. Dr. Hermann Nitsche, his superior at the Leipzig clinic who also served the killing program as a chief medical examiner, promoted his candidacy.

Dr. Renno was a man who set store by income, title, and security. He had sought his position at the psychiatric clinic in Dösen, a job he assumed in November 1933, not because of "excessive interest in psychiatry . . . but rather because I found a secure government position opportune."[36] The same primary considerations led him to express to Viktor Brack a reluctance to abandon his position at the Leipzig clinic to assume responsibilities under the euthanasia program, as ordered by the Interior Military. Brack curtly pointed out that he was "ultimately, a government official and must submit."[37] Ever mindful of his professional standing, when Dr. Werner Heyde, another of the medical examiners, informed him "the euthanasia would be carried out with the help of carbon monoxide gas," Renno replied that he "had not studied medicine in order to turn on the gas spigot." Heyde reportedly assured him "he was solely interested in having a doctor skilled in psychiatry" on the scene in Linz to confirm the judgments of the medical commission in the presence of the patients scheduled for shipment to Hartheim.[38] Under investigation two decades later, Dr. Renno would deny having turned the spigot, although he admitted having checked to make sure the door to the gas chamber was tightly sealed and that the attendants, "primitive" types as he termed them, allowed the gas to flow long enough to kill all the patients. "Turning the spigot was no great matter," he noted. "Detailed instructions were unnecessary."[39]

Renno was in Hartheim from May 1940 until August 1941, and then again from the summer of 1943. He was at Hartheim when, commencing in April 1944, the second wave of inmates from Mauthausen were killed at Hartheim. Reno disingenuously claimed, however, that although he lived in the castle at the time, and played his flute there, he was unaware of the killing of inmates.[40]

Dr. Renno also worked closely with Hartheim's director, Dr. Rudolf Lonauer. Lonauer, the same age as Renno, was a member of the SS, attaining the rank of SS-Obersturmbannführer in September 1938. He was born in Linz, had a psychiatric practice in the city, and was also in charge of Linz's Niedernhart hospital, which served as a holding station for persons scheduled for destruction in Hartheim. At the hospital he also administered lethal medications. Rudolf Lonauer committed suicide on 5 May 1945.[41]

Lonauer and Renno arranged the transport of patients to Hartheim, and carried out their final inspection before they were led into the gas chamber. In August 1941, they also assisted commandant Ziereis and SS physicians in Mauthausen in the selection of the first inmates to be shipped to Hartheim.[42] Neither Lonauer nor Renno were strangers to Mauthausen. On one occasion, Dr. Renno took advantage of a visit to the concentration camp to have his hair cut by an inmate barber just before he and other Hartheim staffers attended a party held in the officers' club room.[43]

The *Gau*, or Nazi administrative district, directorate in Linz carried out the selection of rank-and-file employees. The chief officers in charge of the selection process were *Gau* inspector Stefan Schachermayr, a highly decorated party veteran, and his successor, Franz Peterseil. It was the *Gau* inspector's job to screen potential candidates for employment from lists his superior, *Gauleiter* Eigruber, supplied. He was told to weed out any persons with a criminal record.[44] Employees needed to have no special training or qualifications to work in Hartheim. However, their selection was not haphazard. The inspectorate sought local Nazi party members, many of whom had personal connections to leading figures from Upper Austria and who could be assumed to be dependable. Job openings were often discovered through word of mouth among party leaders and their acquaintances or relations. With personnel decisions centered in Linz, the operation in Hartheim took on a distinctly local cast.

Many of the persons employed in Castle Hartheim, initially unaware of their future involvement in a killing operation, did actively seek their positions. In so doing they exploited connections with staff members already working in party bureaus. This seems to have been common among the castle secretaries. In 1940 Margit Troller, whose mother worked at the district directorate, was a seventeen year-old employee of an insurance firm in Linz. She remarked that "for some time" she had wished to leave the city. One day that summer she found her opportunity. She stated that "through someone I learned that the *Gau* inspector, Schachermayr, needed someone for an outlying post." In August 1940 she approached Schachermayr and asked for such a job. "Schachermayr agreed that in a few days I would receive a position, but that I should be ready to travel immediately." Gertraud Dirnberger similarly noted that "a Frau Lehner from the district directorate with whom I was acquainted arranged it for me." Later, Frau Dirnberger claimed she had reproached this acquaintance who yet denied knowing what was going on in Hartheim. Helene Hintersteiner, then a thirty year-old bookkeeper for a baking powder company in Linz, noted that Gustav Adolf Kaufmann from the Führer chancellery recruited her with the promise of an administrative job in Hartheim. Kaufmann was an acquaintance whom she had met before 1938 through her brother, an SA-Sturmführer.[45]

Two other secretaries arrived at their positions because of their acquaintance with the Gau inspector. Elisabeth Lego noted that "Schachermayr, who knew me from before, said that reliable personnel were sought for the vicinity of Linz, and promised me favorable conditions." Karoline Burner mentioned that she got her job in a similar way. "I came to Hartheim by way of Schachermayr, whom I knew from earlier. At that time I was a party member and hoped to earn more than previously."[46]

This pattern of acquaintance and contact was quite common in the recruitment of personnel for the euthanasia program. Dieter Allers, a lawyer who worked in the program's main Berlin office, got his post after his mother met Warner Blankenburg, a top deputy in the Führer Chancellery, "in the street." Allers concluded: "I was always of the opinion that most people got in through connections. They would hear of the job as being 'attached to the Führer Chancellery' and that sounded good.

Then of course these jobs carried extra pay; and it meant not having to go to the front."[47] Herr Allers' wife also served in the program, working in Berlin and, for six weeks, in Hartheim as well. She agreed with her husband's opinion, and cited her own recruitment as confirmation: "I was working in a fashion boutique and I was desperate to do something more useful for my country. A friend told me she thought she might be able to help me get into the Führer Chancellery where she was working as a secretary. 'Secret work,' she said. Well, that sounded very exciting, so I went. And got in. I had no idea what it was until I was in there."[48]

✓The promise of a good income was surely a lure. In 1939 Vinzenz Nohel was a low-paid, skilled mechanic earning only 100 marks a month, barely enough to sustain his family. In need of higher paying work, he turned to his brother, an SA-Brigadeführer who had recently returned to Linz. His brother arranged for him to have an interview with party leaders in Linz. When he appeared before them, they laughed when he told them how little he was making. He and several others were then informed that they would be posted to Hartheim, and were sworn to secrecy. Beginning work on 2 April 1940, Nohel's salary jumped to 170 marks per month, plus room and board. He also received a 35-mark monthly allowance for service as a crematory attendant.[49]

Nohel became something of an expert in the field of human disposal. As he recalled, the procedure was as follows. After being led into the reception room, the victims were cursorily inspected by the doctor and 3 or 4 assistants. Victims were individually stamped with a 1.2 inch registration number, led into a studio where their pictures were taken, and returned to the reception room. With all the victims stamped, photographed, and a mark placed on their backs to indicate the presence of gold teeth, they were led into the gas chamber which lay adjacent to the reception room. They entered the chamber through a steel door. The chamber contained 3 shower heads. (The floor, at first covered with wood, was later cemented.) Walls and ceiling were covered with oil, and in time tiles were added. Another door, which was walled-in, faced the hallway. This door was outfitted with a spy hole through which observers could follow what was happening inside the chamber. Another steel door led to a room containing carbon monoxide flasks connected to a steel pipe by means of a rubber funnel. When a doctor turned on the gas, it flowed from the bottle into a .6–.8 inch iron pipe leading to the chamber. The gassing was over in a short time, he noted, but the ventilation of the chamber took another 1½ hours.[50]

Serving as part of a four-man team[51] operating on alternating 12-hour shifts, the attendants dragged the dead from the gas chamber to an adjoining room where they were stacked, awaiting disposal in the coal-fired oven. The dead were then lifted from the mortuary, slid into a nearby oven, and roasted 2 to 8 at a time. "The work continued, as needed, day and night."[52]

After the war Nohel would speak to investigators about the paving best suited for dragging a body. He discovered that for this purpose a cement floor was somewhat better than wood; tiles sloshed with water were best of all. He learned that women burned better than men: lighter skeletons and greater fat accelerated incineration. He knew what it took to put one's hand inside the cavity of a dead man's mouth; a ghoulish prospector, his fingers had probed the oral cavity for fillings of gold. He discovered that the extraction of the fillings was extremely difficult for one such as he who lacked sensation in one hand, and he was therefore excused from this task. Still, Nohel touched the dead; he knew the heft of a corpse; he knew how hard it was to pry the bodies apart when they were packed into the gas chamber as many as 150 at a time. A daily ration of a quarter-liter of Schnaps helped see the men through tasks which were, as he said, "extremely nerve-wracking."[53]

From May 1940 until December 1944, for four and one-half years, Vinzenz Nohel was a living man among the dead. With his bare hands he helped strip them of their earthly form: his were the hands that separated them, stacked them for storage, shoved them into the oven, burned flesh to ash, and sifted excess chunks of bone for grinding in an electric mill. Busy with a thousand other details, the other staff members remained unspattered with waste or blood, free of contact with lifeless flesh. They had merely seen to it that the dead would pass through hands other than their own—those of Nohel and his luckless companions.

Months after the end of the killings, Nohel was plagued with the sight of his deeds. "Even today I suffer from bad dreams," he noted in September 1945. "On such occasions many of the dead appear before me in my mind, and many is the time I believe I am going insane." Were the others whose tasks kept at a remove, and whose hands remained clean, spared similar imaginings?

Like the doctors, at least some of the castle personnel undoubtedly shared the ideological assumptions underlying the original killing project. Such agreement might well have soothed an otherwise restless conscience. Frau Elisabeth Lego revealed a significant detail about her own family history that sheds some light on her willingness to carry out her duties as a secretary in Castle Hartheim. "My aunt Pauline Lego, my father's sister who was active in a cloister as a teacher, had suffered a 'nervous breakdown' and then came to Niedernhart where she was a patient for many years," she recalled. "From time to time she had lucid moments. I often visited her in Niedernhart. My visits to my aunt . . . gave me cause to form thoughts about the mentally ill and, to be sure, that a mentally ill person is for his relatives something totally frightful."[54] There was some uncertainty in her mind how weighty this consideration was in her willingness to participate in the euthanasia operation, yet conceded it eased her choice to at least cooperate in the "distanced" tasks of an office worker.[55]

Most of the staff members were not assigned to Hartheim at random. Nearly all belonged to the Nazi party, and many exploited their party connections to acquire their jobs. But while party membership or acquaintance with party leaders opened up professional opportunities, they soon learned it also led them to participation in organized murder. Because they were deemed politically reliable, in the eyes of their employers they were already suitable for such work. Nazi party affiliation was not a shield from horror, but rather an invitation to engage in it.

In general, persons chosen as candidates for employment in Hartheim received unexpected notification from the *Gau* directorate or labor office that they were to prepare themselves for a change of employment. Often they were then summoned to the offices of the directorate in Linz for an interview. From the testimony of some of the employees it appears that the interviews were rather superficial. Some time later individuals who had been selected would be picked up and driven to the castle to begin their assignments.[56]

Until their arrival at Hartheim new employees were uninformed as to the true nature and purpose of their assignment. Despite their suspicions, some of those first assigned to assist with the construction of the gas chamber and ovens did not know for certain that the fixtures were designed to kill until, upon completion of their labors, the castle director, Captain Christian Wirth, informed them directly.[57] Once operations were under way, however, all new employees were led directly to Captain Wirth. He immediately swore them to an oath of silence regarding all matters in the castle. Wirth always stated that the penalty for failing to maintain the oath of silence was either internment in a concentration camp or execution. Often the oath was administered in the form of a written statement the staff member had to sign. In some instances, but not always, he told the new employees directly that the purpose of the operations in Castle Hartheim was to provide a "mercy death" for the incurably ill. Out of regard to the consciences of the arriving employees, Captain Wirth sometimes attempted to provide a legal veneer to the procedure, stressing that it was being carried out according to a secret law promulgated in Berlin, to be published after the war. Sometimes he also mentioned that he would assume responsibility, ✷ allowing the employees simply to fulfill their assignments.

Once employees were inside the castle, little effort was made to conceal from them the meaning of the work for which they had been recruited. Among the first to learn of the castle's new mission under its National Socialist administrators were the workmen who carried out the remodeling of the castle interior. Although some of the men were initially kept in the dark concerning the purpose of the work, it did not take long before their suspicion turned to certainty.

One of these men was Heinrich Barbl. A tinsmith and plumber by training, Barbl was also a member of the SS, employed at the nitrogen works in Linz as a gas and waterpipe fitter. By the time of his transfer to Castle Hartheim, work on installation of the gas chamber was "already in progress." He recorded that at the time it was said the work was being carried out "under contract from Berlin." He noted the other workers were German plumbers who at first did not let on about the ultimate purpose of the enterprise. Following the orders of Captain Wirth, he set to work on cutting screws and sealing pipes, stressing that "at first I did not know what it was all about." He did hear that the new equipment was to be used to "convey poison gas," but when he asked a co-worker about the matter directly he received the evasive yet ominous response that he would understand "soon enough." He recalled, too, that they had constructed one room with pipe openings "such as those used with shower facilities." Yet it was not until after the deadly gassing began, he maintained, that he knew for sure the purpose of the work.[58]

With the installation work completed, Barbl was given a new task that brought him into constant, daily contact with evidence of the functioning of the death machinery. He and two others worked as stampers, punching out name plates to be affixed to urns bearing the ashes of victims. The device used for the plates was a type or letter case. He estimates they were turning out some 20 plates on a given day, or perhaps 400 to 500 per month. The labeling of the ashes was largely a sham. The ashes that "lay in a big heap" were indiscriminately scooped into various urns without any effort to match individual remains to the names fastened to the containers.[59]

Another maintenance man, Matthias Buchberger, explained how he came to be enlisted as a construction worker on the remodeling team. Buchberger recalled that at the beginning of 1940 he received a written notice informing him he was to report to the *Gauleitung Oberdonau* in

Linz. Arriving there, he found himself ushered into the company of Dr. Lonauer, from the Niedernhart hospital, and Captain Wirth. He believed that *Gauinspektor* Schachermayr may also have been on hand. "The above-mentioned gentlemen only looked at me, yet asked no questions. I heard Dr. Lonauer say, 'Well, let's take him, he lives just a bit too close to the castle.' " However superficial the interview, Buchberger, who claimed not to have volunteered his services, speculated that his selection "may perhaps be traceable to the fact that I was a member of the National Socialist Party."[60]

Fourteen days later, Buchberger was told to report officially to the castle on 28 March to assume his duties. Several others started work with him that day, including six men who later became crematory attendants. When he arrived, Captain Wirth informed him he was to assist workers already engaged in renovating the castle. He found the existing oven in the castle bakery, as well as a nearby mortuary, "partially demolished and rebuilt." The crematorium was being constructed in the old bakery. The gas chamber, outfitted as "shower and bath room," was installed in the existing mortuary. He believed the renovations had lasted "a total of three months."[61]

According to Buchberger, "after the completion of the renovation work Captain Wirth had all the workers and other personnel called together in one room" and in a "detailed lesson" explained that the gas chamber and crematorium were designed to dispose of the mentally ill. Vinzenz Nohel, who like Barbl and Buchberger began work during the remodeling phase, confirmed Buchberger's account of Wirth's speech to the staff. Yet Nohel dated it in mid-April 1940—just before, not after, construction of the crematorium began. "Comrades," he recalled Wirth announcing,

> I have called you together today in order to explain to you the present situation here in the castle [and] what will now take place. I have received the assignment from the Reich Chancellery to direct what follows here in the castle. I as captain have everything under my command. We have to build a crematorium here in order to burn the mentally ill from the *Ostmark*.[62] Five doctors are designated to examine the mentally ill to determine whatever is to be saved and what is not to be saved. Whatever is not to be saved comes into the crematorium and will be burned. The mentally ill are a burden for Germany, and we want only healthy persons. The mentally ill are only a burden for the state. Several men will be designated who will have to work in the crematorium. Above all, this means silence on pain of the death penalty. Whoever does not keep silent will go to a concentration camp or will be shot.[63]

While several of the original workers, including Barbl and Nohel, went on to become crematorium attendants, Buchberger succeeded in avoiding this most odious of tasks. He emphasized that he explicitly refused to serve in this function when asked. "Right at the beginning of my activity in Hartheim Dr. Lonauer approached me one day with the unreasonable request to function as a burner. When I explained to Dr. Lonauer that because of my abhorrence of corpses I was not suited, he did not push me further, and in the future when it came to such offers left me in peace."[64]

✗While admitting to having known in detail facts about the workings of the killing operation, Buchberger nevertheless most heartily distanced himself from responsibility. For him the line separating innocence and complicity lay at the point of being on hand to view the mass executions. By remaining absent when persons were killed and their corpses disposed of, Buchberger kept his conscience clear. He stressed one incident in which he deliberately turned down the opportunity to view the killings, expressing his objections to the operations:

> I could have had opportunity to convince myself personally of everything which took place in Hartheim. With that I want to say that without hesitation I could have been present at the gassing procedure. But I always consciously failed to do this because the actions of my superiors against the defenseless victims I found distasteful to the core and I, although a National Socialist, decidedly rejected this. At no time did I participate in a gassing, and never was given the task of burning the corpses.[65]

Mindful to avoid the gas chamber area, Buchberger stayed on in the castle as errand runner and maintenance man. Freed from the unpleasant chore of disposing of the dead, he contented himself with the day-to-day tasks of keeping the castle tidy and in working order. He went about his duties, ever cautious never to cross the imaginery line separating his common functions from those involved in killing, and in covering up the traces of murder: "I myself, as already mentioned, had nothing to do with either the killing or the burning of the mentally ill. Because of my working knowledge of agriculture, I was used as a man Friday. I had to keep the courtyard clean, clean out the cow stall, and in winter service the central heating."[66]

Transportation workers were also needed to drive the buses full of victims from other hospitals and the railway station to the killing center. Like the installation workers, these men possessed a simple skill that could be applied to the killing operation. Similarly, Nazi party affiliation was a precondition to their recruitment. Like the others, they understood the meaning of their new assignments only after arrival at the castle.

One of the drivers, Franz Hödl, stated that he arrived in Hartheim after he and two other men, out of five who had been summoned to the *Gauleitung*, were told to prepare themselves for unspecified duties in Alkoven.[67] Though he too apparently did not volunteer for work in Hartheim, his loyalty to the party made him a suitable candidate. Hödl had joined the Nazi party in October 1937 and as of February 1938 was a member of the SS. At the same time, he was employed as a bus driver for the postal department on the line connecting Linz and Passau.

Hödl took over supervision of the castle motor pool, including three new Mercedes buses that had been painted gray with their windows sprayed over in blue. Accompanied by transport directors, the bus operators picked up victims from various institutions in Austria, such as Niedernhart, Ybbs, and Neuhofen a. d. Krems, and on occasion from institutions in Germany and Czechoslovakia as well. They then drove most of the patients to the Niedernhart hospital in Linz, where the victims often would wait a few days before being shuttled to Hartheim for extermination. Others, especially those from very large institutions, came by train and arrived at the railway station in Linz. Here the procedure was for the police to cordon off the area. Arriving at the station, Dr. Renno then boarded and walked through the wagons, examining the passengers and their case histories, and sorting the patients. The most serious cases, as well as those who, in Dr. Renno's words, "behaved most disorderly" or for whom the written diagnosis was "100% certain," were sent immediately to the castle. The rest were transferred to waiting buses and, depending on the volume of arrivals and the backlog of bodies awaiting processing in the castle crematorium, were also driven either directly to Hartheim, or to a holding area at Niedernhart.[68]

After reaching the castle the buses drove to a side entrance protected from view by a wooden canopy. Here the nurses took the victims from the buses and escorted them inside. The victims were then undressed and the doctors inspected them in preparation for their extermination. This was also the point at which the drivers' official contact with the victims ceased. Driver Hödl stressed this in taking moral refuge behind the limited scope of his technical duties. While acknowledging his participation in transporting the patients, he maintained that his responsibility for the victims ended at the castle entrance. "In no way did I have anything to do with the actual events in Hartheim," he stated. "Also, we vehicle drivers were never given the assignment of undressing the arriving mental patients."[69] Another driver, Franz Mayrhuber, claimed to have nothing to say about what happened to his passengers after they entered the building, "since I was never interested in observing these things. I only know that the patients were undressed in a certain room, but I never saw that myself."[70]

One of the drivers, however, did admit showing an interest in the fate of the victims. Once the buses pulled up to the entrance, the nurses took over. After they had seen the patients off the vehicles, the drivers "immediately drove the buses back into the garage yard." Nevertheless, this particular driver, Johann Lothaller, noted that

> out of curiosity I occasionally tried to see in detail what happened to the patients who were brought in. I saw that they entered a room in which they had to undress. I also observed that they were photographed once again. Once more the patients were presented to the doctors. I saw the doctors in white smocks at the processing of the transports; and, to be sure, Dr. Lonauer and Dr. Renno. I do not know in detail what the doctors did with the patients because when one attempted to observe events for any length of time one was chased away by Captain Wirth who was also on hand at the processing of the transports.[71]

The porter of a castle, if not by nature, then by training and assignment, is likely to be an observant figure. He, if anyone, would have been certain to notice some of the suspicious goings-on in Hartheim. Yet, it comes as no surprise that a porter may also choose to overlook things occurring outside his limited sphere of authority. Rudolf Loidl was an employee of a once-Jewish liquor firm taken over by another company owned by deputy *Gau* inspector Peterseil. When his position was threatened because of the wartime allocation of spirits, he was reassigned to the porter's lodge at Castle Hartheim where he also worked the switchboard. Another factor in his selection for this new assignment (one that likely influenced his circumspection with regard to certain happenings in the castle) was his ineligibility for army service because of a childhood spinal defect that left him with a damaged leg.

From his vantage point inside the porter's lodge, he saw the buses pass by on their way to the unloading entrance. He also saw many other people, including the doctors, come and go through his door. Yet, he claimed not to have paid much attention to the passengers. "That mentally ill were in there was generally known. I cannot say if concentration camp inmates were also among them. I did not bother myself about who was brought to Hartheim." He insisted his perspective was limited. After all, "the castle had several entrances. Past my gate death candidates were neither driven in, nor were their ashes driven out."[72]

Castle Hartheim required a staff of secretaries to carry out the daily load of correspondence. This work not only consisted of exchanges with authorities in Berlin and other institutions, but also with cemetery officials and, most importantly, relatives of the victims who had to be informed of their deaths. The issuance of death notices served both to deceive relatives of the inevitability and normality of the death of their loved ones (they were told that medical science had done its best), and to reassure the secretaries of the propriety of the operation. Notification of the next of kin was the final stage in a procedure involving the bureaucratization of murder. A uniform trail of office correspondence covered the victims' movements from selection to death.[73]

For Elisabeth Lego, who indicated she was one of 10 to 12 secretaries in the office,[74] filling out these forms occupied a daily routine in which, in her own mind, she remained at a safe remove from the killing. While conceding that she participated in the operations in Hartheim, she characterized her own work as "distanced, office-type cooperation." As she noted,

> My work consisted of writing the death certificates apportioned to me and correspondence notifying relatives of the persons gassed, as well as informing the proper cemetery administration. I simply received the file and had to fill out the above-named written materials. The cause of death was written in advance by the physician, Dr. Lonauer, by means of a pencil notation. In most cases it was a matter of pneumonia and heart failure. There were also other indications which, because they involved medical expressions, I can no longer remember.[75]

Echoing the statements of the maintenance man, Buchberger, the bus drivers, Hödl and Mayrhuber, and the porter, Loidl, Fraulein Lego stressed that her work in the office did not bring her into contact with either the workings of the killing procedure or its victims. Speculating that it might have been Dr. Lonauer who activated the gassing apparatus, she insisted she never went near the device. "I never came into this wing of the castle, and I cannot say anything at all about it." So removed was she, she claimed, that "only a single time did I see mentally ill in the castle."[76] Another secretary, Margit Troller, similarly maintained that she "never caught sight of" them.[77] Nevertheless, Helene Hintersteiner, who directed the activities of the other women in the office, admitted to having participated "two or three times in the undressing of persons selected for gassing" when the nursing staff was short-handed.[78]

It is still safe to say that the secretaries, however they sought to come to terms with their role in the killing procedure, knew the victims were arriving in the castle to be killed. In fact, they had occasion to see them arriving, as the victims passed from the bus drop-off along the arcade corridor that was partially visible from the hallway outside their office upstairs. Karoline Burner, employed in the administrative office from the spring of 1940 until the spring of 1943,[79] saw the gray buses and the arrival of their human cargo: "several times I observed how the transports were delivered. I only know that the persons who were brought in were killed." People spoke about the new category of arrivals. "It was pointed out to me by others employed in Hartheim that now concentration camp inmates were delivered too." She could see them, but admitted lacking interest in looking "because that sickened me."[80]

Gertraud Dirnberger, employed as an office worker from August 1940 until August 1943, confirmed "it was a matter of general discussion that concentration camp inmates were also killed in Hartheim." By stepping out of her office into the hallway on the second floor, she could look down across the courtyard to the arcade passage where the victims walked, accompanied by the nurses and Dr. Renno. After they had walked "about a third of the way" down the passage, however, a "boarded wall" obscured her view so that she "never saw what happened."[81]

On occasion, however, the secretaries were called upon to assist directly in the processing of the incoming patients, bringing office workers face to face with the victims. As Frau Dirnberger recalled:

> Once, late in the evening a transport arrived. It involved a transport of women. Captain Wirth called upon the female office personnel to help in the processing of the transport. We had to go down into the arcade passageway. The clothes were tied up, laid on a big table and overlaid with a name plate. Then the arrivals were led to both doctors, Dr. Lonauer and Dr. Renno, who were in a special room. We no longer caught sight of the arrivals; they were apparently killed after presentation before the doctors. The arrivals belonged to the category of the mentally ill. That one could determine without difficulty from their behavior.[82]

The experience was so unpleasant she never wanted to repeat it. "After dispatching this transport I informed Captain Wirth that I was emotionally incapable of such things. He then no longer drafted me for such purposes. Whether my female colleagues were drafted again I would not know."[83]

A notable exception to the usual practice of accepting politically reliable or well-connected insiders was the enlistment in October 1940 of a small group of nurses from the Ybbs mental facility. They stressed that they did not seek their positions, nor did their political backgrounds indicate suitability for work in this sensitive area.

Two of the nurses, Anna Griessenberger and Maria Hammelsböck, insisted that their involvement with Castle Hartheim was involuntary and so disagreeable that they attempted to be transferred. Frau Griessenberger noted that she had been employed in the Ybbs facility since 1934 after having completed a nursing course. She described how one day in October 1940 she was called into the office along with 10 other nurses. "A man in uniform" told them that volunteers were needed for war service. When none of the women volunteered, she and two others were selected "because we were the youngest and still unmarried. He did not say where we were going, yet we learned that we would be enlisted into compulsory emergency service." They were given a day to prepare for their transfer.[84]

Frau Hammelsböck and the other nurses chosen were first driven to Hartheim at night. The next morning they received an oath, holding them to strictest silence, on pain of "incarceration in a concentration camp or immediate shooting." They were also informed that the purpose of Hartheim was to gas the mentally ill. Evidently, "they did not want to stay." Wirth responded with the assurance "that he alone bears responsibility and we only would have to obey his orders."[85]

One of the tasks of the nurses was to travel with and care for victims on the buses, and assist in their arrival at the castle. In this capacity they came into direct contact with victims. Nonetheless, the nurses were spared the horrible sight of their execution and disposal. Frau Griessenberger and Frau Hammelsböck both accompanied patients on journeys from homes and hospitals to Hartheim. Griessenberger remembered doing this on only four or five occasions; Hammelsböck did so at least 10, if not dozens of times.[86] Their mission included undressing victims in preparation for final inspection. The disrobing, as she remembered it, always seems to have gone smoothly.[87]

The nurses also had the unpleasant chore of cleaning the rooms through which the victims passed. Yet here too the castle administrators protected the women from viewing the killing. "At any given time after a wind-up of a transport we nurses still had to clean the photo room, not the gassing room. The gassing room was cleaned by the men." As a result, like others who worked in the castle for years, Frau Hammelsböck could claim never to have seen the gas chamber: "Wirth took strict care seeing to it that we not come in contact with these things."[88] Hermine Pimpl, another nurse transferred from the Ybbs hospital to Hartheim in

October 1940, accompanied transports of victims from hospitals in Ybbs, Mauer-Öhling, and Feldhof. She too remained with the victims no further than the point at which they were led in to the doctors. Her assignment ended, she was spared the sight of the extermination:

> The pick-up did not last long, and we drove back to Hartheim. There the patients had to leave the bus. They were led into a room where they had to undress for bathing. I myself helped the patients in undressing. Then I had nothing more to do, but men came from the other side. I still saw how the patients were led in to the doctor. I knew that there would be gassing there. Who loaded and operated the gas apparatus, that I do not know.[89]

Although spared the worst sight, some of the women did express feelings of discomfort at viewing the arrivals. Like Frau Dirnberger, who asked to be excused from undressing the arriving patients, Frau Hammelsböck recalled being disturbed at the sight of concentration camp inmates brought to the castle to die. "I know that transports came to Hartheim from Mauthausen and Dachau," she noted. "I only observed one transport, but from what was said I knew that several transports had arrived. When the concentration camp inmates were unloaded, they left a wretched impression on me. I found that especially burdensome. For that reason even today the proceeding is still well in memory."[90]

Unpleasant as she may have found the sight of the inmates, she noted that it was dissatisfaction with the menial nature of the work that was decisive in her efforts to be freed from duty in Hartheim. The janitorial task of cleaning up struck Frau Hammelsböck as undignified for a nurse. For this reason, she noted, she sought reassignment on two occasions: in 1941 when she volunteered for service on the Russian front, and in the fall of 1943 when she asked to go to the Rhineland to participate in relief work following air raids.[91]

Aside from asking Wirth directly, there were other ways one could seek release from duty in Castle Hartheim. One method available to the women was to become pregnant. Frau Griessenberger said she took advantage of a visit by her husband to do just that. The plan did succeed for a time, but unfortunately the child of this union died after three months. Because she was still needed as a cook, she was forced to stay on in Hartheim. Repeated appeals to Captain Wirth were rebuffed.[92]

According to their testimony, the secretaries and nurses were intimidated and fearful. The source of that intimidation, they repeatedly indicated, was their superior, the rough-talking Captain Christian Wirth. For them the terror apparatus of the Nazi state took on a personal appearance in this domineering, threatening male figure. For these women, and for some of the men as well, defense of their continuing cooperation in the killing procedure rested not only on the requirement to follow orders and a sworn oath of silence, but also upon the simple dread of the consequences of not obeying this man.

Employees maintained they did not want to obey, and in fact strove to be relieved of their posts; yet, fearful for their personal safety, obey they did. As one secretary noted, "Captain Wirth, to whom we were subordinated, was a horrible person who permitted no contradiction whatsoever, and always immediately threatened us with a concentration camp and shooting."[93] She also noted that, in the privacy of their common lodgings, they talked of their predicament: "I slept in a room first with Hintersteiner and then Troller. She complained greatly that she had to be there. But, like everyone, she knew of Captain Wirth, that there was no getting away there."[94]

Dr. Renno confirmed that Wirth acted brusquely toward the secretaries and the staff in general. When occasionally entering the secretarial bureau to seat himself at a typewriter, or meeting with Wirth to go over pick-up schedules for fresh victims, Dr. Renno had occasion to notice Wirth's overbearing attitude toward his subordinates. "I can remember that sometimes Wirth dealt too militarily with the stenographers, and correspondingly with the entire personnel," Renno stated, "and that the personnel complained to Dr. Lonauer about him. Tension arose between Wirth and the administrative director. Lonauer then tried to smooth out the tensions with Wirth."[95]

Wirth was also rough toward men who showed weakness in their duties. His remedy for an employee discomforted by the unpleasant odor of burning corpses was to have him handed a bottle of Schnaps. When later the man still sought release from his duties, Wirth resorted to his usual threats to execute him or send him to a concentration camp. Bruno Bruckner's job was to photograph victims immediately before they were led into the gas chamber. Shortly after he arrived, he complained to Wirth about the terrible odor that made him sick to his stomach, stating "he could not eat a thing 'because his nose was so full of the burning odor.' He also announced this at lunch to Captain Wirth, who immediately had him supplied with Schnaps, so that even in the daytime he had to be brought to bed heavily drunk." Still, "much sickened by the continuing odor of burning flesh," he again approached Wirth, indicating that "for medical reasons he wanted to be let go." Wirth shot back at him an unmistakable threat: "Bruckner, for you there are three possibilities. 1) Mauthausen. 2) be sent to the wall; or 3) you remain here."

Soberly, a report on Bruckner's testimony noted his reaction to these choices: "for Bruckner this expression was clear enough and he preferred to adapt to the situation."[96]

Employees found it convenient to place responsibility for their acts on Wirth's shoulders. Yet people like Bruckner and the others preferred to overlook the fact that they would never have found themselves in this situation had they not already demonstrated to the personnel directors in Linz their eagerness to serve the party. Many of them were already known to the Gau directorate, and judged likely to cooperate and honor the oath to remain silent once they had been initiated into the killing project in Hartheim. Bruckner, for example, a man who had been unemployed for four years before finally landing a job in August 1938 as a porter in the Linz slaughterhouse, had distinguished himself as an enthusiastic member of the SA at the Nürnberg party rallies, and was an "ardent supporter of national socialist ideology."[97]

For all his rough and threatening talk, employees still accepted Wirth as a boon companion during staff get-togethers. Noting that "on the job Wirth was relentless," Bruckner remarked that "on the other hand, Wirth was popular with the staff, joined all the drinking bouts, doubtlessly had intimate relations with the female employees of the establishment. In this regard a good number of all the employees in Hartheim were intimate with one another. This may be attributable to the strict seclusion. There was never much fuss made about this."[98]

In so deporting themselves, staff members in Hartheim only mirrored the behavior of some of their superiors in the euthanasia program. Doctors from the medical commission in Berlin are said to have arranged liaisons with the women on the staff of the killing centers. One exasperated hotel keeper tossed several comission members out of his establishment because their goings-on had aroused a scandal.[99] Celebrations took place in castle Hartheim, sometimes with concentration camp officers from Mauthausen on hand, or with staff members of the T4 headquarters in Berlin. For most, even the ever-present odor of death did not hinder the festivities. One young woman from the T4 headquarters who arrived with Berlin staffers for a candlelight supper in Hartheim, however, shut herself up in a guest room rather than participate. She recalled first noticing a group of inmates, some "30–40 persons with shorn heads" and dressed in outfits "similar to that of prison clothing" enter the interior courtyard of the castle. Perceiving the unmistakable smell of smoke filling the castle interior a short while later, she avoided the gathering, only to be implored by one of the celebrants to return to the party.[100]

To be sure, the deeds of the maintenance staff, bus drivers, secretaries, and nurses were ordered and coordinated by administrators who were their superiors. It is difficult indeed to imagine that persons working in a setting that constantly set before them awareness of routine acts of murder against innocents would have participated voluntarily in this process. Yet, once involved, none risked the threatened penalties by flat refusal to participate, or by running away, or attempting to sabotage the operations.

In fact, if the experience of the employees in Castle Hartheim tells us anything, it is that when acting under coercion and fear of personal harm individuals are capable of doing their jobs with diligence, insuring in no small way that the plans of their superiors are carried out fully. It also becomes clear that under these circumstances persons can effectively satisfy their conscience through a conviction that their cooperation has been forced contrary to their personal will. Some took refuge in a type of fatalism, best summarized in the words of one of the secretaries: "there was nothing to be done." Resignation led to a belief in helplessness, the ultimate inner justification of submission.

Persons who worked in Hartheim maintained years afterward that they wanted to leave but were unable to do so. In explaining their inability to extract themselves from their predicament, they explained that all such efforts were "pointless" or "without result." They wanted to leave, they said, but all attempts they characterized as hopeless. The phrases themselves, common to bureaucratic procedure and authority, once assimilated, absorbed, and given expression in common speech, reinforced passivity. These expressions comprised a framework and guide to mental categories of moral paralysis. Protected thereby from thoughts of individual responsibility, the employees appeared for work day after day.

Though fearful, each stuck to his assigned tasks, taking refuge in the limited technical routine of his labor. The bus driver concerned himself with his vehicles, the maintenance man with his chores and equipment, the secretary with her dictation and correspondence, the nurse with assisting her "patients." If their individual acts struck the employees as innocent, it was because in themselves these tasks, viewed in isolation from the goal of the enterprise—in this case the murder of human beings—*looked like*, and indeed did not differ in any technical way from, similar routines in countless other business establishments. The secretaries who first sought their jobs in Castle Hartheim expected to work in offices similar to those in which they had previously trained and worked. They doubtless would have preferred to serve in a routine party or government office where they would have taken dictation and prepared correspondence just as they did in Hartheim. Such an assignment, divorced from the direct purpose served, did not differ from what these women were assigned to do in the killing center. Had they not been delegated to Hartheim they would have likely lived through the war without major event or participation in harm to others.

Some of the nurses, involuntarily selected for their assignments in Hartheim, were better able than the secretaries to maintain their underlying unwillingness to participate. Yet they too swiftly became enmeshed in the cogs of the death apparatus. Once engaged, they found it too late to beg off or escape. In their eyes as well, if anyone was guilty, they implied, then it was the cruel, browbeating, threatening Captain Wirth; or the "Reich Germans," other native German nurses who, they said, actively participated in preparing the victims for the gas chamber, were always privileged to ride the buses, and spared the menial tasks of cleaning up and sorting the laundry. The German women received the easier, "cleaner" tasks, while the Austrian nurses were assigned "most of the dirty work" of sorting clothing and cleaning up.[101] In effect, she was saying that, contrasted with the sorting of the victims' laundry, riding on the transports and deceiving the victims was comparatively clean.

Castle employees found a common defense in the imaginary line they drew between those carrying out routine functions and those operating the gas chamber and the ovens. It was as if responsibility was most direct, most unmistakable at the point of transition where human beings became corpses. In this sense the employees shared a common delusion that their individual actions were not instrumental to the entire process. Even those who, day in and day out, saw to it that the victims arrived at their ultimate destination, avoided seeing or touching them in the moment of death. This avoidance, they believed, freed them of responsibility. Murder was thus localized, in a workshop of destruction. Even within the castle, it formed a secluded realm whose frontiers were marked by the closed steel door leading to the chamber and the mouth of the coke-fired oven into which the victims vanished. After each group of "visitors" crossed the threshold the stench of roasting flesh filled the castle. Yet each employee was left free to deny that his turn of the steering wheel, snap of the camera shutter, or clacking of typewriter keys had anything to do with the unpleasant atmospheric conditions.

They refused to acknowledge that these living beings were made into corpses and then billowing ash in part because they helped process them along the way. Everyone, from Captain Wirth, Dr. Lonauer, and Dr. Renno who organized the transports, made on-the-spot final checks of the victims, consigning them to the gas chamber and supervising the introduction of the deadly gas, to the custodians, bus drivers, nurses and secretaries, distanced themselves from the "*Schleppers*" and "burners" who handled the cramped, lifeless corpses. The real filth of the operation was visible only at the end; and the end product which was death was the domain of the drunken team of men who disposed of the victims. Only here, so it seemed to the castle staff, was the actual taint attaching to what each of them helped create unavoidably visible. It is not surprising that the only member of the castle staff to be executed shortly after the war for his participation in the operation in Hartheim was one of the crematory attendants, Vinzenz Nohel.[102]

In this regard the insistence of maintenance man Buchberger that he refused to view the gassing of patients or serve as a cremation attendant is most significant. Direct personal responsibility for the killing seemed to attach only at the moment when one came into contact with the dead or dying. This was the logical and intended result of a bureaucratically organized system of mass murder comprised of a series of coordinated, separate, divisible steps implemented by individuals with little personal regard, not to say indifference, for the victims they helped create.[103]

Chapter 4

Into the Valley of Redl-Zipf

[handwritten: missile technology]

In 1938 the topics of space travel, rocketry, and journeying to the stars still belonged to the realm of fantasy. The local newspapers in and around Linz sometimes carried features mocking such possibilities.[1] Yet, the war had a way of forging the fantastic and upsetting accepted notions of the possible. Discoveries were being made in the sphere of technology, as well as in that of inhumanity, and by 1943 new developments in rocketry and equally revolutionary developments in the weaponry of human destruction came to converge. One site of their convergence was Redl-Zipf, a small farming community located between Vöcklamarkt and Frankenberg in Upper Austria. Its selection extended the reach of the Mauthausen camp complex deeper into the countryside and into the population's awareness.

The fate of this remote locale was decided on 7 July 1943 when Adolf Hitler, who had earlier expressed skepticism about the feasibility of missile technology, entered his private movie theater to view one of the first successful tests of the V-2 rocket. On hand were Albert Speer and a staff of rocket experts, including Walter Dornberger, director of the missile testing program in Peenemünde on the Baltic coast, and Werner von Braun, the young rocket specialist. Speer noted that "after a brief introduction the room was darkened and a color film shown. For the first

time Hitler saw the majestic spectacle of a great rocket rising from its pad
and disappearing into the stratosphere. Without a trace of timidity and
with a boyish sounding enthusiasm, von Braun explained his theory.
There could be no question about it: From that moment on, Hitler had
been finally won over."[2]

After retreating to his bunker, Hitler, whose "imagination had
been kindled," was "ecstatic about the possibilities of the project," and
ordered advanced production of the weapon he was convinced could
"decide the war."[3] His only concern was to keep the undertaking as
secret as possible; hence, in his view "only Germans" were suitable for
the tasks. However, just "six weeks later" Himmler, anxious as always to
press his influence, convinced Hitler that "If the entire work force were
concentration camp prisoners, all contact with the outside world would
be eliminated."[4] Hitler concurred, and in so doing set the stage for
combining missile technology with the slave labor of the concentration
camps.

Bombardment from the sky forced a shift in the site of operations.
Following the attack of the Royal Air Force on Peenemünde in August
1943, Hitler called for the transfer of rocket development to outlying
sites in "secured locations" affording "the greatest possible utilization of
caves and otherwise suitable bunker emplacements."[5] In the autumn of
1943 the Nazis chose as one of the sites for the development of the rocket
a thinly populated locale in Upper Austria. The site lay approximately 45
miles southwest of Mauthausen. Though somewhat remote, it lay within
reachable distance of Attnang-Puchheim, a principal rail junction along
the main line connecting Salzburg, Linz, and Vienna. The area was not
well suited to farming, yet it was characterized by rolling wooded hills
providing camouflage, and a mineral composition of the ground offering
both a somewhat "elastic" resistance to bombardment and properties
suited for the construction of underground tunnels.[6] The operation in
Zipf was given the deliberately misleading name of Rock Quarry Processing Corp., Operation Schlier. To disguise the activity there as a quarry
operation, the word "Schlier," referring to the stone or mineral composition of the area, was prominently displayed in the official dealings of
the corporation.[7]

Operation of the Schlier corporation began in the autumn of 1943.
Principal locations chosen for its activities were a brewery, a parcel of
land belonging to a local farmer, and a section of wooded land above the
brewery atop a mountain directly behind it. On 30 September 1943 a
major discussion was held in Zipf, with *Gauleiter* Eigruber in attendance,
in which the Schlier corporation laid claim to two-thirds of the cellar

space in the Zipf brewery. Despite the difficulties resulting from this interference, the brewery was assigned the task of continuing its production of beer, presumably to maintain the desired cover for the engine testing. Work began on 4 October 1943.[8]

The Schlier, or Rock Quarry Processing Corporation, also succeeded in gaining control of a parcel of forest land behind the brewery and atop a hill from the hands of a locally prominent citizen, Baron Wilhelm Limbeck-Lilienau. Property was also acquired on a nearby farm owned by the family of Theresia S. These latter sites may have suggested themselves to local authorities as especially worthy of confiscation since both Baron Limbeck-Lilienau and the members of this family were known to be unsympathetic to the regime.[9] The new operation also required the construction of a special railway link of some one and one-half miles connecting the facility to the Salzburg-Vienna rail line at Redl-Zipf. As many as 45 to 50 wagons bearing freight eventually rolled along this new stretch of track each day. Furthermore, bunkers were erected: one topped with an iron-reinforced cement cover ten feet thick; a second, whose iron cover was twice as thick as the first, sat atop the wooded mountain above the brewery; another bunker, on the grounds of the S. farm, housed an electrical transformer station, supplying the work-site with electricity by means of underground cables. The transformer was so large that a special 16-axle wagon rolled along tracks leading into the station bunker was needed to bring in one of the transformer's larger parts. This third bunker was camouflaged with a roof and painted windows on its sides to make it look like a farm house.[10] In addition to the bunkers, nine tunnels were constructed. An elevator shaft 130 feet deep was carved inside the mountain behind the brewery and connected with a concrete engine testing stand.[11]

To create this facility quickly and secretly, concentration camp inmates from Mauthausen were brought to the site. At its maximum strength the camp at Redl-Zipf held 1,488 inmates; during the 16 months of its existence nearly 300 inmates are recorded as having died there. These figures do not include those who had outlived their usefulness and, according to common practice in the satellite camps, were shipped back to Mauthausen to be killed.

The work site at Redl-Zipf was designed to carry out experiments on "a rocket propellant which resulted from the liquefaction of air by means of heavy compression machines." On the mountain itself stood a "large testing stand" that was linked to the underground factory by means of "a shaft (freight and personnel elevator)" as well as "through gas pipes." The fuel, consisting of "a mixture of methyl alcohol and liquid oxygen was introduced into the propulsion aggregates. Each V-2 rocket engine was tested individually. It had to endure the pressure of the firing. In the process four thousand liters of liquid air and 96% alcohol were brought to ignition and forced through the engines, so that in the vicinity a one-minute thundering could be heard." Zipf functioned exclusively as a fuel-production and testing facility; those components deemed satisfactory were "embossed [with] an eagle [measuring] five millimeters . . . and a number" in preparation for shipment.[12]

The site was built under the authority of a construction directorate led by an SS *Oberstürmführer*, or first lieutenant, from Mauthausen. There also existed a technical administration and a business directorate. The operation was assigned a six-member team from the Security Service (SD), who served as agents and informers while disguised as laborers. A guard company of some 50–70 men also secured the area, guarding the entry roads and protecting against possible parachute attacks or acts of sabotage. Besides engineers who were assigned to the testing area, a group of young women with recent *Gymnasium* certificates were assigned as secretaries and as assistants to record the results of the engine testing.[13]

At first the engine trails were a triumph. The force of the propellant resulted in an enormous release of energy. An inmate recorded that during one test, "The earth shook and the mountains rethundered [the blast] with a chorus of tardy echoes. Nearby . . . tree branches fell and a skyful of paralyzed birds showered to the ground. Then all was quiet, and the stench of ozone hung in the atmosphere. The SS scientists smiled at each other. Success! And the work to finish the underground factory went on."[14] "By night it looked as if the mountain belched forth fire," Frau S. noted. "There were enormous pillars of flame."[15] A German photographer who worked at the test site likened such eruptions to an epiphany: "One said . . . when the (noise) went forth . . . for God's sake, what on earth can that be. It is the Holy Ghost."[16]

In the first week of October 1943, 100 inmates from concentration camp Mauthausen made their way inside a boxcar "whose locomotive crawled tediously through Upper Austria. After many dark and uncomfortable hours," one of the voyagers noted, at last "we were unloaded into a glaring autumn sun. When our eyes became accustomed to the brightness, we saw a small town whose railway station sign announced it to be 'Redl-Zipf.' " The inmates glimpsed a world beyond the cordon, beyond the "ugly fortress Mauthausen and the hole of Wiener Graben."[17] Long accustomed to the dark of the freight wagon, their eyes were dazzled by light. Their mission was to build a new camp, thereby reconstructing with their own hands the darkness they had left behind at Mauthausen.

As they marched from the station, the inmates beheld a terrain as yet unspoiled by the presence of a camp. There was no division between inside and out, between the free and the condemned, the living and the dying. The inmate was open to the sensations of nature. The landscape was still green, there were trees and lawns, meadows and brooks. At this moment the town struck these wretched pioneers as an idyll of natural majesty. "Autumn claimed the beautiful country-side. Burnished forests clung to the boulder biceps of the hills and some peaks rose like a vision from the earth's core to hold up the sky, while Redl-Zipf snuggled warmly in the valley." So too, they "passed through a section of cottages surrounded by gardens and orderly orchards, rusted by autumn nip. The charm of the town was marred only by posters which were nailed to every post, fence, and even to the trees: "Psst!, der Feind hört mit [the enemy is listening]."[18] There were secrets to be kept; the forest had ears.

The town of Redl-Zipf consisted of "about fifty dwellings." The most significant cluster comprised the Zipf brewery, centering upon "a large white house with open windows where the barley was dried. There was a red brick building with a tall chimney w[h]ere the brew was boiled and behind it were two storehouses for barrels, hops, grains, and bottles. On the slope of the nearby hill were two large wooden doors which opened into huge cellars where the beer was aged."[19] The brewery was the source of the town's reputation and pride. When Austrians thought of Zipf they thought of its beer.

As in any small town, strangers drew attention. The inmates' arrival did not escape the notice of town residents. The first inmates and their 20 guards settled beside their "temporary sleeping quarters," a "thatched roof house, which was situated by a brook." The inmates were aware of the eyes observing them: "As we relaxed that evening on the pleasant ground around the house, women and children of the town gaped in curiosity. The alternating gray and blue stripes of the prisoners' uniforms seemed to amuse them."[20]

The evening of relaxation was no more than a momentary respite from terror. Lest they forget why they had come, a guard shouted they were there to work; for them Redl-Zipf was not, as he chose to remind them, a resort. As work began, the camp arose from "an innocent meadow. . . . Stakes were thumped into the ground with sledge hammers and . . . trucks rumbled over the hummocks bringing new, prefabricated barracks" whose "lumber was new and pungent, smelling fresh." In just "a few days the camp was finished," complete with the familiar "network of barbed fencing and machine-gun towers." The alien complex pretended to be at one with the land: "The barracks were painted a dark green, making them less visible from the sky." As work shifted to "the quaint old brewery" the sunlight vanished: the sky turned overcast, as at first a "convenient fog" enshrouded "the activity of the valley. Day and night, trucks brought drilling machines, cement mixers, pipes, rails, wire, cement, iron, glass to the brewery courtyard." On the hill beside the old brewery "the emerald slope was torn open and boulders [were] ripped from [their] billion-years-old foundations. The fresh dew was sullied with smoke and soot, staining the green foliage a dirty gray."[21]

The brewery was painted black, and its cellars, dug into the mountain behind it, became the center of activity for the inmates. In alternating shifts they marched past the darkened brewery into "a brightly lit, large tunnel." Inside was a chaotic underground realm, cluttered with a tangle of hoses, pipes, cables, struts, tracks, wagons, and machinery. Armed guards stood at "every few paces." Also on hand, busy, nervous, shouting orders to the hapless inmate-slaves, were the supervisors, who included work-detail leaders drawn from the inmate ranks as well as civilian mechanics. In their brutality toward the inmate laborers some of these civilian foremen were hardly distinguishable from the capos. They shouted their orders in a crude and colloquial German, often incomprehensible to the new inmates, most of whom were foreign. Those who failed to respond immediately were struck "with a food or fist or even with a hammer if at the moment they had one in hand."[22]

As in the quarry, so too in the tunnels the inmates were oppressed with heavy weights. One onerous task involved shifting a "huge cauldron," which was "overloaded with sundry materials," through the maze of cluttered passageways. It was particularly difficult to balance the cauldron on its base as they maneuvered it around corners where the shafts adjoined. Also hindering their efforts were the clutter of implements and the activities of other work crews, each overseen by detail leaders, all of whom worked furiously and single-mindedly toward the accomplishment of their own tasks, without regard to those of the others. Another weighty assignment was to haul through the tunnels a winch weighing more than 440 pounds. Six weak inmates on the ends shouldered the brunt of this enormous weight, with others arrayed along the sides pulling up the slack. The greatest danger came when one of the men was shoved, or "heart . . . beating insanely . . . knees beginning to tremble" proved unable to bear the strain and stumbled, buckled, and fell. A man could easily have his legs crushed beneath the instrument. Worse still, the capo would exploit the delay to lash out at the pitiful inmate whom he deemed responsible for the mishap.[23]

Work went on in twelve-hour shifts that alternated at 7 o'clock each morning and evening. Frequently, before exiting the tunnels, the assembled slaves had to strip and be searched for stolen items: woe to the man who was found with a bit of wire, a small nail, a scrap of paper "torn from a filthy cement bag" with which he might hope to wrap his feet. Such thefts were severely punished. Enduring the inspection, the naked men stood in the damp tunnel as cold water ran down from the ceiling onto their exposed bodies and their "naked ribs were struck by the blows of the capos and soldiers."[24]

Brutality yielded pain and humiliation. Amid the din of the reckless enterprise, there was painful silence as well. In the tunnels even the foreign labor conscripts acted as if the concentration camp inmates did not exist: "We inmates often tried to speak with them, but they shunned all conversation, because they feared being brought into the camp. One saw in them that they had more to fear than we; we at last had nothing more to lose." And when opportunity brought the inmate in contact with the residents of the town, the silence was as great. "We were strictly forbidden to speak to them, and according to all appearances they too with us. Never did a German citizen enter into a conversation with us in public, unless it was in the course of duty."[25]

The inmates were on intimate terms with the darkness. They knew it as the shadow through which they passed by day as well as by night. All the more were they dazzled by any sign of light, whether experienced when emerging suddenly from a boxcar, or from the tunnels where they slaved day in and day out. Their shift ended, the day workers would set out from the main cavern into the darkness. Some straggled behind, their legs refusing to budge or hopelessly stuck in the snow. Once more the guards lashed out with their clubs. Looking back on the agonies of that winter of 1943/44 an inmate recalled that their exhausted column brought to mind a procession of "ghosts" or "wrapped skeletons." He sensed they passed unseen. As they marched back from the tunnels to the camp "not a living soul" from the town was present. Still, after a day in the tunnels, the night landscape appeared to him strikingly bright: "round about, everything was white: the sky, the woods, the streets; only in our hearts grew black hatred."[26]

The futile inmate search for townspeople, or for an acknowledgment of their own presence, added to their abiding sense of isolation. The townspeople sensed the existence of the inmates nearby in the darkness but denied their reality. Whereas an inmate's eyes widened to absorb whatever was luminous amid the black, the residents wove of this darkness a blindfold to conceal the inmates, the living dead. Internalizing their invisibility, the inmates came to identify themselves as men without substance or shadow. In their own eyes they had become beings as unreal as their rulers said they were.

Outside, marching through the no-man's land between the tunnels and the camp they were as ghosts. Once inside the barracks, the inmates were thrust into the glare of a harsh and probing light. Each night following work they submitted to the indignity of the louse inspection, the *Lausjagd,* a "hunt" for lice on their bodies and clothing. Forced to strip once again, the inmates had to line up for inspection, "shirt in one hand, underwear in the other," and "step up to the block leader." In a motion that resembled the mounting of a gallows, the inmate "had to climb upon a chair in front of the leader who illuminated [him] with a powerful electrical lamp which he held in his hand." The inmate, so invisible to the outside world, here yielded to a scrutiny in which "one had to position oneself and bend, assuming all possible attitudes, moving in all directions, while [the block leader] examined every bodily crease."[27]

In the service of producing the rocket propellant, the inmates' bodies slowly and excruciatingly broke down in the damp and dirt of the tunnels. When the inmate noted, "Our tunnel resembled a giant, old-fashioned laundry in which the wash was pounded. From all sides sounded rumbling and banging," he understood that he and his comrades were the objects so rudely laundered. They had been turned into little more than the "wet rags" with which they had covered themselves. At the end of the day the inmates returned to camp with their uniforms saturated with the cold water from the walls of the caves. For fear of theft they dared not dry their drenched uniforms in the open, but rather were forced to place them beneath their straw mattresses. Compelled to stand in the damp caverns twelve hours at a time, their legs stiffened into "pillars." Some 90 percent of the inmates suffered from limb infections. Abscesses filled with pus; the blood of these slaves became a watery, infected mix. If an inmate pressed against the swelling a cavity formed that only slowly refilled with contaminated fluids. The pain was worst at the beginning and end of the day. The walk "to and from the tunnels" was "unspeakable agony."[28]

Worlds intersected routinely. The residents were up and about on their daily rounds. Inevitably, the paths of townspeople crossed those of the inmates and guards. As in Mauthausen, residents of Redl-Zipf learned to adapt to the frightening spectacle. In the dark of night it was easy to uphold the illusion of the inmates' invisibility. To what lengths needed one to go in order to veil their presence by day?

Children and young persons in their teens occupied a privileged position as bystanders. They alone were allowed to approach the camp area, to linger while viewing the prisoners, to make contact with overseers and even inmates. The guards had a patience and tolerance with them they displayed with no other age group.

The youngsters were especially curious about the changes the new camp brought to the town. Herr B., then a boy of 14 or 15, and others of his age were allowed to approach the camp, and even to climb into nearby trees to watch its activities. At their age, however, they were at the outer range of childhood bordering on adulthood and the regime's distrust. Those who were older, beginning with 16 and 17-year-old youths, the SS kept clear of the camp area.[29] From his tree vantage point and from his home, near which the inmates passed, B. was able to make out details of the inmates' condition and appearance. He saw their poor physical state, and the rough way they were treated. He saw them in their uniforms, undernourished, with their feet wrapped in "paper and woolen rags." He recognized triangles of "six or seven different colors" on their clothing. He recalled that the "SS had dogs"; he knew that "when an inmate took off the camp siren sounded," and "fleeing inmates were shot. He also saw how the SS beat the inmates with their clubs." He noted that "the capos were the most brutal, they had no weapons, but lashed out with their sticks."[30]

The image of the camp entrance impressed itself upon B.'s memory. Four armed SS entries stood continual watch before the entrance. The work details consisted of 10 to 15 men with a pair of SS guards as overseers. Perhaps because of the general air of bustle and crowding in the camp, it brought to his mind the image of "an ant hill." In the fall of 1943, he recalled, the town changed: besides the presence of inmates and "many outsiders" in town, "for camouflage the houses were painted black."[31]

Anna K., then around 14 years old, came close enough to observe camp practices. A group of 10 inmates, guarded by two SS men and two capos, worked on her parents' property. She also saw them at work picking up bricks and loading containers at the railway station. One of the capos there was especially rough, and whipped the inmates as they attempted to lift the heavy containers. "The inmates [wore] striped blue and white [uniforms], with the middle section of their hair shaved away, and wore wooden shoes, with scraps of newspaper on their feet in winter. . . . On their striped jackets they had symbols. The criminal inmates green, the political inmates red. The green ones were the capos."

With the approval of the SS overseers, inmates working on Frau K.'s property sometimes did get extra food from the family. The SS were given Schnaps. Frau K. got to know a Polish inmate who told her "that inmates were sometimes hanged in the camp by their arms until they sweated blood. Then they died. Sometimes they screamed from the torture into the early hours." She knew too that inmates who fled and were later captured were shot. In the case of one, she knew that "he was brought back into the camp, and had to show the place where he got through, and there he was shot down. She herself saw a truck that transported the bodies—she says to Ebensee. The bodies were in wood boxes. From some of them ran blood."[32]

Frau Theresia S. was 15 years old when the inmates arrived and the concentration camp was built. The cement bunker used to house the large electrical transformer needed for operation of the test site was erected only 330 yards from her home. The construction required engineers and men from civilian firms, but the concentration camp inmates did the heavy work of lifting and carrying. The engineers and local laborers arrived first, followed by the inmates. A barrack was constructed. In general, the engineers were quartered with town residents. Two of the engineers and six to eight foremen lived in Frau S.'s home. Construction of the bunker proceeded from the summer of 1943 until the following spring. During the construction, an electrified barbed-wire fence and four watch towers were installed. The owners had no say in the use to which their land was put. The military simply arrived, confiscated their property, and began surveying.[33]

Local farmers had to contribute carts, plows, oxen, and horses for the camp. Frau S.'s step-father owned a small transport concession located in the farmhouse. The firm was pressed into assisting the work. Frau S. was obliged to ride a wagon hauling gravel and iron. This brought her up to, though never beyond, the camp gate. She was able to get a close look at the inmates, whom she saw "every day," and observed their treatment by the overseers. She saw the inmates driven on with whips. Some of the capos beat inmates and so did SS men with their clubs.[34]

From one of the capos Theresia S. received an early lesson in the behavior expected of a civilian working in proximity to the inmates. He enjoined her "that I need not . . . look to the left, I need not look to the right, I need not see."[35] She was simply to do her work. As in Mauthausen, the bystander wore blinders, kept a stiff neck, and peered straight ahead. Sideward motion of the head drew suspicion. The angle of noninvolvement was forward.

In spite of the warning, Theresia S. was unavoidably aware of the pitiful condition of the inmates she saw. She noticed their hands and feet were uncovered, and attempted to leave behind cloth as well as food for them to pick up beside the road. After being spotted by a guard with "a bit of rag for their feet," she was summoned before an SS lieutenant who threatened to send her to a concentration camp. In consideration of her age, and the work she had been doing on behalf of the new enterprise, he relented.[36]

She regularly saw and heard inmates being beaten. She saw that those inmates who fell and did not immediately arise were struck repeatedly. From a nearby building, a sports facility, she "often heard" the sounds of inmates being struck with a cane, as well as screams of agony. "My God, now they're beating another one again," she remembered thinking to herself.[37]

Most residents resigned themselves to the evidence of brutality. They sensed "one [simply] cannot help, one may not help, and also one could not [do so]. One was no longer so sensitive when one [of the inmates] was beaten." Several days laborers from the railway worked part-time on her family's farm, and took meals with them. The laborers expressed the view that if the inmates had not broken the law in some way they would not have ended up in a concentration camp. They sought to defend themselves against identification with the inmates by pointing to the logic of crime and punishment, yet failed to see that the Nazis had long ago undermined any rational correspondence between the two. The residents feared that any interference on their part could lead to their own arrest and imprisonment. The presence of the camp in their home town was a daily reminder of the extremes to which the regime was capable of subjecting a person. Still, the farmhands, like most of their fellow citizens, welcomed the rationale of inmate criminality as an excuse to remain uninvolved. In the interest of their own "survival," they believed it best to remain aloof. They did not look at the inmates, rather they looked out for themselves and narrowed their angle of vision to exclude the horror. The less one saw at the time, the less one recalled years later. Theresia S. noted forty years afterwards that many of her fellow residents "forgot everything." At best, their memories were spotted with an occasional benign recollection. They spoke of having noticed the inmates "marching and singing" on their way to work. "They always said that Zipf was so camouflaged, so secret. Each one simply knew: he was not permitted to see and not permitted to hear. It was just best to get through it."[38]

Some townspeople strongly disapproved of what they saw taking place, yet they too held their tongues. Herr Be., 38 years old at the time, was a shoemaker ordered to Zipf in 1943 by the shoemaker's trade association. During the camp's existence he worked in a barrack making shoes for the civilian employees. He did not make shoes for the inmates, who (when fortunate) wore wooden shoes. He shared the barrack with a barber.[39]

Herr Be. was of the view that "all the Zipfer knew what was going on in the operation and in the concentration camp; that the inmates were poor devils; one saw, for example, how the inmates dragged their colleagues home. He saw the inmates on the brewery-factory grounds go by, [there was] much hunger. . . . Capos were often swine, the guard detail did less."[40] Herr Be. admitted his disgust at what he witnessed, but honestly conveyed that in the prevailing "climate of fear, mistrust, and repression," he held his tongue and acted blind.[41]

If Herr Be. represented the silent, yet watchful, observer, Frau E. characterized the type of bystander who, though unable not to see what was happening in the nearby camp, chose not to look, or inquire. "She embodie[d] the type [of resident] who made [the] regime possible: not speaking, not looking, not even asking afterward, not once curious, for in her close position next to the camp she could learn more than most other residents."[42] Frau E.'s house was situated "directly next to the camp," affording her an excellent observation point. To be sure, she recalled aspects of the camp's appearance: there were "watch towers, lit by night, atop which were guards. She heard screams [coming] from the camp." The guards had weapons, and the inmates were "without strength, visibly foaming," and were "carried back into the camp by their comrades." Frau E. worked in the armaments operation as a cleaning woman inside the administrative building. She was simply told to do her work and not look around. An "SS man or Gestapo man in civil dress came and warned against passing on talk. An SS man conceded that the inmates were from Mauthausen and were brought back there."[43]

Frau E.'s reluctance to inquire about events in the nearby camp might reflect the fact that in the home she shared with her mother and son were quartered an SS man (who struck her as "peculiar") and his family, as well as two civilian technicians from the Schlier firm, with whom "she never spoke" concerning "their work and tasks." During the rocket tests, she noticed how "there was a roar and the house shook," and "fire-light was visible at the bunker up above." One of the technicians living with her family was killed in an explosion at the test site. Afterwards, his belongings were removed from the house. Fearing for the safety of her mother and son, she maintained silence: "everyone in the locality held his distance."[44]

Frau Dorothea H., like Frau E., submitted to the advice and warnings of her superiors to keep quiet and mind her tasks. In the Schlier administration she served as a girl Friday, telephone operator, and bookkeeper. She had studied at a trade academy in Salzburg and received her *Matura* certificate in 1943.[45]

She said that in Zipf there was "an unwritten law: do not talk, do not ask." Yet there was some clandestine discussion concerning the fate of the inmates. "Cases of death among the inmates were rumored about. Some were very thin and sick. One often said: this one will not survive the winter. The winter of 1943–44 was a severe winter, and the inmates had to clear snow."[46] She knew the inmates had been working on the cellars at the brewery. Though echoing the statement of others that "the capos were mostly worse than the SS people," she recalled that her mother, cooking soup, asked one capo if she might give inmates working near her home something to eat. The capo responded by indicating she could do so, "that he sees nothing, and so the inmates slurped the soup away at zooming speed."[47] Despite her mother's gesture, Frau H. feared the inmates and if possible avoided the vicinity of the camp: "if one did not absolutely have to go past the camp, one preferred a longer detour."[48]

Fear and mistrust gripped civilians living outside the camp and sufficed to close off one principal source of information about life within the gates—camp personnel. Together, the townspeople and the individuals working in the camp and the test facilities shared an unspoken commitment to silence. "It was not only that the persons employed in Zipf passed on nothing of the scope and corresponding perceptions of their duties, but on their own part the residents hardly posed any questions, because they already knew the answer, that is, the silence. In other words, [there was] a kind of still and silent agreement in daily life."[49] A potential channel of exchange and communication was consciously blocked and ignored.

An SS man trained in Mauthausen who arrived in Zipf on 16 October 1943 did not talk about the camp with civilians with whom he had contact. "Not a word, not a sound, there it was dark," he remarked. In the SS barrack he shared with five to seven other men, relationships were cool and wary, making discussion difficult even among peers. Mistrust was enhanced by the mixture of SS men from different backgrounds: Austrians, Germans, Sudeten Germans, and Germans from other lands

[*Volksdeutsche*]. In addition, personnel were frequently rotated, precluding close personal bonds among the men.[50]

His disinterest in affairs outside the narrow scope of his assignments was reinforced during "his training to become an SS private in Mauthausen." Although this is doubtful, he claimed that "he was afforded no sight of the inmates and the rock quarry, since the SS barrack was outside the camp by the [SS] swimming pool." He insisted that he neither clearly saw, nor did he pay attention to what went on in the concentration camp. Rather, he learned not to ask certain questions: "On the basis of bad experience ('the next time it will cost you your head') one appropriate[d] a self-behavior mechanism; disinterest." Even if one were interested, "one could not learn the truth anyway."[51]

Along with camp personnel, the local party chief, *Ortsgruppenleiter* Z., was in a position to learn a good deal about the concentration camp, but he too remained narrowly focused on his own duties. He remembered that an SS man came to demand confiscation of space at the brewery, but he claimed that at first he was not aware that the facility was to be converted into an outpost of the Mauthausen concentration camp. Nevertheless, he admitted that "in time everything became known." Herr Z. had contact with the secretaries, young women from the League of German Girls, who worked in the Schlier office. They were quartered in private homes and villas in the area. "For some time," in fact, one of them stayed in his own home, "but [there were] no discussions about Schlier, since officially the *Ortsgruppeneiter* had nothing to do with Schlier." Furthermore, though he knew that "the inmates were poor dogs, that one saw," he recalled no instances of "torture, death of inmates." Besides, there was a general rule forbidding communication with the inmates.[52]

Meinhard H., an engineer assigned as a photographer to the testing station in Zipf, explained his limited contacts with both resident civilians and inmates. He was one of the many outsiders who came to Zipf to work on the rocket program, yet who remained strangers in the town, too preoccupied with their own assignments to pay heed to the camp. Overburdened with long working hours, he insisted there was no time to make contacts with civilians in Vöcklamarkt, where he lived for a time, and Zipf. "I had to get up mornings around seven, six o'clock. Around seven o'clock away, and evenings back late. I did not recognize Vöcklamarkt at all. It was always dark, dark, dark."[53] Working 12-hour days, except Sunday, left Herr H. little time for the cultivation of outside contacts. Long hours made one too tired to think about others. In any event, he kept quiet about matters concerning Zipf: "I was a bearer of secrets. I was not permitted to speak."[54]

Engineer H. did in fact have some access to inmates who did certain odd jobs for him. Like practically everyone else in Zipf, though his contact with the inmates was limited, he had seen them "when they had to do something for me. They had to pick up some coal, or some piece of furniture or chest, and [perform] similar tasks."[55] In any event, Herr H., whose job at the test site involved photographing measurements registered on the pressure gauge, had a sharp eye for the things that interested him. The delicacies of nature, for example, drew his attention, and years later came easily to mind. Speaking of the testing zone, he remembered how "up there there were wonderful blueberries. I searched for blueberries. Even today I see them still." Yet he seemed convinced that on the whole "the inmates were very well treated."[56]

Some of the residents in Zipf were genuinely disturbed by what they saw of the treatment of the inmates. A woman who lived a little more than a mile from the camp, recalled the effect on her family of witnessing events associated with the camp:

> My father was at the time a warehouse man at the railway station Redl-Zipf, the reloading point for the armaments construction just beginning. Ever new, terrifying reports came home of terror by the SS and the unimaginable condition of the prisoners who were assigned to the work details. Here they were also unloaded, and after they were incapable of work . . . they were loaded for shipment back to Mauthausen. The wagons were . . . prepared like other cattle or freight transports. We always lived in fear that one day he could not return home, because at the beginning he indeed tried to mix in, which was life-threatening. I know of his anger, helpless rage and desperation over what he experienced.[57]

Similarly, the young son of a locomotive engineer, Franz E., noted that "his father reported to him that he often saw how laboring inmates inside the works grounds were mistreated."[58]

The realization of what was happening in and to the town took little time. In the beginning the residents showed simple interest in all the activity going on. Soon enough followed the understanding that their town had become the site of a concentration camp:

> The initial curiosity about the construction activities—work went on day and night—soon transformed itself into distress, as one was suddenly confronted with the reality of the concentration camp and the SS guards. My

terrifying experience was [to observe] the laying of cable along the street from Zipf . . . in deepest winter and in all weather conditions. Everything had to be done by hand, dug out with only clamps and shovels, without appropriate shoe covering or mittens, [dressed] only in the usual striped outfit, [with] head shorn even when the cap was missing. The housewives there attempted to bring the inmates tea or something to eat, which was strictly forbidden and unconditionally prohibited by the guards. There were exceptions.[59]

Herr S., a fireman, made a terrifying discovery concerning the fate of the inmates when his curiosity provoked him. Once a driver who had stopped at the fire department gasoline pump behaved "quite impetuously," arousing Herr S.'s interest. He then took advantage of an unguarded moment to peek inside the truck. "In the vehicle lay inmates, all dead (presumably destined for Mauthausen)."[60]

Whether curious or not, whether desiring it or not, residents could not avoid knowledge of the concentration camp, the brutality of the overseers, and the maltreatment of the inmates. The camp had massively altered the physical and moral landscape of this small rural community. The ground was torn open, cables set into the ground, cement was poured, new rails laid; barbed wire enclosures and guard towers appeared, followed by the engineers, the laborers, the young women, and the guards, the capos, and the inmates. One not only saw these changes, but one heard sounds unusual and frightening for this area. A dozen times a day booming noises emanated from the mountain where the rocket tests occurred. At any time of day one might unexpectedly hear something else approaching from the distance. Franz E. recalled that "he was outside with his mother when he heard a peculiar noise that came ever nearer. Then a large column of inmates appeared in marching rows. Some carried food in tin buckets."[61] The presence of the inmates, their labors, and their treatment were daily sights in and around the town. Although the Nazis had the buildings in the town painted black in an effort to conceal all this, the dark silhouettes remained. Though the town became invisible from the sky, the blackness could not hide the horror visible on the ground below.

Chapter 5

Outside the Monastery

No structure so dominates and typifies the town of Melk, situated some 48 miles downriver from Mauthausen, as its beautiful Benedictine abbey. Rising from a granite promontory 187 feet in height, the Melk monastery towers over the landscape, overlooking both the Danube and the town of Melk nestled directly below. The Benedictines have occupied this awesome setting since 1089, the year Leopold II called the Benedictine order to Melk.[1] The structure's colossal, ocher-colored facade is dotted with more than a thousand windows that both look out upon and admit the world, suffusing the interior with light. A pair of architectural ranges, one of whose famed corridors has been likened to "a baroque railway tunnel" that "in either direction . . . stretches away seemingly to infinity,"[2] encompass the complex and culminate on one side in the renowned monastic library, stocked with 85,000 books and "1,200 manuscripts from the 9th to the 15th centuries."[3] Opposite the library lies the magnificent *Marmorsaal*, or marble dining hall. The two rooms are joined by a great terrace affording a commanding view of the river, the railway, the town, and the hills and fields round about.[4]

Clasped like a jewel within the embrace of this magnificence lies the abbey's splendid baroque church whose twin steeples rise yet another 207 feet from the rock toward the heavens. The visitor to Melk will crane his neck upward to take in its riches. Upon the ceiling of the dining hall the eighteenth-century Tyrolean artist Paul Troger has painted Pallas Athena riding out of the clouds "on a chariot drawn by lions," sailing "from the kingdom of darkness, evil, and brutality into the kingdom of light, goodness, and beauty which is to prepare the way for science and art." The theme is echoed on the central vault of the church where one finds depicted St. Benedict, founder of the holy order, "surrounded by the allegorical illustrations of the battle against evil." On the church's high altar, beneath a golden papal crown, the biblical prophets stand arrayed to the left and right of Peter and Paul. The crown points toward Christ above, and "the sign of victory, the Cross, towers over all." Beneath the cross, "to the left before God the Father stands the majestic figure of Moses. The earthly leader of God's people points to the tablets of the Ten Commandments. . . . Correspondingly, . . . on the other side to the right of God the Father we find Aaron, the spiritual leader of God's people, and behind him in the ceiling fresco a representation of the church, which incites Christian fervor. Above all this Veronica's veil acts as a banner for the spiritual domain."[5] The entire complex is a confident celebration of light, learning, and faith triumphant.[6]

For centuries the abbey had dominated the town below. It alone displayed unmatched magnificence; no adjacent structure dared challenge its splendor and power. Secured to the granite beneath which "the land falls away in sheer cliffs on every side," the abbey held sway over the Danube's rushing waters and dwarfed the buildings and lanes of the town. The abbey bore its dominance over the inhabitants below with the benevolence of a guardian. In times of trouble "the people knew that true safety was only to be found inside the abbey walls. They lived in the keeping, in the shadow, and in the refulgence of the abbey."[7]

Over the years Melk had welcomed famous guests: emperors and empresses, musicians and generals. Young Mozart had stopped here, and in 1805 and 1809 so did Napoleon Bonaparte. Staying at the monastery, he is said to have sampled wine from its cellar, walked with the prior in the abbey garden, and enjoyed the view.[8] More than a century later, on 14 March 1938, fresh from his enthusiastic reception in Linz, Adolf Hitler briefly halted in the town of Melk on his triumphant ride to Vienna.

A news report spoke of the "thousands upon thousands [who] surround[ed] the car" in the square, the "flowers upon flowers handed to the Führer" who "had to grasp countless hands." So pressing was the crush of well-wishers, "the SS men and soldiers from Germany and Austria were able to clear only a narrow alley for the Führer's vehicle."[9] Standing in the automobile, wrapped in a trench coat, he rose above the crowd and lifted an ungloved hand to acknowledge their greeting.

"People were thrilled. They were wildly thrilled when they first set eyes on Hitler," recalled a woman who claimed to have seen him on the main square that day. "We looked upon him as a god. Like a god. He had thoroughly light skin—he had eaten no meat—and light blue eyes. Blue eyes, yes, beautiful, such beautiful blue eyes! Really. That one time on the main square I got such a really good look at him. People really just fell at his feet." Women dressed in traditional *Dirndl*, or apron dresses, "broke out in tears. Yes, at that time he was very, very beloved." She summarized the mood at that time as "simply a jubilation."[10] Another woman who was on hand wrote of the excitement of rejoicing at the arrival of the Führer. "The March days of 1938 were indeed unforgettable. One could see great manifestations of joy. Ringing with enthusiasm, we were on hand for the welcoming of the Führer in Melk. Afterwards I went to visit the *Ortsgruppenleiter* [local party group leader], Wedl, a school colleague of my son. His young wife showed me the cup she [had] presented to the Führer, and when I tried to sip from it, she said she had already licked it up on all sides."[11] Another Melk resident, who recalled being in the hospital in Melk that day for an appendix operation, spoke of the "frighteningly loud" shouting coming from the town center. "The people screamed and were as frenzied as madmen."[12]

To see and to touch and to shout with joy; to be as near as the outstretched hand or even the tongue can bring one near; to be within sight of him, to catch the reflection of light from his eyes, or the brightness of his skin: those who jammed into the town square in Melk that day in March 1938 were united in their wish to be close. They *wanted* to see; they not only lifted their arms and opened their mouths, they swiveled their necks and raised up their eyes. In their intoxication, amid the "ringing of bells" and the "roar and tumult of shouts of *Heil*,"[13] the townspeople formed a wild chorus. No less were they an attentive and ecstatic audience whose vision was singularly focused.

High above, distant yet still bound to the delirious mass, stood privileged spectators: Benedictine monks who stepped out onto the abbey terrace to enjoy a bird's eye view. Perched above the scene, the monks experienced no jostling, no rubbing of shoulders with the host below. To enhance their splendid vantage, one of the monks had brought a pair of binoculars. "[We] looked down, saw how the people were set up, and all of a sudden the auto arrived with Hitler." Father R., one of the monks, recalled that in the face of this event he "had been speechless, inwardly speechless as well [*sprachlos gewesen, auch innerlich sprachlos*]," but added, "I was full of hope, surely full of expectation."[14]

Six years after this unforgettable celebration such excitement must have seemed light years distant. Much had changed. Hope had been transformed to anxiety and apprehension. Enemy aircraft flew overhead on their way to bomb targets in the area; the eastern front was drawing nearer to the borders of the Reich. And on a hill just beyond the railroad tracks, about 650 yards from the terrace of the monastery, a concentration camp had been established.

The concentration camp of Melk was founded on 20 April 1944, Adolf Hitler's 55th birthday. It lasted nearly a year; in the final weeks of the war the camp was forced to disband, and the guards and prisoners were shunted westward between April 11 and 15, 1945. The camp occupied the premises of the Freiherr von Birago-Pioneer-Kaserne, a barrack for the Austrian Corps of Engineers built before World War I, located atop a hill just south of and astride the railway artery connecting Salzburg, Linz, and Vienna.

The Melk camp was built to accommodate inmates drawn from many nations—France, Germany, Austria, Russia, Poland, Yugoslavia, Italy, Spain, and Greece—who had been exiled to Mauthausen. Some 1,100 French political inmates from Mauthausen were among the first to arrive by 23 April 1944.[15] In addition came thousands of Hungarian Jews, part of some 7,500 first sent to Mauthausen from Auschwitz on four transports in May and June 1944. Those deemed unfit for work were immediately selected for extermination at Mauthausen; the remainder were largely routed to the satellite camps.[16] In Melk the inmates were set to work primarily in the underground factories of the German armaments industry, producing ball-bearings for tanks and aircraft. The inmates themselves dug these underground factories from a mountain known as the Wachberg. The tunnels were situated outside Melk near the town of Roggendorf, some 3 miles distant. Inmates were also engaged in such projects as flood protection, the collection of wood, laying of cable, and canal construction.[17]

The Melk concentration camp bore the code-name "Quarz," derived from the soft quartz sand native to the region. It was through this shifting sand that the inmates had to dig the underground tunnels. The work was especially dangerous, because the disturbance of the sand led to frequent cave-ins.[18] The inmates reached the tunnels by train. Each day they were marched through the town in shifts to a loading area just beyond the railway station, and then transported by rail to the tunnels. The return journey followed the same route.[19]

The inmates were poorly nourished and clothed. Housed in primitive wooden barracks, sleeping four to a bunk, they were exposed to cold and disease. As the camp grew, conditions worsened. Of 10,000 men not more than 1,000 to 1,200 were outfitted with shirts; only half possessed shoes.[20] Their deficient diet consisted of coffee, watery animal feed stew, 10.5 ounces of ersatz bread, and just under an ounce of both margarine and sausage per day.[21]

During the single year of the camp's existence nearly 5,000 of the camp's more than 14,000 registered inmates died of beatings, shootings, and work accidents. To these deaths should be added those among the 1,544 inmates, many badly weakened and ill, sent from Melk to their destruction in Mauthausen and Castle Hartheim. In January 1945 alone, 1,221 inmates were recorded as having died, nearly 40 per day. This was the highest total recorded for any single month. In November 1944 a crematorium was put in operation in Melk. Until then, those inmates who died in Melk were also transported to Mauthausen for disposal.[22]

Inmates steadily arrived in Melk, beginning as early as 11 April 1944, when a contingent of 500 began work on shelters for inmates and guards. Arrivals continued throughout the camp's existence, and by the end of January 1945 the camp recorded its highest total of the war, 10,314 inmates. This figure was more than three times the figure of 2,898 persons recorded as comprising the town's population in 1934. The inmates were watched by SS guards whose numbers rose from 150 at the beginning to as many as 800. The number of inmates in the camp sank toward the total of 7,478 listed on the rolls when the dissolution of the camp began on 11 April 1945.[23]

Inmates who moved from Mauthausen to its outlying camps journeyed from the darkness of one enclosure to the darkness of another. Between camp and camp lay the routes of passage: footpaths, roads, and rail lines intersecting the terrain of the bystanders. For some 500 inmates selected to enter the new camp in Melk, such a journey began before dawn on 23 April 1944. "Under the watchful light of the searchlights," noted René Gille, a French veteran of this crossing, they marched through the darkened prisoner compound amid "the silence of the camp." Fittingly, they were attired in the garments of night. They wore "these famous vertically striped, light gray and blue costumes . . . which bring to mind pajamas," appropriately sewn of a material "resembling mattress fabric." With the town's permanent dwellers in the shadow, they passed through the gates of the camp beneath the "black banner of the overlord, luminous, struck with the double SS stylized in white."[24]

Once beyond the threshold, Gille and his fellows encountered the world with keen eyes. "As soon as we [left] the outskirts of the camp . . . as soon as the high wall of the camp [slipped] from view we [were] in the midst of greenery. The meadows [were] veritable fields of dandelions, on all sides as far as the eye can see." They walked past the town of Mauthausen skirting the rushing waters of the Danube swollen with melted snow.[25]

The townspeople were "still asleep." Oblivious to the marchers, they soon would be up and about. Reaching the railway station, the inmates encountered some early risers. These were the station employees. They seemed preoccupied and indifferent. The inmates' "arrival arouse[d] not the least curiosity among the personnel." Long accustomed to the sight of inmates, they "[went] about their work in the most natural fashion."[26]

In bright daylight[27] the inmates boarded the train and departed. The route to the new camp took them eastward past the nearby cities of St. Valentin and Amstetten. They saw the spring landscape dotted with pleasant features; traveling along the Danube, they were "able to admire, with melancholy, the smart villages with their roadside inns and their arbors at the edge of the river."[28] After traversing the Austrian countryside, "toward noon" the train halted to disgorge the striped voyagers. They had arrived in Melk, and its famed Benedictine monastery, situated some 400 yards from the station, rose up before their eyes upon the heights. It was a sight, noted Gille, he would "pass every day for nine months morning and evening!"[29]

They reached their ultimate destination, "a big ocher-colored caserne"[30] via "an uphill path" that cut "between the meadows and villas, so neat and so cheerful, with their orchards in blossom." Two days earlier another shipment of inmates had reached Melk. On arrival Gille found these men "already at work, installing the barbed wire."[31]

In addition to preparing the camp, the inmates quickly attended to the vital tasks of digging tunnels for the ball-bearing works located underground in Roggendorf. To facilitate the movement of inmates from Melk to Roggendorf by rail, the inmates immediately began the construction of immense loading platforms, each some 250 yards long and 18–23 feet wide, situated astride the tracks in Melk as well as outside the tunnels at Roggendorf. By the end of May 1944, about 985 yards of platform were completed, at which time stairways were added.[32] Upon these platforms some 7,000 men a day climbed in and out of the railway wagons leading to and from the tunnels.

Inmates recalled the wait for the trains atop these boards as having been among their worst moments. Helpless, exposed to the elements, they waited for the transports that would take them to the tunnels. Contrary to initial impressions, the weather proved to be punishing. They suffered under the hot sun, the wind and rain, frost and snow, as well as "the harsh Austrian wind [that] lash[ed] their weakened and poorly clothed bodies."[33] Adding force to nature's blasts, Stuttgart-bound express trains roared past at more than 80 miles an hour, whipping up "glacial whirlwinds of snow, in a violent wind." Frequent delays only intensified their agony, and "For many, the extended waiting for several hours, standing in the cold on these elevated platforms [was] the beginning of a fatal pneumonia."[34] After a torturous winter, there was a brief thaw at the beginning of February 1945, "but soon the rain [made] its reappearance on this Danube plain, open to all the winds of the east and west indifferently bringing us snow or rain, according to the season. And, as in the spring and preceding autumn, we again [began] to wear clothes for weeks at a time which never [had] a chance to dry."[35]

Every inmate assigned to the caves descended and ascended this path twice a day. Those who died in the tunnels were dragged one final time up the hill. Each day was a struggle to remain standing. Torment settled into the extremities. "We march in step, dragging our more or less dismantled wooden shoes, wounding our damaged feet."[36] "The climb up to the camp is hard, each day a veritable Golgotha. The Austrian roads are simple paved paths where the ruts . . . are deep. In dry weather our feet, heavy with fatigue and edemas, shift clouds of dust. In bad weather we wallow in thick mud. . . . In winter the snow, beaten and compressed by 7,000 men who take the route two times a day, quickly becomes a thick ice, a skating rink, a glazed frost upon which we slide, carrying away with us all our comrades in the row, possibly playing ninepins with the other rows [as well]."[37]

"That the people of Melk didn't at all know that in Melk there was a concentration camp is notorious nonsense and a lie," noted Dr. Hans E., another survivor of the Melk concentration camp.[38] Each day the inmates were brought to the vicinity of the railway station from where, after loading onto a freight wagon stationed on a side track, they were brought to their work-site by train. On their way to the station the inmates marched through the town. Hiking to and from the station in two shifts, columns of inmates appeared in the town four times each day.[39] Residents would have seen the inmates visibly exhausted and in poor condition. As the men trudged back from work those still able bore "the dying, or those already dead, into the camp on crossed beams which they had somewhere acquired."[40]

Although the loading area was on a side track that was somewhat isolated from the main station area, and the civilian populace could not get a direct view of the proceeding, Dr. E. believes that they surely knew of the repeated daily comings and goings of the inmates: "We marched through the town, we were at the railway station and there . . . stood a freight train, and the inmates were already on the ramp. . . . The civilian population would not have had the possibility at all even to see how we were loaded in the wagons. That was outside the area somehow. But they knew, that is, the inmates are coming there, and coming back again. That is certainly completely clear. Unmistakably."[41]

Town residents confirm Dr. E.'s assertion that they were aware of the presence of the inmates near the station. Father R. one of 8 to 10 monks who stayed on at the Melk monastery during the war, recalled both the construction and existence of a separate location where the inmates boarded the trains: "one saw it. Vis-à-vis the train a separate boarding place was built outside of Melk."[42] When asked if he had seen how it was actually built, or only saw it afterwards when it was standing, he replied: "Yes. I saw that. Both. Perhaps during construction there was a platform. That was nothing special. A kind of platform where the train halted, where they then climbed in, and then were led to the work site."[43]

Frau Erika S. also recalled the existence of the loading area: "Earlier the inmates climbed in at the railway station, at the freight station. The train waited for them. And so many residents of Melk went there to look. They went to look. You know how people are. They're just stupid. And then on the other side a wooden building was constructed. It must have been a barn or something like it. They climbed in over there so that one did not see over it."[44]

Even without directly viewing the scenes taking place by the railway, nearby residents were thoroughly frightened by the sounds they could hear coming from the area. "You know, a big staircase was there. They built it over there in front of the railroad," recalled Frau Maria R., then a postal employee in Melk. "And these inmates were driven up it. But the neighbors heard shouts. They said they shook with fear, shook through their whole body, you know. And the inmates went there so often. They were very thin, didn't get much to eat. One left them a little piece of bread, with a little bit of something on it. But left hidden, so that they found a little bit of something."[45] Hearing these sounds coming from the direction of the steps, neighbors of Frau R. living near the staircase were too fearful to go and look. "No one dared, you know." Instead, they yelled to the guards from their windows. "They certainly shouted a couple times: 'Quiet down! Quiet down!' Because the guards beat the inmates rather often."[46]

Curious onlookers came to gape at the inmates not only at the loading area, but also near the camp itself. "There were indeed people in Melk who went on up. Then they positioned themselves behind the caserne near the woods, and looked in on what was happening in the camp," noted Erika S.[47] She indicated that she did not join them: "How can I do such a thing? I certainly can't help. I couldn't do that at all. That was an impossibility. One can't do such a thing."[48]

Another woman, Frau G. S., remembers having walked by the buildings on the side of the camp facing the street. She said she could look inside and see the inmates and their simple bunk beds. Walking by this building in 1983, she pointed inside, remarking, "So, the inmates were in there. They were in there. . . . The people walked by on the street. They could look in and see the inmates. Yes, yes. One saw everything, indeed so."[49]

Some town residents saw the inmates marching to work, or engaged in construction projects in local areas. "One saw how these emaciated inmates walked. It filled one with pity, you know," recalled Frau R. Nearby, and even in the town center, one came across them, "because they had to build a canal. Over there in Pielach[50] a canal was built. . . . And one saw them working. And in the evenings, around six or seven, they marched back home to the barracks."[51] It was in fact difficult to pass through the area near the camp, whether on foot or on bicycle, without coming in contact with columns of inmates and their overseers. As yet another woman, Frau Ri., noted, "In the war I was employed at the health office, and my daily route was past the concentration camp. A single time, one of them was beaten, and that was on a Sunday. That I only heard, and didn't look. . . . I was under way. My parent's home was three miles distant from Melk. . . . And then at the end of '44, when the tunnels were built there—the inmates had to make them—I saw them daily. Almost daily. They were so completely exhausted, accompanied by two or three overseers with weapons. And now and again one was carried by four others. This one was carried because of exhaustion. That is indeed in my memory. That was '44 and the beginning of '45. In May, '45, everything was over."[52]

Monks from the Benedictine monastery also saw the inmates passing by in work columns. "One was able to see them from the monastery. Naturally that was from a distance," noted Father R. "One saw them more closely in the final years—in '44, '45, that is, '44, the air attacks had already begun—and even before then one saw how they marched down by the Danube. In an entire group, a big group, but there were guard personnel there. Well, yes, one was not able to see easily from the monastery, but somehow one was able to observe them. We knew. And by chance once I saw them there on the street. I remember that a couple of times I saw them on the street there. I saw that they carried a dead man. They had a kind of stretcher on their shoulders upon which they carried a dead man."[53]

Men from Melk who were enlisted into the home defense forces, the *Volkssturm*, certainly became aware of the existence of the camp. Indeed, H.E., a forester who served in the home guard, knew of the existence of the concentration camp immediately after it was established. Only two days after returning from an outing on the Königssee on 19 April 1944, he noted in his diary. "On the twenty-first I see the concentration camp, substitute camp, in the caserne. The corps of engineers are transferred on account of the concentration camp to Krems.[54]

During attempted escapes the local militia was pressed into the search for fleeing inmates. The forester took part in some of these patrols. He recorded that on 2 July 1944 he was awakened in the middle of the night and summoned to the police. Two inmates had escaped, and he and others were made to patrol until five in the morning. On 6 August, he was again called out to participate in a search for an inmate who had fled, his diary reporting this in a brief notation: "inmate-catching."[55] Citizens could not help being aware of the chase, as escaped inmates being hunted by the patrols on occasion passed directly by the homes of town residents. The forester indicated that on 6 November "around midnight a guard shoots at a fleeing inmate who wanted to get in at our garden gate, and hits the wall next to our left bedroom window. The bullet pierces and breaks the window frame and the window."[56]

Soldiers who returned on leave also had contact with the columns of prisoners they could see marching under guard. Gustav M., son of the town's mayor, came home to Melk once after serving two years in Russia. He said he was in civilian clothes at the time he came across a column of several hundred inmates coming from the camp on their way to work. He recalled how one of the guards noticed him watching and shouted at him, "Don't come too close, or you'll have difficulties." This confrontation with the inmates came as a disturbing surprise. It was "the first time I saw the misery as they marched toward me, and they were in part also dragged along by their comrades when they were no longer fully capable of walking."[57]

Herr M. was disturbed enough by what he had seen that he spoke about it later both with his fellow soldiers, and with his father and mother. They told him it was impermissible to talk of these things, adding that the inmates "were all opponents of Hitler, and people who were to be seen as traitors to the German people."[58]

Local residents were not the only ones to see the inmates. Passengers on trains passing through Melk were able to get a close look, especially when the trains halted. Passengers could distinctly make out the violet-striped uniforms and the characteristic, narrow razor-cut on the heads of the inmates. A teacher who traveled from Scheibbs to her home in Prinzersdorf, a neighboring village just outside St. Pölten, could "remember very well the prisoners who were led down in such large divisions, eight to a row. On this ramp, approximately where today the sugar beets are loaded on the railway, they had to line up, and on the ramp were these guard people. And the inmates were shorn, with a stripe, so they could not escape. That I remember very precisely."[59]

As one veteran of the platforms and the tunnels recalled, the long wait beside the tracks would end with the arrival of the transport, an "old locomotive . . . followed by 20 freight wagons," he writes. "We climb up two by two, we must hold one another by the arm to facilitate the count. We are crowded on each side of the central door to which we must turn our backs, and above all not try to turn our heads, the cudgel of the capo is watching."[60]

The trains bearing the inmates halted before the entrance to the tunnels. In April 1944, the setting still appeared deceptively pleasant. Inmates arriving in Roggendorf to lay the groundwork for digging the tunnels found themselves "in the midst of a green valley, fresh rye bordering a village of apple trees in blossom, cherry and peach trees."[61] In January 1945, the underground works long in operation, another inmate assigned to the tunnels could still admire a bit of the winter landscape from the platform outside, noting "the red sun which appears above the horizon toward the little pine forest, down there, on the hill which covers the subterranean factory hollowed out of its flank. It is there we go to work." Then the image shifts abruptly to the sight of the dead: "Our comrades of the night shift are aligned to the left of the cement path. At the head, three cadavers on stretchers." Before work begins, the labor consignments are checked. "The foremen of the German firms entrusted with the work are there. Each capo takes his count of men in accord with the civilian boss."[62]

Life-threatening climates prevail in the underground cavities. Meteorologists of death, the men know which of the several tunnels afford the best and worst conditions for survival. The caves are divided into six galleries, labeled A through F. "C is the hottest gallery. . . . E . . . is humid; along with F this is the worst gallery," for in the latter "the water drips everywhere, and the pumps do not manage to dry the large pools of water. Many of our comrades there caught the last blows needed to demolish their frail carcasses. The capos there were cynical assassins."[63]

Even those inmates privileged to work as specialists in the "better" tunnels were subject to assault without provocation. Should a power failure halt the assembly line, simultaneously causing the lights to fail, an inmate knew "the civilian foreman will not hesitate to let loose a volley of blows of [his] iron cudgel." Equally unrestrained, the SS were on hand to strike the inmate in charge of the power "twenty-five blows to the buttocks if, at this moment, busy at the bottom of the gallery, [he did] not rapidly catch sight of the breakdown."[64]

The overseers needed little excuse to vent their fury. When it was discovered that two inmates were missing at the end of the shift enraged capos went back into the tunnels. Finding a pair of Hungarian Jews who had apparently "fallen asleep" inside, the head capo "hurls himself upon them" and "successively" strikes them "on the head with two truncheons." After they fall to the ground he proceeds to kick them hard in the abdomen and about the face. Frenzied, the guards join in. "Powerless, we are only able to mark our disapproval by turning our heads a little to the other side," recalled one of the inmates who witnessed the spectacle. Under these circumstances, the turning of the head, the averted gaze, signaled not indifference, but a humane response. "The blood spurts. They no longer utter cries." All that is left to do is haul their remains back to the camp where their comrades deposit them in the bottom of the sick bay "with the cadavers."[65]

The telltale odor of smoke coming from the crematorium left no doubt in the minds of the Melk citizenry that inmates were being burned in the camp. "In any case, when we went walking down there, that is, over there, one smelled the skin, the way it irritates. It has this peculiar odor. And the hair, one smelled that. That smells so. That is from the chimney there," recalled Frau G.S.[66] Yet, in the mind of this woman there was something almost matter-of-fact about this perception. Believing the inmates to have died of exhaustion and starvation, rather than having been deliberately mistreated and killed, she regarded their disposal in this way as routine. She noticed the odor as she strolled, but the sensation was easily explained away. "I said, 'uh huh, someone is being burned again.' One smells that, you know. That is, I believe none were shot in Melk. They often simply died of hunger or something. They often died of weakness."[67]

Frau Erika S. also recalled the smoke from the crematorium. "Oh, yes, we noticed that, especially when the wind blew back. We always said, when the wind reverses, and the lower wind blew, it blew upward, but when the west wind blew we had the whole stink inside here."[68]

Frau Maria R. was also certain that she sensed the crematorium in operation. "Yes, that one certainly knew. That one certainly knew. One said then, 'Holy Lord God, it has smoked again. They have burned again.' "[69] The employee in the health bureau who passed by the camp on her bicycle to and from work could not forget the sensation either. "One smelled it, when the crematorium was in operation there."[70]

Among the strongest recollections of town residents is the fear they felt before the uniformed men who guarded the prisoners. That fear succeeded above all in enforcing silence and obedience. People explicitly expressed their fear of being drawn into the system of terror in which they would share the experience of the inmates. The repeated threat of the guards to force those who aided the inmates, or who tarried too long in their presence, to "come right along" was effective. It alone sufficed to check acts of assistance or displays of sympathy.

In addition, townspeople believed that resistance was in itself a crime, a form of lawlessness that brought upon the perpetrator the taint of guilt and criminality. The Nazi's standard explanation that those who were thrown into the concentration camps were indeed criminals was internalized by many of the civilians.

Frau Maria R. stated that she refused to join the others flocking to the main square on the day Hitler rode through Melk in March 1938. Yet, as a postal employee she was obliged to attend local party assemblies held in the town's movie house. She described how these gatherings were preceded by an announcement delivered by a party functionary who knocked on her door, reminding her and her husband of their duty to attend. She did so, although she found these meetings depressing affairs from which she departed in quiet despair. In the assemblies the speakers sometimes spoke of the persecution of the Jews. "We were unable to say anything at all. Not a thing at all. Just walk away keeping still, silent and sad. I was inwardly sad that one had to bear that so. That we have this regime." Her fear of failing to obey was reinforced by the threat of the concentration camps. "One heard that there was a concentration camp, and one heard right after the change of regime, right after Hitler marched in, that many persons disappeared. One found oneself having to deal with fear, you understand."[71]

Acts of kindness were confined to the surreptitious dropping of fruit or potatoes along the route of march. This kind of assistance usually involved some degree of forethought. While riding home from work at around six o'clock in the evening Frau R. often passed the inmates. She said that she opened a hole in the bag or satchel she carried on her bicycle. Through the hole she was able to drop apples and peaches to be found by the inmates. Once, a guard discovered the objects falling from the bag, saying, "You're losing your apples!" to which she replied, "They belong to all of you." She appears to have surprised herself through the audacity she displayed in daring to respond to him that way. She quickly left the scene. "I rode on with my bicycle. Rode on fast. But perhaps he was a man who was not so rough."[72] She returned home following this incident, and recalled praying, "Dear God, an end. Please make an end of it all, because I must never look at that."[73] For Maria R., the burden of witnessing was itself a form of torment. One simply did not want to look at or think about such things. One "must never look" precisely because to see was to raise unwanted questions of choice and action.

Residents indeed knew the general condition of the inmates. On occasion, they were able to display their sympathy with them by leaving food, yet ultimately their fear of the regime was strong enough to force them into a position of observant passivity. Others deliberately looked away even as though they knew the inmates were suffering. Frau Erika S. typifies the civilian who had seen with her own eyes the state of the prisoners, but who dared do nothing for fear of bringing harm to herself or her family. She carried on as normally as possible, keeping her head down and avoiding trouble. She knew that through silence and minding her own business she would survive. Whatever pity she felt for the inmates was dissolved by the fear of violating the SS injunction against interference. She shunned the temptation succumbed to by others who approached the camp area to get a good look, and thus learn more than was unavoidable to know. She felt able to carry on with her daily chores, conducted in the immediate vicinity of the camp, without endangering herself or her family.

Erika S. had a small market garden, located near the camp, where she grew potatoes. When going to the garden, she instructed her children to walk ahead and keep from drawing attention. "Just go right by the barracks, don't look, don't listen. Just go straight on your way, you know the plot. That is only 20 steps up the hill, and don't take long. Don't mix in. The people don't concern you."[74] Her potato garden was her own secure island. To this island of safety her children could come if they needed her. The garden afforded an unwelcome view of the inmates, but that did not mean she or the children had to become involved. "I went up, worked my plot, and left again."[75]

Still, the sight of the inmates was sometimes unavoidable. One day she was confronted with a sight that remains embedded in her memory. On the street a large group of inmates was coming toward her. Their number was so great that she was forced to turn sideways with her back to the street as they passed. She could go no further. "There were so many. . . . They all had to march in row and formation. Those who could not walk they attached and dragged. I don't like to talk about it at all."[76]

One of the unfortunate inmates in particular drew her attention. He had great difficulty moving forward. His feet were bare, and he advanced only with great pain, forced along by the whippings of the guards. "Honestly spoken, as truly as I sit here, I pitied him, but secretly I had to laugh so as I saw him hop and jump. He had nothing on. There was a shirt and his long underwear down with the ends hanging, and barefoot. He was perhaps 22, 23 years old . . . and [with] beautiful black hair. That is, a typical Jew."[77] She believed that he had been working in Roggendorf where she knew the inmates labored in the underground tunnels. She noted his confused and exhausted state. "In such a desolate condition, he did not know how he should walk, because it really hurt him." She recalled that the healthier prisoners were able to march forward, but those, like this prisoner, who were unable to advance were left behind where she was standing. These slower inmates became entangled, holding up the column. The guards screamed at them to come forward, which they did as best they could "because they had to keep tempo, you know."[78]

Viewing this spectacle, Frau S. said that for her to offer the inmates food was out of the question. "I could have given bread. I did have it, but too little. . . . For my part, I would have given the whole piece, but then I would be imprisoned, and then out there for a couple of years. I know how that was. That was terrifying."[79]

After returning home, she told her husband what she had just seen. "Says my husband, 'What are you laughing about?' I said, well, because I saw a Jew jumping so. He came forward like a circus horse. . . . How else was he to come forward on the street? I mean, he would have needed two hours, except that he was whipped from behind so that he went faster."[80] Her husband, however, was not interested in learning more. "My husband said, 'Please stop with the thing. I hear so much.' Because my husband had to go into the barracks and inspect, because he supervised the masons there. But he did not say a word."[81]

With the exception of talking to her husband, Erika S. maintained the strictest silence concerning events associated with the camp. "I never, I never—that could have been my best friend—I never spoke to

anyone about the concentration camp. On my own I rejected doing
so. . . . I had only to keep silent, because I'm not foolish, you know.
And I spoke to no one about it." Accordingly, she also instructed her
children to remain silent as well. "The children were not permitted to
speak about the concentration camp. Children will also have spoken
among themselves, because one can well think that with your children.
And perhaps they also went to look. That's also possible, isn't it? But I
said, not at home."[82]

The silence concerning events in and around the camp usually
extended to local establishments where people gathered in their off hours.
Erika S. frequented a brewery tavern located just down the street from
her apartment. There she often came in contact with soldiers who were
assigned to the camp. "Well, mind you, I played cards with the soldiers
I knew, when we were together in the 'Brewery.' They looked on, you
know, but the concentration camp was never spoken about, not at all.
Neither by us civilians, nor by the soldiers. Only one was a little more
critical." Referring to the camp, he once dared tell her privately, "You
have no idea of the injustice that is going on up there."[83]

Yet, Frau S. remained silent. She neither spoke, nor sought to look.
When someone asked her to come along and watch, she refused. It was
best to pretend it never happened at all. "I am happy when I hear
nothing and see nothing of it. As far as I am concerned, they aren't
interned. That's it. Over. It does not interest me at all."[84]

Frau S. faces a choice and makes a choice: though she sees, she will
look away and ignore what her eyes tell her. In her narrative uncon-
trolled laughter at the sight of the jumping Jew contrasts with her self-
willed blindness and silence in the face of the camp. She could not help
herself in laughing, yet she exercised rigid control over her public utter-
ances. Items of nourishment—the bread she thinks she might have given
to the passing inmates, but did not give for she had "too little," the
potatoes she cultivated at the risk of drawing the suspicion of the
authorities—these embody her concerns. She circumspectly tended her
garden, thought of her children, and endeavored to sweep the camp from
her mind. She took additional comfort in the belief that to assist the
inmates was not only punishable, but indeed a crime.

By the summer of 1944 Melk was repeatedly overflown by American
aircraft on their way to attack sites in the area. The town was under peril
of bombardment, and people had their own lives and property to worry
about. Warning sirens wailed, flares went up, and the sound of flak was
heard. Town residents gathered in the cellar of the monastery for pro-

The Quarry: Shortly after the German annexation of Austria in March 1938, SS chieftain Heinrich Himmler selected this stone quarry in Mauthausen, Upper Austria, as the site of a new concentration camp. (Dokumentationsarchiv des Österreichischen Widerstandes—DÖW)

Mauthausen under Construction: In the summer of 1938, construction began on the camp at Mauthausen. Among the camp's first structures were 20 inmate barracks surrounded by a perimeter of barbed wire fencing and a stone wall eight feet high. The inmates also built guard towers, housing, and administrative facilities for the SS. (DÖW)

Castle Hartheim: In the spring of 1940, this castle just west of Linz was remodeled and outfitted with a gas chamber and crematorium. Operating first as a death center for the mentally ill and handicapped, it also received 7,600 inmates from Mauthausen and Dachau who were to die at Castle Hartheim. (DÖW)

Hitler in Melk: Some 40 miles east of Mauthausen stands the Benedictine monastery of Melk. Adolf Hitler briefly halted in Melk on a triumphant automobile journey to Vienna and was wildly cheered by the Austrian citizenry.

The Melk Concentration Camp: A military installation within view of the monastery was converted into one of Mauthausen's largest satellite camps. A cremation facility became operational at Melk in November 1944. "When the west wind blew we had the whole stink inside here," noted one woman from Melk. (Yad Vashem)

Escape from Mauthausen: Two inmates killed for attempting to flee from the camp. In numerous instances, the SS forced inmates to approach the wire, providing the guards an excuse to open fire. However, on 2 February 1945, roughly 400 men succeeded in breaching the outer perimeter of the camp; they were hunted down and shot by the SS acting in conjunction with the local residents. (DÖW)

The Faces of Rescue: Of those who managed to escape, only three are known to have been protected by people living in the vicinity. Maria and Johann Langthaler, from a nearby town, sheltered two of the escapees from Mauthausen. (DÖW)

Liberation Came in May: On 7 May 1945, troops from the 11th Armored Division of the U.S. Third Army entered the camp to be greeted by surviving inmates. Overhead, Spanish inmates displayed a banner of greeting for their liberators. (National Archives)

Inside the Camp After the Liberation: A priest from the nearby town, Father Franz Loidl (on the left) was among the first persons to speak with survivors of the liberated concentration camp of Ebensee, a satellite camp located about 45 miles south of Mauthausen. Entering the camp after the arrival of the U.S. Army, Father Loidl wrote of having been appalled at the sight and smell of the dead stacked in the crematorium. (DÖW)

(Above and facing page) *Civilians Forced to Assist in the Burial*: In the seven years of the camp's existence, more than 100,000 inmates died in Mauthausen and its network of satellite camps in Austria. In the wake of the liberation, civilians from the vicinity of the camps were made to assist in the burial of the dead. At Mauthausen tractors were brought in to dig long trenches into which the bodies were stacked by layers and covered with earth. As each layer was filled, a priest recited a blessing. (DÖW; Yad Vashem)

Photos of the Atrocities Made Public: A group of civilians on a square in Linz in June 1945 gather around a display of photographs taken at Mauthausen after its liberation. Many Austrians preferred to deflect responsibility for Nazi crimes onto their more powerful neighbor, Germany. An American soldier who observed people viewing the display recalled one man approaching him to say, "We never dreamed that the Germans were doing such things." (National Archives)

tection. In an attack on 23 August, six persons from Melk and the vicinity, including a 12-year-old boy, were killed, and 30 were injured.[85]

On the morning of 8 July 1944 American bombers attacked Melk, hitting the concentration camp and, according to the forester's account, killing 300 inmates and 25 soldiers.[86] He recorded that, following a siren alarm, bombers at first passed over, then some of them wheeled around to bomb the barracks.[87] Inmate accounts recalling the bombardment also speak of "several hundred deaths" or "at least 200 deaths" and an undetermined number of injured among the prison population, in addition to "numerous victims among the SS and other military."[88]

That the attackers knew the site was filled with concentration camp inmates seems unlikely. Melk was only a secondary site chosen after the presence of aircraft from another formation diverted the attack unit from its briefed target of taxi strips and a disposal area at Markersdorf. The unit's mission report, noting that the assault was conducted from a height of 23,500 feet, made no mention of a concentration camp and concluded only that "direct hits were obtained on buildings appearing to be of a military nature." In addition, it was noted that "hits strung out and fell into the river. Possible hits were obtained on the railroad lines running along the bank of the river to the North of the area bombed."[89]

Other civilians witnessed the aftermath of the attack including Frau G.S. "My sister and I, we wanted to help," she recalled, thinking, "There they need all the help they can get because of the emergency." To offer their assistance they approached a local physician. "He said, no, don't go, it's insane. Of the inmates not a single one ran away, because they were so upset that they were bombed by the Americans. . . . The Americans couldn't have known. They believed it was a military installation. From above they couldn't make it out."[90] The evening following the bombardment, inmates returning from a labor detail in Amstetten, 25 miles west of Melk, arrived at the camp and found several limbs of the victims hanging from the trees, and saw "numerous vehicles" loaded with the dead and wounded ready for transport back to Mauthausen to be disposed of in the crematory.[91] Frau G.S. said she counted eighteen trucks filled with the dead driven away. There was blood flowing from the last two vehicles. She saw a dead inmate in the back, "completely blood-soaked. They were all dead," she remarked.[92] Frau Erika S. saw bodies piled onto "big vehicles" with "canvas over them, and where [the bodies] were slumped a hand appeared. It wasn't very skillful, the way they threw them, and the blood dripped directly down."[93]

Vengeance was quick to follow. Above all, the Jews were to pay for

the humiliation of the attack. On the night of 9–10 July, under a black-
ened, storm-threatening sky the inmates were roused from their bunks,
beaten and "chased from the barracks barefoot and in their shirts, and
literally thrown down the steps" onto the roll call square. There they
assembled before the SS and "their hired assassins equipped with flashlights or miners' lamps which dance[d] in the night."

The Jews, some 2,000 in all, were separated from the other inmates. "Completely terror-stricken," their ranks wavered and dissolved
into "indescribable disorder" amid what one French inmate described as
"an unleashing of brutal furor, of violence, of sadism":

> The thunder rumbles and great flashes of lightning split the night. A
> deluge of water falls on us, adding to the deluge of blows which fall upon
> the Jews. Someone shouts for us to grip each other tightly, we who are
> without clothing, in our shirts, most without shoes. Beneath the pouring
> torrent which augments the fury of the soldiers and the capos, the blows
> redouble and become harder on the Jews who are flung to the ground,
> trampled underfoot and struck, struck again and again. With each flash of
> lightning one sees the blood flow, swiftly bathed by the downpour. In the
> thunder one hears the howling of terror and pain, the cries of rage of the
> torturers. When will they then grow tired? . . .
>
> How many poor Jews will die of the blows they received? Following
> this scene of terror many will have to be transported to their block. For
> many days afterward in the camp we encounter the swollen faces, the
> cracked skulls, the clothing spotted with blood, painful testimony to the
> acts of savagery of this Danteesque night."[94]

It was crucial to the citizens' perception of their relation to the
Melk concentration camp that, oblivious to this night of terror, the one
time they witnessed a group of inmates lying dead en masse was when the
Americans bombed the camp. This sight caused civilians to associate the
camp and its horrors with the general destruction of the war. The residents' own feelings of guilt were assuaged by the knowledge that the
Americans had caused the deaths of hundreds of inmates through this
bombardment. "Why they bombed the barracks was a riddle to us all,"
remarked Maria R., "because the prisoners were in there. They certainly
knew, you know, because as strict as this whole regime was, still so much
leaked out into the world, you know." Again, she insisted, "The foreign
countries knew everything, and so they had to know that this barracks
was also full of prisoners. Why they did that, I do not know to this
day."[95]

By now the war had reached such a point that all misery took on a single, horrid unity. The sight of refugees from the East passing through the town, the threats of the authorities, the sight of the exhausted and beaten inmates passing to and from the railway area, the bombings in and around Melk accompanied by the wail of sirens, the bloody aftermath of the raid on 8 July, the fear of speaking out, and the terrifying stories of atrocities committed by the approaching Russians all worked to create an impression that this war was hell. Within this series of overlapping images of horror, the concentration camp inmates were seen as only one category of victims, albeit especially threatened, but victims nonetheless like everyone else among the civilian population. People viewed the violence with a "symmetric vision" that equated the destructiveness of the concentration camp with that of Allied bombing and the approaching Red Army.[96] They could recognize the inmates as victims, but of whom? The Germans? The Americans? Moreover, they would argue, were not ordinary townspeople under mortal threat as well?

Like town residents who were well aware of the existence of the camp, the monks also knew what lay behind the gray walls nearby. The principal structures of the caserne upon whose grounds the camp was built were easily visible from the terrace of the monastery.

The Nazis allowed the monastery to function on a small scale after 1938. Father R. was one of the monks permitted to remain in the monastery during the war. The monastery *Gymnasium* in which Father R. and the others had taught, however, was dissolved and replaced with a state high school under Nazi direction.[97] They also moved state employment and financial offices into the monastery, confining the remaining monks to a restricted area. They were allowed to carry on with their routine of prayer and administration of the monastic holdings. They were watched, but permitted to carry on.[98]

Father R. was placed in charge of bookkeeping in the monastery's central administrative bureau. He kept track of the monastery's forest and other holdings, and in the course of his duties traveled a circuit, visiting the outlying parishes of the order. Within his sphere of work he had a large degree of independence, he noted, setting his own working hours.[99]

In the monastery there was some discussion about the inmates, but the talk was confidential and cautious. "Well, mind you," the monk noted, opinions on the subject were of a "rejecting, judgmental" nature. "But [expressed] only in the closest circles, in the closest circles. Didn't know if one would be denounced or not."[100]

News of the camp's existence also traveled to the outlying parishes. On a visit to Matzleinsdorf, Father R. learned from the local priest that he had been approached by a civilian working as a mason in the Melk camp complex. The mason asked the priest if he would agree to secretly supply wafers for the celebration of the host ritual by French inmates. During the visit, the priest asked Father R. what he would do if so asked. He said he would certainly supply the wafers, whereupon the priest told him he had already done so.[101] Beyond such assistance, Father R. saw little hope for aiding the inmates. The monks spoke of aiding them, but in the end, he noted, they were unable to help: "It was not possible to do something, was not possible."[102] The monks may have spoken prayers for the inmates, but if they did so it was never in common or in public, only in private: "That can be, that was for each his own concern. Mind you, in the prayers much occurs anyway that is appropriate, that was added."[103] This silence apparently extended to the townspeople who came to the monastery seeking shelter during air raids, or for the Sunday mass. According to Father R., they did not speak to the monks about the camp because to do so "would have made no sense."[104]

Like others who lived so close to the camps, after the war Father R. did not attempt to clarify his understanding of what happened in the camp. He maintained that, following the liberation, inmates who had experienced other camps had said that Melk was among the "most humane" of all.[105] Still, he had no desire to test this assumption on his own. In a clipped manner he pointed out that the responsibility for such investigation lies elsewhere. Admitting to not having either the "interest" or the "opportunity" to explore the matter, he remarked, "It made no sense that I, how can I, I can at most somehow speak of only a tiny, little bit of it."[106]

Father R. occasionally left the monastery on foot, or on a bicycle, to visit a friend, another priest living in the wooded country to the north, known as the Waldviertel. In Father R.'s words:

> I myself had an experience with Jews, but not here in Melk directly. The provisioning was bad, somehow [I] was starving [irgendwie schon verhungert], one can indeed say. A good friend, a priest, a colleague, was in the Waldviertel up above. I went up there during vacation, also by foot, up there so. I hiked the whole day. At the same time, it was very beautiful. In any case, I rode down by bicycle. And I also had given me things that one can prepare at home: some flour, and a few eggs, then sugar . . . and then poppy seed."[107]

He was returning from the visit to his friend, laden with small foodstuffs in his jacket pockets. He was on his bicycle when he noticed damage to a tire. Stopping near a rock quarry in Spitz an der Donau to make repairs, he found himself at first approached by a woman. He asked her for assistance. She was very friendly. He recalled noticing that she was not alone. He soon discovered approaching him a group of some 10 to 20 Jews, averaging in his estimation about 30 years old. "Yes, they were Hungarian Jews. . . . There were children, too. . . . All with the Jewish star."[108] He noted that they were able to speak German.

The woman posed a question to Father R.: "She looked at me so, and said, if you had known who we are, you wouldn't have come to me in here. I didn't say anything in response. She was right: I would not have considered going in."[109] Before leaving, Father R. reached into the side pockets of his ski outfit ("it was winter"), and gave them the eggs he had inside. "They were totally joyous," he noted.[110] He then repaired his tire, and departed. "I rode on, rode up and over there to the monastery."[111]

The monk's account of this encounter has a narrative texture. The same may be said of his recollection of the discussion with the priest concerning the procurement of holy wafers for the inmates. One senses he has recounted these events and given them shape. Clearly, they are important to him. His brief encounter with the Jews, he noted, is something he is reminded of often. The narrative begins with anticipation of a welcome journey, promising pleasure in the out-of-doors, renewal of a friendship, and the longed-for satisfaction of hunger. On returning, an unexpected event, the discovery of flat tire, leads to a chance meeting near a quarry. The conflict centers upon his hidden admission of weakness, not to say shame, exposed when the monk silently acknowledges that had he immediately recognized the true identity of those whom he encountered, he would have never dared approach them. From his viewpoint, the central and redeeming moment upon which the narrative pivots occurs when he lifts the eggs from his pockets, offers them to the Jews, and senses their happiness. Eggs are symbolic of life, and in sharing these items, all the more precious in a time of want, he knows he performed a graceful deed.

Father R.'s account crystallizes a moment of choice. It was as if for but an instant he stood encircled within the spotlight of moral decision. All the more necessary was it for him to have displayed an act of kindness. Yet, Father R. did not recognize the mortal danger to which the Hungarian Jews were exposed. In the final year of the war thousands of them died on Austrian soil.[112] Speculating on the possibility of their fleeing, he remarked, "Where then should they have gone?"[113] The comment leaves no room for doubt concerning other possible choices for the bystander: returning on another occasion to provide them with more food, inquiring with the authorities about the state of their care, or providing a place of safety or hiding for some of them. Within the afterthought, "where then should they have gone," lies a question directed to the bystander, as well as the victim.

Bystanders' recollections underscore the very involuntary nature of their awareness of the mistreatment of the inmates. The townspeople cannot help but see. Here one spots inmates at work on a ditch, there one sees them assemble on the loading ramps, there the inmates carry a dead man on a stretcher. The recollections point toward a haphazard and unwanted acquaintance with the camp. Such sight does not necessarily lead to insight; it may as easily lead to fright or a blank response.

Turning one's back, pretending that nothing is happening even when one sees the inmates mistreated is the expression of the ultimate wish not to know.[114] Yet the other senses are engaged. Sound travels, and if one is close enough one hears inmates being beaten. "Quiet down! Quiet down!" someone shouts, hoping to restore the silence. Smell travels great distances. The wind carries odor across town, up into the nostrils. Through interpretation the meaning of the senses is scrambled. People were dying and the dead must be disposed of. But the understanding that they are dying not through some slip-up, some disruption in supply or organization brought on by the war, but through deliberate policy is denied. All the senses may work perfectly, indeed combine, flooding the brain with all the proper signals, but the stimuli are subject to interpretation: this is smoke, this is caused by the cremation of the dead, it comes from the camp, it is carried by the breeze. But the meaningful conclusion is not drawn, cannot be drawn: people are being killed by the thousands before one's eyes and ears, under one's nose.

What is lacking in most instances is the vision or look that signifies recognition and bespeaks care for one's fellow man. Such concern would mean wanting to see and know in order not to turn one's back, or shout for quiet, or pedal away. Such a vision of concern entails an openness not only to the unexpected encounter—the sudden appearance of a column of inmates before one's eyes, the smell of the smoke as one walks by the river—but a desire to see, a choice of preparing oneself to see in order to make contact, at the least to leave a morsel by the roadside or toss an apple into the ranks. The concerned vision seizes the opportunity to act.

To look with solicitude is to express a choice; without a word spoken, sight has the power to break through the divide between those banished from humanity's midst and those who walk freely, as if in another world. One overcomes a divide in those moments when "the person we look at, or feels he is being looked at, looks at us in turn."[115]

In a few instances this happened. René Gille, fortunate enough to enjoy for many months assignment to one of the better labor details in Amstetten, thereby avoiding for a long time the murderous tunnels in Roggendorf, recalled passengers of passing trains looking at the men "with compassion." In Amstetten he noticed as well a young woman and an old man, a grandmother, a daughter and her children who watched them sympathetically from their windows each day as they marched to work.[116] Another inmate whose work detail inside the camp shielded him from the agonizing exposure to the elements along the route to and from the tunnels, noted how Austrian workmen used their vantage atop the scaffolding to alert the inmates below when they need work hard, or when it was safe to let up.[117] As assuredly as those who looked away, these rare civilians exercised a choice: they wanted to see, and in using their eyes communicated their concern. However isolated the encounter, however little an understanding glance contributed to the saving of a life, someone chose to look and in so doing allowed light to enter the darkness of their existence.

In the labor process, the inmate is reduced to an interchangeable part. As an object, the inmate is something that "stands against" and "affronts"[118] the one who stands by. Even when near, the inmate is boxed in, roped off, striped and cordoned from the observer. From head to toe, from the 1.5 inch stripe shaved over the curve of his skull to the stripes down the leg of his trousers, the inmate wears the mark of his confinement and separation. The cordon is portable. Even as he marched in the midst of the onlookers he was encased within a perimeter. Were a bystander to brush up against an inmate, he would touch a boundary. The bystander asked himself: what would it take for me to slip between the lines? Thus did Erika S., seeing the inmates approach, turn her back in order to avoid being swept into their ranks.

Laughter accompanies blindness. It displaces horror, dissolving it into Schadenfreude, malicious pleasure. Humor also displaces shame. Under the circumstances, laughter and anecdote served to divide, to separate, to distance the onlooker from the victim. These ragged costumes, the pajamas the inmates wore even by day, made their wearers look comical. Frau S.'s recollection of the hopping Jew brings to mind a random, supposedly harmless incident that occurred in the camp. A teen-aged inmate named Lewkowitz was made to stand still and open his mouth wide while his tormenter, a sergeant Otto Striegel, promised to toss bread into his open mouth. "I have always liked jokes, [ever] since

I was a child," Striegel stated after the war. Hence, he found it amusing, in a mockery of nourishment, to hurl not bread, but stones and chips of coal into the open cavity. Inmate Lewkowitz recalled, "While he tossed stones and coal into my mouth I had to keep my eyes open. Woe if I closed them. Striegel was a sadist."[119]

Bad humor also undermined horror in the recollections of an engineer involved in the operations in Melk. Serving as director of the Vienna office of a Steyr-Daimler-Puch subsidiary he was in charge of negotiations with building contractors, the analysis of the economic performance of the inmates, and requests to the SS for their lease. Deflecting attention from the brutal working conditions, he chose to recall an incident expressing the inmates' hopes and presumed forgiveness:

> Personally I had nothing to do with the work at the building site, since that was a matter for the local construction director and indeed I also had gotten to know a concentration camp operation in Wiener Neudorf and, without wanting to gloss over anything, may say the [camp] in Melk was quite well organized and hence, so far as one could avoid roughness it was in fact avoided. I do not know if an anecdote speaks to you, we had a director from the concentration camp, an officer, who heard that in the concentration camp a quartet had formed and when once a couple of friends were visiting him, he called them in and requested they should play something. After they asked what [they should] then [in fact] [play], he said that does not matter to him and the four of them arranged themselves and began [to play], "everything blows over, everything passes ["es geht alles vorüber, es geht alles vorbei"], but he did not take offense at them.[120]

As criminal, as clown, the inmate did not seem quite real; he was not near, but far. A stranger at best, he did not seem to belong to the community of man. And if he died, it was not because the camp was designed to insure his death: one person could still assert that Melk was "quite well organized"; another imply the inmates simply died as a result of hunger or weakness. In the end, the inmate was no one's responsibility. He was not a neighbor; not a fellow being. He was at a remove, and one turned one's back on him.

In so doing the onlooker perceived in the inmate a distorted image of the human. Decked out in his "carnavalesque" attire, the inmate was a "Punch and Judy" figure, "a puppet in the midst of other puppets." Change a man's appearance, and one may alter his state of being. Smile at him in his costume and one smiles at not a man but a marionette. Used up and tossed aside, naked and heaped for burning before the crematorium, the puppet-men woodenly smile back, their faces contorted into "grimaces" that are "at once poignant and ridiculous."[121]

Neither raising his hand to help nor to strike, the bystander considers himself neutral. He abandons the inmates to their fate, forgetting that so removed are the inmates from any state of peace, so debased from the essence of their humanity, that to close one's eyes, to turn one's back upon them is to leave them concealed from the light of existence.

By the spring of 1945 the townspeople looked elsewhere. They turned, in fact, to the greatest dwelling they knew. The town retreated into the bosom of the abbey, the rock and savior of Melk and the Melker. As they gathered to attend mass or huddled in the cellar of the monastery as the bombers passed overhead, they felt a special protection knowing that between them and the Flying Fortresses stood St. Benedict doing battle with the forces of evil, Pallas Athena on her lion-drawn chariot rolling toward the brighter clouds. They turned to the abbey atop the rock, the granite, the stone of strength. They were close to God, close to the Savior who would as ever protect them from the threat from the skies, and from the hordes they saw descending on the town from the East. They hid in the safety of the abbey, comforted "to know for certain", as St. Benedict said, "that God sees one everywhere." And the abbey, in sheltering them, gave living expression to that other essential guideline of St. Benedict's rule: "Let all guests who come be received as Christ would be, because He will say, 'I was a stranger, and ye took me in.' "[122]

Chapter 6

Escape from Mauthausen

"The night of 2 February 1945 was a night of warm breezes with a soft presentiment of spring," recorded the police chronicle of Schwertberg, the town immediately neighboring Mauthausen to the north. "The moon played hide and seek behind white balls of cloud. Everything was peaceful, not even the searchlights of the flak batteries scanned the sky. Then suddenly around 2 o'clock in the concentration camp all hell broke loose."[1] The inconceivable had occurred. Hundreds of inmates had scaled the wall of Mauthausen, crossing the line that separated the camp from the community. Four hundred and ninety-five prisoners, Soviet officers condemned to slow death under specific order, managed a last, desperate attempt to survive. In a spectacular escape, they broke out during the night, scattering across the landscape, and seeking refuge throughout the area. They came right up to the doors and windows of civilian homes. In some cases, they quietly entered, awakening residents from their sleep. Startled in the early morning hours, townsfolk were astonished to find starved, emaciated inmates in their barns, bedrooms, and kitchens.

The inmates who staged the outbreak were the last remnant of a group of some 4,700 Soviet officers sent to concentration camp Mauthausen under a secret order issued by Gen. Wilhelm Keitel, Chief of the

124

High Command of the Armed Forces, on 2 March 1944. The operation was directed toward the physical elimination of captured Soviet officers who had previously attempted to escape. Also included under the terms of the order were non-commissioned officers who did not or would not work. The order fully reflected the exceptional severity the army leadership reserved for its Soviet enemy. Specifically exempting British and American prisoners of war from the terms of the order, the decree underscored the ideological nature of Germany's war against the Soviet Union. In Mauthausen the men were crowded into an isolation barrack and subjected to a tormenting regimen of abuse leading to near mass extermination. This regimen of brutal abuse included periodic withdrawal of their minimal food rations; cold showers and endless standing outdoors; the forcing of inmates to lie down and be trampled upon by their overseers; and sleeping in winter on the floor of a recently flooded barrack (the bodies of those who failed to rise were disposed of the following morning). In the summer their barracks were kept unbearably hot with the windows shut, and their soup was so heavily salted that those who dared drink it risked losing their senses from thirst. During the winter of 1944–45 these inmates were dying at a rate of 20 to 30 every day.[2] An additional several hundred Russian and Polish inmates, as well as a few French, Belgians, and Germans were also sent from Gestapo prisons in Linz and Vienna to Mauthausen to be disposed of under provisions of the Keitel decree.[3]

So effective was this torture that by the night of their attempted escape only 570 badly weakened inmates remained of the thousands of Russian officers who had entered Mauthausen. Only escape might have offered this remnant a slim chance of survival. Seventeen Russian officers, admitted to Mauthausen following an unsuccessful escape from a prisoner-of-war camp near Karlsbad, are believed to have engineered the break. The 495 who were fit to make the attempt did so.[4] Seventy-five who were too weak stayed behind after giving their clothing to their escaping comrades.

The break began with the storming of a watch tower. The men pelted the guards with floorboards, wooden shoes, rocks and other objects, and finally overpowered them with the foam spray from two fire-extinguishers. The inmates then disarmed the electrically charged wire fence by short-circuiting it with wet blankets. A second guard tower was overtaken with the aid of weapons captured in the initial assault. Despite this stunning success, many of the fleeing inmates were too weak to advance more than a few yards from the camp's exterior wall. The next morning inmates on their way to work found the area traversed by the

Russian escapees littered with carnage. "One saw the dead lying in the fields right down toward the forest below. They were only skin and bones, completely starved, badly clothed, without shoes. Their feet were partially covered with rags. One can say that if they had gone further they would not have endured the hardships."[5] According to a report issued by the Criminal Police[6] in Linz on 3 February, only 419 inmates succeeded in making their way past the outer perimeter of the camp into the surrounding area of Mauthausen. The day following the outbreak more than 300 of them had already been caught, yet only 57 of those retaken were still alive.[7] The bodies were returned to Mauthausen for disposal. "Then we saw how during the day the farm wagons, that is, horse-drawn rack-wagons, were brought into the camp full of corpses," noted an inmate. "And the dead were brought to the crematorium. That went on for about two days."[8]

An escape of this magnitude was a unique event in the history of the camp.[9] The Russian prisoners' hopes of survival in the event of a successful escape had been raised by the belief that the Red Army had already advanced to the gates of Budapest, and the nearness of Czechoslovakia offered a refuge where they could expect sympathy from the civilian population. They also hoped that at this late date they might find among the Austrian population persons who no longer supported the Hitler regime who would take them in.[10] Yet, only a dozen of those 419 inmates who were able to advance beyond the camp perimeter into the countryside are known to have survived the escape. Of these, two were saved by three laborers, a pair of fellow Russians and a Pole who worked as servants for the mayor of Holzleiten, a town in the vicinity. The servants managed to hide the inmates for two weeks in the mayor's attic without his knowledge. Afterwards, the two escapees had to make their way further. One of them was later retaken, but was able to pass himself off as a laborer, thereby avoiding a return to Mauthausen. The other succeeded in reaching Czechoslovakia where he eventually made it to the safety of the Soviet lines. Another inmate also succeeded in reaching Czechoslovakia where a Czech family protected him. Two others reached the *Waldviertel*, a hilly, wooded region that begins about 30 miles northeast of Mauthausen, where they hid until their liberation in the spring. Another survivor used a different name when captured, and was taken to a prisoner of war camp, not to Mauthausen. At least four more men survived after being hidden by three Austrian families in the vicinity of Schwertberg and Perg, both lying within a 6-mile radius of the camp.[11]

In the wake of the outbreak the police were besieged by frightened farmers who awoke to find concentration camp inmates on their property and even in their homes. "The farm women and men came out of their houses and related to us how they were frightened when suddenly someone was in the room or even next to the bed," noted police commander Johann Kohout in the police record of Schwertberg. Yet the escaped inmates themselves were similarly fearful of the strangers whose homes they quietly slipped into or sought to enter in the middle of the night. The shock of first sight was mutual. A Frau W. remembered having been up very early in the morning when she first saw one of the inmates appear before her. "I got up at five-thirty and was just in the process of heating the oven. All at once someone knocked on the door. The door opened and an inmate stood there. I was so frightened. He must have been too. He turned around and disappeared again."[12]

The escaped inmates acted decently toward the populace. Their worst crimes appear to have been trespassing and petty thievery. In some instances farmers complained of the theft of small items such as cheese and bread, hats and shoes, and the police dutifully recorded these.[13] In one instance inmates who had escaped with a gun or a pipe had displayed these objects before some residents in a threatening way, but no assaults by inmates against the citizens were registered. The police in Mauthausen concluded that the inmates "behaved very properly toward the populace, no acts of violence such as murder, arson, and so forth were undertaken. They were concerned solely with attaining food to still their hunger and civilian clothing to facilitate their advance. In pursuance of this aim naturally many thefts were committed."[14] The same opinion was echoed by Schwertberg police commander Kohout who remarked,

> How easy it would have been, instead of preferring raw turnips and potatoes, had the escapees robbed the farmers, slain them, and been able to take possession of food, civilian clothing, as well as vehicles. The flight to Czechoslovakia would have been favorable for them. Even if they were already worn down as a result of hunger and cold, the drive for self-preservation would have yet strengthened them as far. But they trusted that the Austrian civilian population which allegedly wanted nothing more to do with the Hitler system would help them further.[15]

Frau J. S. remembered the fateful night of the outbreak: "On the evening of 1 February we were in the cinema in Mauthausen. We went home past the camp. We had just lain down in bed when we heard shots. My mother said, 'What are they shooting out there like that!' We look out the window, my mother forces me away from the window and calls out, they are shooting at our house. For a moment, we did not know what was going on. . . . We hid ourselves, since because of the shooting it was impossible to step in front of the house without being hit." Later they found two dead inmates who had stopped at their neighbor's home. One lay with a pot of pig fat under his arm, the other with his mouth stuffed full. "The inmates were terribly hungry. They harmed nobody." She also noted that in the area 30 inmates had been shot. "In Marbach Castle, in which the SS lived, the inmates ran directly into the hands of the SS."[16]

Another woman in Mauthausen, Anna K., was awakened at four in the morning. She went to a small window in her apartment and shouted to someone she noticed outside: " 'What do you want?' A man answered me saying we want to protect you. And I thought to myself that is an SS-man." When she asked why this protection was necessary, "the SS-man answered me, saying, because so many broke out of the camp. . . . Yes we want to protect you, many have gone into hiding, was his answer." With this, she returned to bed. "Then I go back to sleep. You can sleep peacefully," she recalled.[17] Similarly, it was from the second story of the town hall in Ried in der Riedmarkt, two and one-half miles north of Mauthausen, that Josef R., the town secretary, watched the loading of bodies of inmates whose escape had ended in failure: "From the window of my apartment I could see how the dead lay on a truck. Two of them who had been captured [alive] had to lay down upon the dead with outstretched arms; and like this they were driven away."[18]

If at night or early in the morning fear held the citizenry close to home, still their windows offered a glimpse into the terror outside. The indoors was a scant refuge from the sight of the killing. One woman continued her chores within plain view of a mounting heap of the dead and dying:

> At the time I was employed in a restaurant in Katzdorf. The windows of the kitchen opened out onto the square. There stood a truck upon which they hurled the dead and half-dead from the day. The blood ran down. The whole day one heard the whimpering of those who were not dead and lay up on the wagon. After the conclusion of work I went home. There I had to go by the chapel. There three dead ones lay. Today I no longer know if they had been beaten or shot. It was simply terrible to see this.[19]

So too a maid employed at the SS family residence in Castle Marbach reported having witnessed the capture and execution of an inmate routed from a hayloft:

> I saw directly how they shot him. . . . There they pulled him down, told him he should walk forward, and from behind they shot him. I had just

made the beds, the window was toward the street side. They shot him in the back of the neck. For along time he lay in front of the window. We did not dare go out to look at the dead one. He lay there 8 or 14 days. As a deterrent they left him lying there so long.[20]

Those who ventured out in the early morning hours of 2 February reported coming across frightful scenes of chase and execution. The sight was sometimes so unexpected and sudden it might occur as one rounded a corner. Some onlookers were shocked into silence. Frau Hilde M., an employee of the Hospital of the Merciful Sisters in Linz, described how at five o'clock in the morning she had left the Engelhart inn in Ried where she visited her ailing mother. She was on her way to the railway station to catch an early train to Linz. She passed a school building where she saw several inmates. "One stood in front of the door, in front of the school entryway. I believe it was a young man; he stood there with an apple in his hand. How he stood there, my God, I thought. An SS-man took aim at him. [The shot] had no sooner rung out than the inmate dropped like a sack. I was terribly frightened. I hardly dared to look." She walked on, only to discover a garbage wagon by a side building upon which lay men in striped uniforms. "I saw dead persons, and I saw that some were still moving. . . . That frightened me terribly. It cut me right to the quick. On the way to the station I saw no inmates. I climbed into the train, it was as if I were stupefied. I spoke with no one in the train, I did not dare."[21]

By the morning of 2 February word of what had happened spread fast. Civilians had been spared the fright of inmates approaching their homes or property heard from others what had transpired; in many instances their curiosity drove them to locations such as wooded areas or market squares where inmates were being shot or held captive. Even those who dared not go were told of the extraordinary events. A woman in Oberthal who declined to look ("I did not dare, my children were small, my husband was in the military," she noted) learned of the slaughter from the milkman who arrived to say, "It's already happened, inmates have broken out [and] are crying and pleading for their lives."[22]

On the night of the breakout Josef Z. was working at a crossing on the Danube. "By early in the morning we had heard it said that something was the matter." After duty he "went down" to Hart where he witnessed a search of a house where inmates had recently hidden. The woman there, Frau S., had cooked them some potatoes before they took to the woods. They were later discovered by the *Volkssturm*, or home defense forces, then hunted down by the SS. The SS combed the nearby woods between Hart and Haid, finding and killing 15 to 20 escapees. Herr Z. went to view the dead. "It was ghastly indeed. I was there and took a look at those killed. I went there because people said one should look at what had taken place there."[23]

A number of onlookers came to the market square in Gallneu-kirchen where captured inmates were assembled. A woman who was then a 15-year-old schoolgirl remembered returning from the intermedi-ate school with other children and crossing the square. There she saw the SS driving a group of inmates across the square and into a tavern.

> A number of inquisitive persons ran there. It was being said, they will be shot, the murderers. We waited, in the meantime a truck came. The 5 or 6 emaciated inmates were loaded onto it, and then they were driven away from Gallneukirchen in the direction of Linz. As we were on the home-ward path toward Schweinbach we heard shots coming from the Aigner slope.[24]

Like the children, Aloisa K. remembered joining others going to the square to see the inmates. "I went into the town just like other women, and looked upon that myself. The inmates were loaded onto the truck like cattle. They sat, they stood, many had not the strength to stand."[25] Another woman from Gallneukirchen who went to the square admitted to having been scared of the inmates: "Many of us had a proper fear, we believed they wanted to do us harm." Yet seeing the inmates in their wretched condition, she asked the SS to show pity: "On the market square I saw how they stood barefoot in this cold. The SS drove us away. I said, in God's name, what have they done that they are to be shot? If I did not leave, the SS-man said, I would be taken along." A teenage girl who was among others walking along the main street in Gallneukirchen also recalled how "we were not permitted to remain standing. One woman cried and said to the SS [these were] such poor people. One of these SS-men turned to this woman [and said] she should not cry, it could have consequences."[26]

Similar scenes took place in other nearby towns. Upon word of the roundup, people rushed to get a good look. Frau Resi L. from Linz was working as a housekeeper in Schwertberg. She remembered how on the day the inmates were brought into the town her employer hurried to the site of their capture. "What upset me about the family with which I was employed was that the husband was a real coward. With his wife he hardly dared open his mouth, but in this event he ran quickly to the market square to look."[27] The former town secretary in Ried in der

Riedmarkt, Josef R., said he knew that the inmates were taken to the sporting grounds and shot, and that people hurried to catch a glimpse of the killing. "There were the curious; they were women who rushed to the place of execution, who had to see this 'spectacle' that called forth great lack of judgment among the other residents."[28]

Not all townsfolk chose to witness the round-up and slaughter of escaped inmates. Some chose to avoid the whole scene. Frau L. indicated that by the time she heard of the outbreak she already had a clear idea of the poor treatment the inmates could expect. From working in Schwertberg she was already acquainted with the mistreatment of inmates being brought to the area in shipments. "Oftentimes we heard of inmate transports that came from Germany, that is, from the Reich territory as it was then known, and that inmates were badly treated on these transports and that some died on them." On the morning of 2 February she "heard that they drove the captives together by the fountain on the market square. There by the fountain they gathered the inmates. It was cold and icy. I had to go shopping, but avoided the square, went into a side street because I did not want to see what I had already heard." Nevertheless, it was precisely in the side street she had taken in the hope of steering clear of the activity on the square that Frau L. came across an SS-man leading an inmate. He was wearing a striped uniform, and his feet were left exposed. "I was conscious of the danger resulting from a remark. I could not stop myself, I could not remain silent about what I had seen. 'Barefoot he comes,' I called out. The SS-man replied to me, 'he was also barefoot when he took off.' "[29]

The sight of captured concentration camp inmates being led through town, unpleasant as it was, was only a small measure of the horror that followed. "On the second afternoon they brought the inmates together," recalled Anna K. "With a horse and chain on it they attached the dead inmates and dragged them so over the frozen field. I did not see that myself. The women from Brucknerstöck related that through dragging the whole lower jaw was torn away, and then in the evening they loaded those collected onto a horse-drawn cart."[30]

Throughout the chase, the capture, and the shooting, the SS did not act alone. The civilian populace in and around Mauthausen was called upon to participate. All able-bodied men, young and old, enrolled in the *Volkssturm* and the Hitler Youth received orders to take part in the hunt and the killing. Schwertberg police commander Kohout recorded with regret the many instances in which local civilians carelessly seized the opportunity to kill. They killed without regard for the helplessness of their victims, rejecting the most basic appeals for mercy:

What happened during theses days is all difficult to describe. One pressed a weapon into the hands of many a previously honorable farmer and worker, and now he was supposed to shoot at human beings. In most cases these defenseless human beings fell to their knees before their persecutors and with raised hands pleaded for their lives. At least this much German they could speak. How brutal were our people then. At close range they shot at the poor beings kneeling before them, and then observed with satisfaction their last shudders. Yes, they boasted publicly of their deed, heedless that their children listened to them in astonishment. In their stupidity many became murderers, and the just Judge of all things will know of it; but many fell victim to the intoxication of blood; the slumbering demon inside them broke forth and transformed them into beasts. A clean-up action would have been necessary in any case, but not in such a manner.[31]

For these civilians the restraints which otherwise held individuals from committing acts of brutality had entirely broken down. The leadership encouraged citizen participation, inviting the populace to share responsibility for killings that previously had been the special right of the camp SS. With the approval of the SS and the party, the killing began in earnest. The police noted:

A great commission of murder began—a real bloodbath. The slush on the street was covered with the blood of those shot. Everywhere, however and wherever one came upon them—in dwellings, in the wagon shed, in the cow barn, in the hayloft, in the cellar—if one did not pull them out and dispose of them at the nearest corner, one shot them on the spot, irregardless of whomever was present, whether a pregnant woman or children. Some had their heads split with a hatchet.[32]

On the morning after the breakout, men of the Schwertberg *Volkssturm* assembled in the town square were told that 500 "hardened criminals" had escaped from the concentration camp. "They constitute a great danger for the residents. They must be made harmless immediately. No one may be taken captive, all are to be immediately killed." Alfred Langthaler, a *Volkssturm* man who was present, recalled: "At an assembly of the *Volkssturm* in the park in Schwertberg Director N. said, bring none to me alive, beat them, stab them, and so forth, in no case [bring] a living one."[33] Langthaler underscored that "Many of the *Volkssturm* people were quite roused to indignation, fear had been instilled in them. These [escapees] were hardened criminals. No one knew that they were soldiers."[34]

The party exploited the public's fear of escaped criminals to enforce cooperative passivity in the general populace. A woman who was working that day at the telephone exchange at the police post in Wartberg, 7 miles north of Mauthausen, noted: "I did not go out at all. One shook absolutely as it was said that so many had broken out, that the SS was after them." A man in the same town added, "We were immediately told that the escapees were criminals."[35]

Whether they acted out of fear, or fury, or lust for violence, many residents seized the opportunity to kill. "Near Hartl one heard much shooting," Alfred Langthaler recalled. "Many rejoiced in the continuous shooting. A part of the population was scared, and another part was incensed over the criminals who had broken out."[36] In all this there was much unthinking, stupid brutality by people who clearly enjoyed the sport. From Wartberg comes word of a witness who spoke with a man who boasted of how he had hunted down an inmate and shot him from behind against a tree. The witness asked him, "Do you enjoy that? 'Jawohl,' he said,"[37] A priest in Allerheiligen, 7 miles northeast of Mauthausen, recalled a man who visibly enjoyed participation in the killing. "Laughing, he shot one in the woods who pleaded for his life."[38] Similarly, two residents from Mauthausen remembered a master painter who, upon discovering an inmate in the home of a farmer, seized a pig's leg and beat him. Both residents reported that afterward the painter spoke openly of his deed: "Then he went into a tavern and there boasted that he has now blown the light out of one of them."[39] Frau Maria H. from Tragwein, 7 miles north of Mauthausen, recalled a brutal instance from her town: "They drove a couple home across Tragwein, whereupon the butcher's daughter . . . is supposed to have said, 'Drive them right inside onto the meat bench, we'll cut them right up like the calves.' "[40] The police in Schwertberg recorded the case of a grocer who went into a frenzy of violence when he discovered that seven captured inmates were being held in the municipality building. "Excited and feverish," he demanded of the police, and later of the mayor, that he be given the keys to the cell. Though they did not hand them over, theirs were not the only keys available, and "With the aid of an SS-man . . . he collected his seven victims from their confinement and stood them up in the courtyard of the town hall. One after the other he shot down these poor human beings with his K-98 rifle at some meters distance. Each of them kneeled down before him and with raised hands pleaded for his life. B. had a heart of stone, or had lost his senses."[41] To this the police commander commented: "According to the German law for the protection of animals it was forbidden to allow animals to look on during the slaughter of other animals. With human beings it was allowed; yes, the SS expressed their appreciation for this dreadful, bloody deed."[42] The SS found their task all the easier because time and again citizens who suspected the presence of inmates on their property killed them on their own. Pitchforks, guns, and knives were the instruments of these amateur killers. Discovering an inmate hiding in a feed storage area, one man in Schwertberg stabbed him in the throat. Adding a parting indignity, "his wife leaped near and gave the dying man a slap across the face."[43]

Some *Volkssturm* men and even boys in the Hitler Youth killed inmates under the explicit direction of the SS. When an SS man ordered him to shoot a captured inmate, Franz B., a 46-year-old man from Wartberg o.d. Aist, shot the inmate with his hunting rifle. He later declared with pride: "I did my job and knocked off an inmate."[44] Some Hitler Youths killed a pair of escapees on order from the SS. "Both youths readily shot the inmates down with shots to the back of the head. . . . The three youthful murderers were later praised in Pregarten, and their pictures hung in the display case of the Hitler Youth."[45] The citizen militia were in hot pursuit of their prey. "When we came to Altaist," the police commander noted, "the street was already occupied by the *Volkssturm* from Mauthausen. The people were arrayed as if for a chase." Afterwards, local people appropriately referred to the events surrounding this bloodletting as the "*Mühlviertel* rabbit hunt [*Hasenjagd*]."

The SS behaved with fanatical savagery. "I met an SS man—he already had gray hair—he was so agitated that the foam came out of his mouth. It was weird to look at. In the purest sense of the word, an intoxication of blood had seized the SS," police commander Kohout reported. "Things were very disorderly [*Es ging sehr wüst zu*]. Anything that moved was shot at." In their wild haste to kill, they accidentally shot a Hitler Youth from Naarn.[46]

Beside those who actively did harm to others were the many who stood aside, frightened into passivity, or horrified by the sight of killing. The Schwertberg police commander claimed that he and his men confined themselves to the motions of receiving citizens' complaints about trespassing and thefts by the inmates. When they went out to hunt down the inmates, they avoided finding them, and where possible threw the SS and *Volkssturm* off the trail. Leaving a station masters' house, he wrote, "we found the bloody tracks of persons going barefoot. Probably the frozen snow made bloody their bare feet. On the individual traces one could recognize that rags and strings were tied around the feet. With our boots we made these traces invisible in order to hold back the pursuers and hinder an SS bloodbath. . . . We did not pursue. We would not reconcile it with our conscience and our regulations."[47]

While most people did no direct harm to the escapees, when confronted by the difficult choice of harboring an escapee they found themselves unable to risk their lives to save one. As a highway attendant from Obergaisbach put it: "In desperation, many an inmate would gladly have entered a house in order to hide himself. God forbid, had we done that. We would all have been killed. We would have been placed in a difficult situation if they had come to us. One cannot refuse, but one had to refuse this, since the threat of the SS made it dangerous."[48] So too a retired priest from Arbing admitted his inability to help when faced with the direct appeal of an inmate who approached him on the road. "It was the beginning of February 1945, on the day of the breakout," he related. "I had business to do in Perg. Toward evening I returned from Perg toward Arbing. On the way home a concentration camp inmate addressed me in German, asking if I would possibly provide him a hiding-place. I could not do that, and I also had no possibility. Afterwards we parted."[49]

Near Mauthausen there were two families that were willing to risk their security, their homes, and their lives by providing shelter to a few escapees. These families were the rare exception in an overall pattern of timidity, fear, and frenzied brutality. Long after the war, people in the area recall their bravery. Karl L., a priest from Schwertberg, who noted, "Yes, I was indeed there at that time. . . . One just did not go out of the house, it was so terrible," in the same breath also spoke of these two families, the Langthalers and Mascherbauers, who saved three of the Russian inmates.[50] The highway attendant who admitted that one had to refuse to aid the inmates for fear of the SS knew as well that there were people whose bravery defied common sense: "Our lord God does not allow the trees to grow to heaven. I have often read of the Langthalers; they were heroic, hundreds of others did not risk that."[51]

In 1945 Maria and Johann Langthaler lived along with four of their children[52] in Winden, a village that "lies upon a hillock 4 miles from Mauthausen." On a clear day the chimneys of the camp were visible. From elevated ground behind the Langthaler home, one could look out and see "in the distance the dark-gray walls" of the camp. Johann Langthaler, who worked as a quarry laborer in Mauthausen, had long since communicated to his family his knowledge that Mauthausen was a site of killing. "Yet another transport has arrived," his son, Joseph, recalled him saying once after returning from work. "Children, old people, women. If everyone who had been brought there were still alive, the camp would have to be made of rubber."

After the breakout "sirens sounding at short intervals went off in Mauthausen. Shots were fired in the vicinity. And twice a vehicle rigged with a loudspeaker rode through the village, announcing: 'Several hundred dangerous criminals have fled from the Concentration Camp Mauthausen. They pose a great danger for the population and have to be rendered harmless at once. No one is to be taken captive, all are to be liquidated on the spot.' " Joseph recalled that "even after nearly all the escapees were captured," loudspeakers driving through numerous villages in the area carried a blunt warning to the citizenry: "For hiding—death, for assistance—death!"[53]

To save a life under these circumstances meant allowing an escaped inmate to take refuge in one's barn, attic, or storage area. It meant having to stand by while SS men, soldiers, and local party officials searched one's property, poking through and turning over the hay. One also had to deal with nosy neighbors who asked suspicious questions, and spied upon one's property. When patrols came round again, one needed to divert them by feeding and entertaining them in the kitchen, their dogs at their side. Ultimately, such action involved the risk of sharing the inmates' fate if they were discovered, and bearing the consequences of harm to oneself and one's family.

Those who did help were no less fearful than their neighbors. However, they acted upon a conviction that, despite the raving violence taking place round about, the inmates were persons in need and deserving of the most basic human kindness. Such basic regard and respect for others was unique in this setting and moment. Yet these few persons could help precisely because they saw in the authority of the local regime only a transitory, illegitimate power subordinate to unchanging elementary precepts of care for fellow human beings. "I am a Christian, and as a Christian I am obligated to help when someone is in need," Maria Langthaler simply stated. "The Lord God is for the whole world, not only for the Germans. It is a community and there one must help. I did not ask them to which party they belong, I asked nothing at all; that made no difference to me. Only because they were human beings."[54]

Frau Langthaler knew of the mistreatment to which the inmates had been subject and had determined to help should the opportunity arise. From her son, Alfred, who was in the *Volkssturm*, she learned in detail of the mass escape and the ensuing murders. "At the time he came home he said, mother, you will not believe how miserable [the inmates] are. So helplessly and horribly are they being murdered. They beat this one with a rifle butt so that the blood squirted from him. So horrible, mother." Hearing these words, she thought of her five sons in uniform.

"I always thought, if it also happens like this to my own [children] in the hands of the enemy as it does [to the prisoners] among us, it is terrifying. If any were to come to me, I would not let them be killed. I would save their lives."[55]

She despaired that she would not have a chance to aid one of the inmates. "I thought to myself, no one can I help!" Yet, only moments later she heard a soft knock. "I went to the door, opened it up, and there stood a form outside. He had a blanket draped around him in which he cut a hole where he had stuck his head through." He wore shoes and a hat he had "somewhere got hold of." It was impossible for him to conceal his identity. "He did not want to say that he was an inmate. But I already recognized him by his 'Hitler street.' " (That is, he bore the revealing stripe shaved over his skull). Frau Langthaler ushered him inside. There was no hesitation. "He looked entirely pitiable, and I said, I already know who you are, poor devil—and I took him by the upper arm. I sensed only the bones—come in."[56]

After the inmate entered, he moved first toward the oven, then looked around, his eyes searching to see if they had a portrait of Hitler. "He could not see into us as we were. I could give him food, and then fetch the police. In fact many are supposed to have done that." The man only asked, "No call the police [nicht Polizei sprechen]."

Frau Langthaler's next step was to persuade her husband to allow her to keep and hide the inmate. "Father, you have heard, an inmate has come," she recalled. Fearful of the dread reprisal of internment in a concentration camp or execution for harboring such a person, he immediately replied that to do so was out of the question: "You Blunze [swearword], you idiot, we cannot do that, because we will all be sent to the camp. We will all be executed. We cannot do that." But she persisted, saying that it was to be only for "some days, until the murdering has ended."[57]

Consequently, they kept the inmate hidden among them. And then they sheltered yet another. But one Sunday morning when Frau Langthaler and her daughter were on their way to church, they came upon a troop of some 30 SS men engaged in a search. A tall officer with a dog was leading the search party. Frau Langthaler exchanged perfunctory greetings with the officer: "Guten morgen, guten morgen." At that moment she was seized with fear and doubt, as if suddenly cognizant of the reality of the danger to which she had exposed herself and her family. "When we had passed, I said, father, now it's all over. . . . What shall we do?"[58] She decided to send her daughter back to the house to inform her older sister to hide the inmates in a large quantity of hay and straw.[59]

The child at first cried, shying from the dangerous task. "Anni, you must go, you must save our lives, otherwise it's over with us, it's all over if they are sitting in the ditch and they come up with the dogs." At last she obeyed, running home and passing the SS along the way. By then, the SS had proceeded on to search another building. Seeing it unoccupied, they turned to the Langthaler daughter. "They asked, now little one, does anyone live there? No, she said, and ran on. Breathless, she came home and reported that so many are coming, that the house will be searched."[60]

Frau Langthaler went on to church in Schwertberg. Her fear and anxiety intensified as she poured out her worries in solitude, hiding in a corner of the church, lost in confusion and despair. "Even today I cannot yet relate the state I was in then. I did not know if I was a man or a woman. During the mass I spoke uninterruptedly. Lord God stand by me, and so on. That was the entire mass." Outside the church she met her husband. "I said, father, today I have gone through something. 'You think I haven't?' he responded. . . . Never in our marriage had we gone home [from church] together. [But] this time we went home together. Speechless."[61]

Even then the Langthalers discovered fresh evidence of the fate awaiting those captured. Across from their house stood a restaurant where they saw the SS assemble and then lead away three inmates. Frau Langthaler did not indicate where they had been discovered, only that they "stood barefoot in the snow. One had his head bound. And the SS stood behind them with their weapons aimed at them, ready to press the triggers." Walking round their house, the Langthalers also saw "an SS man with his dog coming down from the hayloft." Alone, he had apparently failed to find the hidden inmates, for the dog did not pick up their scent. Later, one of the two inmates said he had heard the SS man's footsteps. Though concealed, he was able to watch his three captured comrades from out of the hayloft window. As Frau Langthaler remembered, this inmate "moaned like a child" over their loss. "Barefoot they drove the three on the ice-filled street. It was the fourth of February. They shot them in Schwertberg."[62]

Afterwards the Langthaler's brought the two, Michail Rjabtschinski and Nikolaj Zemkalo, into the house, hiding them in the attic. Here they helped them set up a small, sealed apartment, complete with mattresses, a table, and stuffed chairs. It was a small interior space containing the rudiments of civilized existence. In time, the Langthaler's allowed them to come down to work about the farm, carrying out various chores such as chopping wood. This was not without risk, since the neighbors

were curious, indeed nosy and suspicious. Frau Langthaler invented stories to account for the presence of these new farm hands. "I had to lie,"
she recalled. She passed them off as extra help since "father [her hus-
band] was a rock quarry foreman, and he often sent us people, day
laborers." On one occasion several people, all Nazis, walked by and
caught sight of the two Russians chopping wood. "The neighbor asked,
what kind of children do you have out there. I said, I do not know them,
father sent them to us. All lies, always I lied." Remaining with the
Langthalers for three months, inmates Rjabtschinski and Zemkalo lived
to see the liberation in May.[63]

In Schwertberg lived a family that harbored another escaped Russian inmate, Semjon Schakow. Johann and Theresia Mascherbauer lived
with their five children on a farm. Two foreign laborers, a Polish woman
and a Frenchman, as well as an Austrian maid, resided with them.[64]

During the night of the escape she heard a disturbance that turned
out to have been the result of several inmates making their way onto the
Mascherbauer property. Noticing one fumbling about in the bee hives,
she shouted out: "What are you doing there?" He ran off, but afterward
there was a rapping at the window. Another inmate appeared, and she
gave him potatoes, half a loaf of bread, and milk which he instantly
consumed. He joined some 6 or 7 fellow inmates who spent the night
hidden in a wagon hut and a shed on the Mascherbauer's farm. Though
these men apparently disappeared before the SS arrived early the next
morning, this particular inmate was captured and led away by the SS.
Later in the day, another group of armed men arrived to search for
inmates. They first asked Herr Mascherbauer to sift through the hayloft.
When he refused, they went to work, uncovering three men still in
hiding. A local Nazi leader had *Volkssturm* men hurl two of them down
the steps. They picked themselves up, raising their arms in surrender.
Then, again according to Herr Mascherbauer, they were "shot on the
spot." One of them, though wounded, had not been killed and began
moaning. "The *Volkssturm* men had to shoot him again." The third
inmate managed to spring to safety and ran off.[65] Their children were
witness to this scene. "We hid ourselves in the parlor and cried," recalled
one of Masherbauer's sons who was then 14 years old. The French laborer
then removed the bodies with a sled.[66] Eight days later, however, an
inmate showed up. Frau Mascherbauer reports: "I take a look through the
loft window and think to myself, look, there comes a railway worker this
way." But then, as he comes nearer "I see he has an inmate uniform. He
approached looking completely afraid, he had a frozen beet under his
arm. He came asking for matches." Told to wait, he unaccountably

disappeared, after which Frau Mascherbauer pursued him. "I put food together in a basket, and we followed the tracks into the forest. There he was kneeling under an evergreen tree where he had a rag laid out upon which we placed the food before him, and again departed. We had to watch out."[67]

The next day the inmate reappeared. Frau Mascherbauer and the Polish woman working for them prepared milk and heated a brick with which he could warm himself. He left, only to return twice more, before finally requesting to stay. Frau Masherbauer went to her husband, asking his permission. "My husband said, then he should remain and hide himself in the straw." After he settled into the barn, she prepared him more food, indeed too much food, for the thick rabbit soup she served him made him ill. She feared he might die while still in her care.[68] She found him clothing, exchanging some of her sons' things, telling a shop woman with whom she exchanged them that her boys were getting bigger. Under her care, in time he became well, indeed growing "as fat as a brewmaster." He remained with the Mascherbauers three months and eight days.[69]

At first the Mascherbauers even attempted to keep knowledge of the inmate's presence from their young sons. One of them noted how after the camp breakout a neighbor gave the boys a hunting rifle "with the remark, if something comes up, we can defend ourselves." "We boys were 13–14 years old at that time. We ran around with the unloaded rifle and played 'find the Russians.' Our parents scolded us a great deal." However, after the boys entered the barn and discovered human excrement, their parents broke the secret and revealed that they were hiding the inmate. "Our parents were embarrassed, became completely red in the face, and so they confessed to us what was happening." It then became the boys' task to take food to the inmate. Stating that at first "we were really afraid," the son noted how he soon won the boys' friendship, fashioning for them rings and crosses made of aluminum pipe.[70]

Their neighbor, a farm woman, suspected what was going on, and reported the matter to the military police. Two military gendarmes showed up, wanting to know if the Mascherbauers had hidden an inmate. This was only one of several occasions when they had to fend off searches. Whenever a patrol arrived Frau Mascherbauer successfully diverted them from their search with refreshments and conversation. Once, "about a month after the escape" four or five SS men and their dog appeared. She offered them sausages and cider. "They said, for once that's something different," and seated themselves for the meal. The SS man with the dog, a "sullen man," was reluctant to join them, but allowed himself to be persuaded. "I asked the dog leader if the dog was vicious," Frau Mascherbauer noted. "Yes, when I order him, he certainly is," came the reply. Fortunately, the cozy atmosphere kept the SS distracted. They ate and amused themselves talking to Frau Mascherbauer's son. Finally, an air raid occurred and the SS left. But the fear remained. "At that time we really shook," she recalled.[71]

Johann and Theresia Mascherbauer did not attempt to explain their motives in acting to save inmate Schakow. Like the Langthalers they feared for themselves and for their children. Nor were the Mascherbauers punished after inmates were discovered in their barn the day after the breakout. Inmates took up hiding places in farm buildings throughout the area in those first hours after the escape. The men who found and shot those discovered on the Mascherbauer property right after the escape did not hold the Mascherbauers responsible for their presence. Far more dangerous would have been the discovery of an inmate on their property days after the escape. By then the charge of consciously having aided an escaped prisoner would have been compelling. But the searchers never found Nikolaj Zemkalo, Michail Rjabschinski, and Semjon Schakow. Two Austrian families showed that both rescue and survival were possible.[72]

Every escape was an affront to the system of "total domination."[73] Escape signified dispersion, flight, and freedom, an intolerable breach of security and a blow that gave the lie—if only for a moment—to the camp's claim of total power over the life and death of every prisoner. If an inmate succeeded in fleeing, "apocalypse was unleashed."[74] The entire camp population was herded onto the roll call square, and forced to stand hour after hour in all types of weather, sometimes all night long. In the snow and ice, feet froze. Weaker inmates collapsed. Their legs aching, in their heavy stance the rigid and motionless assembly acted as a mass counterweight to the one who dared to flee. Invariably, the escaped inmate was brought back, tortured, and hung before the pitiful congregation. Twisting on the rope, feet suspended above the earth, he was a reminder to all that to leap the perimeter was to die.

In no small measure, the nearly universal indifference, and in numerous instances hostility of the surrounding population contributed to the hopelessness of any such attempt. The vital question was, "To whom could [the inmates] turn for shelter? They were outside the world, men and women made of air."[75] The uniformly wretched and freakish appearance of an escaped inmate was only heightened as a result of hiding in the outdoors; the characteristic haircut immediately gave away the inmate's identity.

For the desperate 400 souls, bursting the cordon proved a life-affirming, if not ultimately a life-protecting, endeavor. Their drive beyond the wall was an expression of defiance in the face of certain death, and a reaching outward toward life. The inmates all escaped in the faint hope that the townsfolk would not simply stand aside but stand by them, nourish them, assist them in their flight. To the contrary, most of the citizenry rejected their pleas, drew up new cordons round their homesteads, and lowered their nets upon all save a very few. In their barns, farmers poked through the hay anxious to discover something live and trembling on the ends of their pitchforks. Captured, the inmates knew they had in fact never escaped the boundaries of Mauthausen. In giving chase to the fugitives, the citizenry made the camp coextensive with their own world.

For a moment, the barriers had fallen. The inmates were no longer strictly confined but were dispersed. They penetrated the forests, the meadows, the market places, the barns, and the kitchens. The citizenry feared the inmates as a foreign and tainted presence in their midst. The official description of the prisoners as hardened criminals reinforced public fears that something safely confined had burst its bonds and now stalked the neighborhood. Yet, the popular designation of the fugitives as "rabbits" offers a clue to a contrasting image that lodged in the mind of the citizenry. Rabbits are wily, elusive, yet ultimately meek and defenseless prey. Images of the hardened criminal escaped from a penitentiary overlapped with those of an amusing and harmless catch, offering the prospect of a sporting chase.

And chase they did. Many responded to the challenge with zeal. They demonstrated initiative and resourcefulness in carrying out the order to root the fugitives from their hideouts. This was a release. Gladly they waded in, smearing themselves in blood. The SS offered the average citizen an opportunity to violate the most ancient of taboos: the killing of one's fellow man. In leaping the bounds of the camp, the inmates paradoxically afforded the onlookers an opportunity to transgress those same moral restraints they had for seven years witnessed the SS violate. Temptation gave way to intoxication. Such recklessness is embodied in the German word *Rausch*, "something that just took hold,"[76] an unleashing of the senses, a drunken madness, an unbridled surge of feeling in which "one loses all hold on things and on reality."[77] Indeed, the SS encouraged people to lose control. The sanction of existing authority sufficed to turn ordinary citizens into man-hunters.

The chase of February 1945 offered the citizenry the license to pursue and kill. The chance to wield the instruments of the hunt fell to the older men and boys organized into the *Volkssturm* and the Hitler Youth, but the women were on hand to point, to inform, to call in the men for the kill. In deputizing the civilian population, the SS counted on their identification with the executioners. The line between perpetrators and onlookers blurred. There was no room for neutrality. Between the Nazi order to hunt them down and the inmates' plea for cover there was no middle ground.

In this final season of the camp's existence, seeing the end coming, the SS would not have overlooked the advantage of having the blood of the victims on the hands of the general population. In deputizing the population the SS and party leaders might well have taken satisfaction in showing that they alone did not bear responsibility for the killing.[78] The order to participate was a call for the general population to make overt their long-standing toleration and indirect, if not direct, support for the camp. Now everyone was a potential executioner. With the citizenry in effect an auxiliary arm of the guard corps, their farms and homes and places of business became extensions of the camp.

Chapter 7

The Death Marches

———

With defeat imminent, in the final weeks of the war the SS was forced to abandon the far-flung outposts of the Mauthausen concentration camp system. The remaining prisoners of the satellite camps closest to the front were forcibly marched toward an interior cluster of camps centered in the core complex in Mauthausen-Gusen, as well as Ebensee, located 45 miles southwest of Mauthausen at the southern tip of Lake Traun in the *Salzkammergut*. From 30 March to 18 April the branch camps of Peggau, Leibnitz, Hinterbrühl, Floridsdorf, Vienna-Sauer-Werke, St. Aegyd, Hirtenberg, Melk, Amstetten, Wiener Neustadt, and Wiener Neudorf were dissolved. By the end of April a similar fate befell the camps of Loibl Pass, Klagenfurt, St. Lambrecht, St. Valentin, and Redl-Zipf. Following an order from Mauthausen camp commandant Ziereis that "not a single inmate may fall into the hands of the enemy," those deemed unfit for the march were either shot or given lethal injections. Under armed guard, all others headed toward the interior. With many of the main thoroughfares clogged with military traffic, the inmate columns proceeded across back roads that nonetheless led through populated areas. Astride the columns the guards hovered like angels of death, beating inmates, shooting any who staggered, lagged behind, or fell. Of the 1,884 inmates in the Hinterbrühl camp, located near the

Vienna suburb of Mödling, more than 50 were executed when the camp was abandoned; no fewer than 150 others were shot during the 8-day, 128-mile-long trek toward Mauthausen.

Also making their way toward Mauthausen at this time were tens of thousands of Hungarian Jews originally assigned to work on fortifications along the Austro-Hungarian border and in factories in Vienna.[1] They were forced westward toward Mauthausen that winter and spring, largely by foot; others were crowded into boats without food and water. To accommodate the influx, those who reached Mauthausen alive were herded into tents assembled outside the main walls. In less than a single week, beginning on 3 April 1945, at least 8,500 Hungarian Jews, including women and children entered the encampment. Those fortunate enough to find shelter inside the crowded tents could barely move. Others were forced to linger on the damp ground outside, exposed to the elements. Dying at a rate of between 150 and 200 per day, in less than three weeks that April an estimated 3,000 Jews failed to leave the tents alive.[2]

Many who managed to survive this ordeal met their deaths almost immediately thereafter. Beginning in mid-April the Jews were marched some 35 miles from Mauthausen to another camp inside the woods near Gunskirchen. The route from Mauthausen, passing through numerous cities, towns, and villages, was soaked in blood. In each one, mass graves were dug. Along the first two and one-half miles of the march, a stretch leading from the main camp to a nearby bridge in Mauthausen, an estimated 800 died. To be sure, "in all, approximately 22,000 prisoners reached Gunskirchen," but there too atrocious conditions awaited them. "There were in all seven large barracks that were not completed, and into each more than 2,000 prisoners were crowded. There was no running water or lavatories on the site. Typhus and dysentery epidemics took a toll of some 200-300 lives per day. Thousands of dead and dying lay around the camp without anyone being able to help them or even bury them." Few survived to witness the liberation when "American army units entered the camp. According to a report by the . . . medical officer, only 5,149 survivors were found alive." Altogether, an estimated 15,000 Jews died either along the route of march or in Gunskirchen itself.[3]

As the war came to a close and the horror of the concentration camps spilled over into ever more towns and villages of Austria, citizens became direct witnesses to mass murder. The inmates were marched through the streets, beaten, and shot before the eyes of the citizenry. The sight was unavoidable. No one honestly could deny knowing what an inmate looked like, and what it meant to be a victim in the hands of the SS.

On these forced marches of the twelfth hour the inmate was no longer an abstraction: his features, though fearfully distorted and other-worldly, were visible for all to see. Witnesses saw too that among the inmates were mothers, fathers, and children, as well as old men. In their recollections, Mauthausen's residents described the beings they saw during those final weeks. "It was a shocking sight," recalled Alois G., who was standing outside a department store on the Kaiser Josef Platz in Wels one morning at the end of April, 1945, "a column of miserable forms . . . only skeletons who could go no farther passed by." Those who sat down, their bones unable to carry them, would be immediately assaulted by the guards. Irmgard G. described the inmates she encountered: "I saw those of shaved heads with faces altogether sunken. Others with eyes framed deep and black. That is, a procession of ghosts, a batch of persons who walked along the edge of the road. And on the road lay corpses that were covered with coats or rags. The inmates were driven on. . . . They staggered, shuffled along, . . . their looks apathetic, downcast." She and five or six companions who "uttered only my God, my God," expressed their helplessness before the image of the passing phantoms: "Twice we saw the column of ghosts. . . . What were we supposed to do? We had neither bread nor other edibles with us."[4]

Observers who watched, staring in amazement and horror at the sight, were often witness to a spectacle in which the living were indistinguishable from the dead. A woman on her way to do her shopping in Enns discovered the road packed with "children, youths, women and men of all ages. The edge of the street which I used for walking was sometimes so blocked by persons lying on the ground that I did not know how I was supposed to get by. I could not determine if, exhausted, they had broken down, or if they were dead, or had to set themselves down on the spot in order to rest up to be able to take part in the continuing march."[5]

Dragging themselves forward along the route of march, eyes dark and hollow, their crumpled shapes strewn upon the ground, the marchers were, in the view of bystanders, like visitors from the realm of the dead. Frau Maria A., wife of the grave-digger and master stonemason in Enns-Lorch, had taken shelter in the cellar of the gravedigger's house in the cemetery. From the window she watched as uniformed men arrived to stack the dead. Under supervision of the SS the men hurled the corpses from carts onto a pile. She watched and she listened:

After some time I heard cries for water that came from the heap of the so-called dead. Thereupon I took a bowl with water and went to the mountain of the "dead," in order to give this to the one who called for water. Immediately an SS guard approached me and with a knout struck the water bowl from my hand. It was a terrible blow. This wrist still hurts me now sometimes. He, the SS man, stepped over to the caller without any regard for me [and] shot him at close range. There was no more crying for water.[6]

More bodies arrived. "Again a mountain of inmate corpses lay in the cemetery. Next to them lay seven to nine soldiers of the German Wehrmacht" executed for desertion. She stated that a physician, Dr. Ferdinand G. of the General Hospital in Enns, came to this site to officially inspect the bodies of the soldiers. On this occasion as well sounds could be heard issuing from the pile of dead inmates. When the SS guard had left, he and Frau A. went over to the bodies. "Dr. G. thought one must do something there. . . . We both together lifted this 'dead one' from out of the heap, dragged him down below into the cellar, into my apartment."[7] Dr. G. determined that the man had a shoulder wound which he treated and bandaged. Frau A. believed that the man was a Jew, and she recalled him displaying a family photo. Although Dr. G. repeatedly returned to care for him, she maintained, he died after only a few days. Their final task was to carry the man, now a heavy corpse, up from the cellar and place him once more among the dead from whence they had pulled him. Altogether 87 Hungarian Jews are known to have been disposed of in the Lorch cemetery.[8]

Some of the most poignant recollections of townspeople who witnessed these marches center upon the discovery of discarded artifacts of the victims' previous existence. More than once a photograph, the memento of family life and home, a representation of the world the victims left behind, was found by the wayside. When the dying Jew hauled from the pile of corpses in the Enns cemetery showed the gravedigger's wife an image of his family, he shared with her a momentary bond of humanity. Such a picture could not help but proclaim that the man whose family was represented in it was human too. Years later a priest remembered having discovered "a family photo that showed a large family, in the background an estate" among the items a group of Jews left behind at a brick works near St. Florian. The picture lay among other objects— pullovers, scarves, and vests—left following the departure of the surviving marchers.[9]

If there were some who through discovery of these signs found a shared humanity with victims who passed by, others surfaced to drive them from toward their deaths. Not only did the SS routinely shoot Jews along the highways, leaving bodies left exposed and unattended, there were civilians who dispatched any Jews who had managed briefly to escape their executioners. A gendarme, Alexander K., related that he was alone at his post in Sierning when a number of Jews being led from Adlwang to Steyr were shot in the cemetery. Two women, one of them quite young, approached to inform him that there were Jews present near the cemetery and "demanded of me that I shoot these Jews, which I refused; whereupon the girl . . . called me a coward."[10]

Efforts to dispose of the victims in cemeteries, however, were inadequate to deal with the numbers left rotting by the wayside. Their presence raised disturbing questions of the responsibility of the living toward the dead. Overwhelmed by the sight of persons brutally murdered and left behind unattended, a priest in Enns addressed a letter of protest to his episcopal superiors in Linz: "In recent days here thousands of inmates, allegedly Hungarian Jews, were led through the streets. Many of them broke down from exhaustion, and were not able to keep up. They were then beaten without hesitation on the open street with rifle butts by the accompanying SS men, or killed through a shot to the head. The columns then moved on without further concerning themselves with the dead." Reporting the public's response to the treatment of the victims, he noted,

> the populace is infuriated by such uncivilized behavior, and I bid His Excellence, the most highly honorable Herr Bishop, to intervene with the Gauleiter for Upper Danube so that such conditions, shameful for the German people, be halted, and that the appropriate offices be reminded of the regulations of the sanitation police. If there are institutions for the removal of animal carcasses which have to remove the bodies from the street, so indeed must human bodies be cared for as corresponds to a civilized people.[11]

In this final stage the terror now poured openly onto the streets, pathways, and meadows. The SS and their accomplices did not shy from committing acts of brutality before the eyes of the civilian population, making men, women, and even children witnesses to their crimes. It was as if in this final spasm of hatred it no longer mattered whether the worst acts of violence were kept from general view. The executioners demanded only that the onlookers keep quiet and refrain from open acts of sympathy toward the victims.

Years later some would maintain that this unavoidable exposure of brutality finally undermined their faith in the party. "The dead shocked persons who otherwise still expected their salvation from the National Socialist regime," wrote a priest from Gunskirchen. "Such coarseness, roughness, cruelty, and mistreatment put off even people of deadened temperament."[12] "Never would we have thought that our affairs would have resulted in something like this," said a man from Wels.[13] Yet, among some there remained the belief, or the wish to believe, that, despite all, Hitler could not have approved of this. A woman recalled seeing "a shocking procession of emaciated figures who had torn clothes and bad footwear. Several went barefoot. We saw how some stepped out of the column and plucked a bit of sparse grass, and stuck it in their mouths. Probably in order to still their thirst." From her daughter's basket, she said, she drew two bread rolls. She threw them to the inmates, and was immediately seen doing so by an SS man. "My daughter was of the opinion that treating these poor persons this way was not right," believing "that Hitler knows nothing about it. He would do away with it immediately."[14]

Some persons rushed to get a good look when they heard that inmates were being marched through the area. "It was the end of April, at that time I was employed in railway master station one," recalled Alois D. from Wels. "There I heard from a roadbed laborer who had worked at signal-box one that terrible looking inmates were driven by. I went to my boss and had myself released from duty. I wanted to see that."[15] Herr D. got on his bicycle and rode out along the Salzburgerstrasse. On the way he saw several groups of inmates making their way under SS guard. He discovered "a group of 30 to 40 Jews, women, children, old bearded men" led by "five or six SS men." Along the Salzburgerstrasse he also found "at least 8 or 10 dead." In addition he came across a large column he estimated as consisting of from 500 to 600 inmates. They were kept off the main roads, and walked through ditches. Those who were able, "bore—or rather, dragged after them"—their "half-dead" comrades.[16]

Herr D. admitted to being disturbed by what he saw. "The whole thing made a horrible and terrifying impression on me." He saw the inmates "full of hunger, with torn clothing that was full of dirt." They bore little bundles, "their last worldly goods." He recalls an old man with a "long black coat," unable to go on. When the man sat down an SS man thrust his rifle butt into the man's back before beating him with the weapon across the back. "It was shocking for everyone who had to look. With their last strength many moved forward, supported and helped by their comrades in suffering. The children cried and were held tight by their mothers. It was a picture that one can never forget."[17]

Sometimes persons retreated toward routine in a confused effort to take refuge from such scenes of terror. A school inspector from St. Florian admitted that she found the sight of the inmates' suffering so unbearable that her response was to distract herself with household tasks. She said she had seen some persons attempt to reach a fountain, only to be pushed on by the SS. She also viewed women carrying children on their shoulders, and other inmates supporting their weaker comrades, dragging them along. It became too much to endure: "After that I slept it off. I was so upset about the whole thing that I began to clean up a room which I had long put off doing."[18]

School children were frightened too, and some avoided venturing out for fear of seeing the inmates. The school inspector recalled asking a couple of absent pupils why they had failed to show up for class one day: "*Ja*, they said, there are so many dead by the side of the road, we became afraid and turned back again." The inspector admitted she too could not bear the sight. While out on her bicycle she found an inmate lying in a ditch with one or two armed guards standing above him. The man was dying. "Then I saw one sitting, gave him a piece of bacon I had with me. I also gave a little sugar that I still had." She came across yet another who "wrapped himself in a blanket and rolled from the street into the ditch. Probably so that no one should see him. What happened with him beyond that I have no idea. I then rode on again." By the next day she did not go out to look; she could not stand the sight. "I did not want to see this tragedy, and was not permitted to help, [was] not able to help."[19]

In these maimed bodies the bystanders unwittingly confronted the irrefutable evidence of mass crime. They also stood in frightened silence as murders were committed before their eyes. A clergyman in Pucking found himself helplessly looking on as an SS man first threatened to kill an inmate, then did so. He heard the SS man say to the inmate, "Just wait a minute. When we get out of the town, then I'll kill you." The priest retreated indoors. "I saw directly from my chancellery outward— today there is a tree in front of it—how he killed him. And, to be sure, he went at him from behind. Thence the man staggered, the SS man shot him in the back of the head, so that [his] little inmate cap flew off. He then fell on his face onto the street and he was dead. A wagon drove up after this column of misery and picked up the dead on the left and right side of the street."[20] Others had heard the SS man issue his threat. One woman apparently had the nerve to tell the SS man, "Don't be so horrid, don't be so inhumane, and they'll die anyway soon," when arguing with him about giving the inmates potatoes. The clergyman noted that "The others anyway did not dare say anything. I as a priest stood there and gave them all general absolution. There was absolutely nothing more one could do."[21]

Assistance might indeed take the form of an appeal for humane treatment directed to the guards. Such appeals, however, could not be certain of hindering overseers determined to commit acts of cruelty. A farmer in Weisskirchen, Hans H., ordered to transport several inmates in his cart, tried to reason with an SS guard who was beating a young Jew:

> I said to the SS man, hey, hey, you don't have to do that. [He asked:] 'You take pity on these people?' Naturally, was my answer. He said; 'There is no mercy,' [and that] I should only take care that I do not become included myself. He took the machine pistol, shot the youth into the ditch, and the eight who lay on the wagon he shot too. Through the shooting my horses became skittish. I had much to do in order to calm them, and drove home.[22]

The townsfolk were close enough to see the victims as individuals, not as "pigs," or "traitors," or "criminals." The guards struck them down within view of the citizenry. Yet, in their recollections, witnesses did not focus on the faces; items of clothing are sometimes mentioned: coats, the ragged covering of the feet, a blanket wrapped around an inmate. For the most part one did not advance description beyond reference to a general likeness to skeletons or ghosts. But if there was one tragic scenario that lodged in the memory of those who, at the least, some quarter century after the events could evoke compassion for the victims, it was the image of parents with their children. Rarely did such recognition prompt a citizen into action. Rather, people stood aside and watched in horror.

One such incident, mentioned by several women, was offered by the wife of a gravedigger from Ansfelden:

> On the death march there were not only men, but women and children. A Jewish woman marched with her child, a small girl. The girl had a sack tied to her back from which a doll looked outward. All of a sudden the mother broke down near the Krems (river) and could no longer get up. Immediately an SS guard stepped over and shot the mother before the eyes of the child. The child cried heart-rendingly for her mother. The woman was carried to the bridge and thrown into the river.[23]

What is the meaning of this doll peeking from the rucksack? Like the little girl, and like the observer of this scene as well, the doll is a helpless witness to a murder. A doll's expression is frozen, it cannot act. The little girl, her doll, indeed the woman who recalls the tragedy are in this way seen as united and bound in their inability to prevent the crime.

A woman from Thalheim recounted a similar incident which she said she learned about from her brother:

> The column of camp inmates were coming from Schleissheim. An old man who could go no further was repeatedly encouraged by his little son, Papa, hold on, Papa support yourself. The father could not carry on. He gasped and with his last strength he tried to move forward with the help of his son. He collapsed. An SS man immediately stepped up to him and struck him as he lay on the ground with the butt of his weapon. The little boy kneeled down before his father and cried. He cried Papa, Papa, again and again. This same SS Man struck the boy dead with the butt and threw the two of them down and over the slope of the road.[24]

As Frau M. from St. Florian reported,

> I know that on the way through town people secretly handed the Jews bread, potatoes, and other things. In town there was not much that one could do, since they were guarded. Guards walked to the side with their weapons fixed. Women walked ahead in the first ranks. Men and women carried children on their shoulders. That is something I still know. I did not go down any more to see the processions, except in passing by. I did not want to see this tragedy, and I was not allowed to help. Had one done otherwise one would have been led away immediately.[25]

A number of bystanders cited danger to themselves as the reason why they were unable to help the inmates by daring to offer the passing inmates food or water. Repeatedly, they point to SS warnings and threats to prove their powerlessness to act. As a woman from Pucking related:

> On one of those days when they marched past we were issued ration cards. We were sitting in the restaurant and naturally were curious about what was going on outside and looked out at the camp inmates marching past. But there an SS man, completely enraged, approached and threatened and screamed at us, if we are unable to close the window that instant we too could immediately join the group. We were not permitted to give anyone a thing.[26]

Nonetheless, some bystanders apparently did leave things by the wayside for the inmates to pick up as they passed. Dr. Stephan Viranyi, survivor of a grueling trek across Austria to Mauthausen and Gunskirchen in the spring of 1945, noted that "In particular villages the Austrian residents placed water pitchers and glasses in front of the garden gates so that we could at least hastily empty a glass in passing. But only a few succeeded, because those who stepped out of the ranks for this purpose were immediately forced back into line with rifle butts. The residents also tossed apples into the ranks, but during the hasty procession only very few could lay hold of one."[27]

To be sure, the SS threatened civilians who dared to offer bread, potatoes, or fruit to the passing inmates. Invariably, the SS shouted they could "come right along" and share the fate of the wretched stragglers; and in some instances the guards gave chase to persons who had offered the inmates food.[28] Yet, while numerous witnesses recall being either the object of such threats, or claimed to know of others who were, none cited any instance in which the SS actually arrested or executed anyone for having dared to assist the inmates in this small way. A woman from Schleissheim claimed to have had a dangerous brush with the SS, yet she lived to relate the incident that follows:

> Then once a transport with woman and children arrived. There I gave milk for a child. It was watered milk. I myself did not have much. There an SS man, a guard, leaps at me and shouts at me. "What are you passing out?" A little milk for the child, was my answer. And already he had drawn his revolver. Around me stands a crowd of children who immediately cling to me. I had five of my own, and some belonging to the refugees [some were quartered in her home, she had noted] were also on hand. He asked, "To whom do these children belong?" To me! He gave me a shove and forced me into the house and slammed the front door shut and left. I believed I was as good as dead.[29]

"The postman," she added, "ran into the village telling people that [I] was shot. He believed I was already dead."[30]

Precisely because courageous acts of direct resistance to the SS were so rare, onlookers recalled unique and striking instances in which such acts forced the SS to retreat from their actions. One bystander remembered seeing a young woman prisoner slap an SS man who had struck her mother. Reeling from this unexpected blow, according to the witness, the SS man ceased his assault.[31] The parish chronicle of Weisskirchen offers a bizarre example of a direct and presumably life-saving challenge to the SS. As the Jews marched by the churchyard, it is said that persons inside waved them over and offered them something to eat. A female

cook offering food drew the attention of one of the guards. The guard
threatened her with joining the marchers. Just as he was about to strike
an inmate, "our big St. Bernard dog, worthy Bari, sprang at this SS man
so ferociously; frightened, the man let up. In the meantime, the inmate
was able to get away and escape the death-blow. Cursing, the inhumane
escort left the churchyard. Meanwhile the inmate fortunately disappeared into the large crowd, saved by faithful Bari."[32]

Those who dared to come to the aid of the Jews had first to accept
the humanity of the victims, seeing past the obviously repellent appearance the persecutors had forced them to assume. In doing so the helping
bystander had to circumvent as best he could the malevolent authority of
those who took the physical wretchedness of the Jews as confirmation of
their dehumanized status. In a fundamental way, under these circumstances, assistance—the offer of bread, of water, or a potato—undermined the basis of the Nazi effort to prove its victims inhuman and
unworthy of life.

Among those guarding the brutal processions were *Volkssturm* men,
teenagers of the Hitler Youth, regular soldiers, police, and firemen. Witnesses including both survivors of the marches and civilian onlookers referred to numerous instances of cruelty on the part of those who did not
belong to the SS. By enlisting the assistance of these other groups, the SS,
wittingly or otherwise, broadened the cohort of potential executioners.
The hastily organized retreat toward Mauthausen paved the way for the
participation of non-professional or amateur killers. A farm woman from
the area of Pucking and Weisskirchen who was then 20 years old noted:

> When I said it was not easy to help these poor people, it was because we
> had a group of flak-soldiers who had withdrawn from Lower Austria quar-
> tered in our village. In spite of the approaching end of the war there were
> quite a number of fanatics in their ranks.
>
> They labeled the Jewish concentration camp inmates as criminals.
> [They said] these are not human beings with whom one may have pity or
> to whom one may give something. One who especially proclaimed this
> attitude was a noncommissioned officer who out of sheer wantonness shot
> one of them with his rifle. This inmate gave him no cause to do so. This
> inmate lay in the ditch by the road with a shot through the lung, and
> begged to be freed from his torment.[33]

Similarly, Alois M. reported from Wels:

> On several evenings when I arrived in Enns by train from work and left for
> home from the railway station between 6 and 7 P.M, it happened that
> transports of Jews coming from Mauthausen crossed my path.

So one time it happened that I was on my way home just as a *Volks-sturm* man shot down a Jewess who carried a small child on her arm. He beat the child with the rifle butt. This *Volkssturm* man is supposed to have been the leader of this transport.[34]

Michael H., from Wels, who at the time was a master craftsman in a machine factory, reported on the reaction of soldiers to the scenes of killing taking place before their eyes. He said he had hitched a ride in an army vehicle heading toward Laakirchen.

On departure from Wels I saw the first Jewish camp inmates who were being forced toward Lambach. I can still remember very precisely on the stretch toward Gunskirchen some twenty corpses lay on the side of the road or in roadside ditches. I saw how two camp inmates dragged along a man in between them. Suddenly a guard went after the three and shot at the one who could not carry on, and then at the other two. What the cause for that was I cannot say. We drove past very slowly. On the army vehicle were also several soldiers who saw all this. "Now, with the war practically over, they should not have to do that any more." The others [said]: "For these pigs it's no loss [*Um diese Schweine ist es kein Schaden*]." There were still such views up until just a few days before the end of the war.[35]

Dr. Rolf Busch-Waldeck, a survivor of the death march from the Wiener Neudorf camp back toward Mauthausen, similarly recalled the brutal remarks of soldiers when their path crossed that of the inmates on 4 April 1945: "It was afternoon. The SS had again untiringly beaten inmates. At an intersection we suddenly had to halt in order to let an endless column of soldiers march past. The soldiers cursed us: 'Traitors to the Fatherland!' 'Bandits!' 'Hang them!' 'Filthy Bastards!' 'Pigs!' and assumed a threatening attitude toward us."[36]

In this moment of indiscriminate murder, civilians tempted by bloodshed found their chance to join in the sport. Dr. Busch-Waldeck likewise recalled that when the camp was abandoned on 2 April, an SS man brought along his girlfriend. In one arm he held his gun at the ready, "on the other arm a vulgarly dressed, made-up, powdered, and giggling prostitute, who in her turn with her free hand casually [led] a dog trained to tear apart human flesh. The SS man and the prostitute laughingly climb[ed] over the corpses. Each time the dog snarl[ed], the hair on its neck ruffled, sniff[ing] at the dead, it [was] jerked along." On the second day out, the woman casually expressed a desire to participate in the killing. She still walked "arm in arm" with her boyfriend, an SS-

Blockführer who had already fired upon the prisoners. Dr. Bush-Waldeck added that "When again a comrade [that is, an inmate] broke down, the woman said: Bubi, you have already made boom-boom so often, now let girly make boom-boom for once." The SS man "laughed. He held the machine pistol fast and let the woman press the trigger. The inmate was badly wounded, but was not dead." Whereupon he "now fired and said to the woman: 'Shooting is something that has to be learned.' "[37]

One of the many stations on the death march of Hungarian Jews lay in Gmünd. In July 1944 around two hundred Jews arrived in Gmünd to be put to work in the local rock quarries, factories, and forestry operations. Their numbers were augmented by nearly 2,000 others who arrived in late December. Poorly fed and sheltered, the inmates suffered a punishing regimen of abuse and neglect that by the winter of 1944–45 resulted in a death rate of 10 persons per day. Between 1 January and 16 February 1945, some 446 persons were recorded as having died. Their basic sanitary needs deliberately neglected, the Jews suffered from an unending plague of lice, diarrhea, infection, and frostbite."[38]

On 23 December 1944 a transport carrying some 1,700 Jews arrived in Gmünd. The new arrivals were rudely herded into a cold grain-storage facility whose pair of iron coke-burning ovens smoked so much they had to be removed, making heating impossible. The inmates had to find space on a cement floor covered with only a thin layer of straw. Outside temperatures stood as low as 10 degrees below zero. "Many hundreds suffered from the worst cases of frostbite, with complete blackening coloration of the hands and feet."[39]

Among those bystanders able and willing to help was a local medical officer, Dr. Arthur Lanc. During the Christmas holidays he received word from the Gmünd police of the presence of "a large transport of Jews . . . housed in the granary" since December 23. He learned as well that "unbelievable sanitary abuses were supposed to prevail there," and that "already some Jews had died."[40] Bicycling to the scene, he discovered some 1,700 inmates crammed into a wooden facility measuring 86 by 21 yards in area and with a height of some 5 yards. With a Jewish physician, the prisoner Dr. Nikolaus Darvas from Budapest as his guide, Dr. Lanc toured the scene. The conditions he discovered were barely describable. His account resembles those of others who share a lasting impression of their encounters with these beings from the world of suffering:

> When he wanted to lead me through the camp in order to show me in spot-check fashion the most blatant cases, in an instant we were sur-rounded by hundreds of these poor people who saw that I gave him a small

grocery packet; and pressed to the floor, with hands uplifted they now shouted at me all their sufferings. Most of them begged for hospital accommodation for themselves or a relative, many for medicines, almost all for something to eat.[41]

He stated that these scenes so weighed upon him that "in the following two months while the camp was lodged in Gmünd again and again I could find no sleep at night."[42]

Hunger and cold had done their work. "Around 200 to 300 persons had the most severe frostbite on their hands and feet. The feet, temporarily wrapped in rags, were mostly colored blue-black up the the ankle joint; because of the mighty swellings and inflammations they no longer wore shoes. On top of that almost all the inmates suffered from the most severe diarrhea." Unable to move due to the effects of their wounds, persons were forced to relieve themselves on the spot. What is more, "all were horribly full of lice. All medicine and means of disinfection were lacking." At a spring near the storage facility those who could washed their shirts, their bodies meanwhile exposed to the cold. On the other hand, "most of them, however, were no longer in a condition to stand, and, whimpering, stretched out their frozen limbs with the imploring request for hospitalization. Many already lay apathetic or in agony. On one spot lay some 5 bodies of those who died during the night."[43]

Dr. Lanc appealed to those in charge to rectify these conditions, only to meet with a crude rebuff. Responding to Lanc's description of what he had just seen in the camp, one official, Hans L.,

explained to me that I could convince myself how animalistic these Jews are. When the transport had arrived there were so many Jews placed on top of the bodies of others who lay on the floor of the wagon (I believe he spoke of 17 bodies). These 'lazy pigs' had left the wagon standing just in front of the grain warehouse and no longer concerned themselves with it. He further related: when they had come to the warehouse these "animals" so forced their way in that the entrance was clogged. Thereupon he took a wooden board and over the ones furthest back smashed away upon the heads of those further up. In this way the passage was made free.[44]

When on another occasion this official complained that he and his colleagues had been forced to witness how "one of these 'pigs' had rolled on his axis, had drawn down his trousers and relieved himself in order to roll back afterwards to his place", Lanc to no avail tried to explain that frostbite would have made the prisoner "incapable of walking even a single step."[45]

Such arguments left L. unchanged in his opinion of the Jews, and he publicly repeated details of this behavior as evidence of their bestiality:

> Some time later an assembly was held in Gmünd in which I also took part in which L., despite my explanation, repeated the above scene anew word for word. At this assembly he also communicated that he could make the joyful announcement that there were already 500 Jews fewer, and he only regretted that their number had not declined yet more. Furthermore, he had to rebuke the local population, because they gave food to the begging Jews. He would rejoice when he hears that these Jews are chased off with one kick. . . .[46]

Despite the interference of party officials determined to further the destruction of the Jews, Dr. Lanc succeeded in providing essential medicines and food. These items, however, could not possibly cover the overwhelming needs of the inmates in Gmünd.[47] Still, Dr. Leopold Fisch, another Hungarian Jewish physician, confirmed, without such assistance the total of 600 deaths in Gmünd might well have been even higher.[48]

Local party officials not only frequently hindered relief efforts, but were also known to have planned and carried out massacres on their own initiative. As had unfortunately been the case with the escaped Soviet officers two months earlier, local men in the home defense forces joined in the slaughter of the Hungarian Jews. That some not only followed orders, but took an active role in staging mass murder emerged from accounts of a massacre near Eisenerz on 8 April 1945. On that afternoon a group of men from the Eisenerz *Volkssturm* received a column of Jews who were passing through Graz and Eisenerz on their way to Mauthausen. Around four o'clock, as the column descended from the Präbichl heights toward Eisenerz, the *Volkssturm* opened fire, and "three-quarters of an hour later 200 members of the transport lay dead or dying in the snow."[49]

Testimony given before a British tribunal in April 1946 made it clear that the leaders of the local *Volkssturm* knew of the impending arrival of the Jews and organized the slaughter in advance. Operating under the direction of the District Leader [*Kreisleiter*] from Leoben and chief commander of the *Volkssturm* in Eisenerz, a special "alarm detachment" was given the assignment to carry out the killing. From the squad leader the order was passed to the leaders of the column and to noncommissioned officers of the detachment. The day before the arrival of the transport, on the occasion of a comradeship evening hosted by local *Volkssturm* officials, the squad leader noted among his after-dinner remarks: "The 'alarm detachment' is assigned to take over a transport of Jews tomorrow on the Präbichl. These dogs and pigs all deserve to be beaten to death together. If tomorrow one of you shows himself a coward I'll kill him myself." Stressing in this way his intention not to hide the deed, but to revel in it, to make of it a public act, he added, boasting, "Tomorrow in Eisenerz something will take place which the Eisenerzer until now have never experienced."[50]

Several *Volkssturm* men admitted having learned in advance what was to happen. When the column of men were under way to the scene of the massacre the following day, the squad leader was heard to proclaim, "Today we're going to have some fun [*heut werden wir eine Hetz haben*]," noting that "in the *Seeau* a shooting exercise aimed at the Jews will be organized."[51] One of the men overheard the *Kreisleiter* saying in his office that some 6,000 Jews were on their way, and adding, "Well, by the time they're among us on the Prebichl there won't be any 6,000 left."[52]

Despite their foreknowledge of the massacre the men proceeded under their commander's direction. To be sure, the men were acting under his repeated threats that he would kill any who proved weak in the execution of the task. Four of the *Volkssturm* men confirmed that on the morning before the massacre the squad leader stated, "and if any of you is cowardly, I will personally kill him." For many, however, the threats were superfluous: they gladly went about their tasks. The man who had overheard the *Kreisleiter's* remark observed a festive mood among those preparing for the expedition, noting "'that it was for the men of the company seemingly a truly special joy to be able to seize the weapons."[53] Extra cigarette rations were promised "for every Jew shot," and they were told they "might excuse" their actions, "claiming that the Jews wanted to flee."[54]

Another witness to the killing was a *Volkssturm* man from Carinthia assigned to the Eisenerz *Volkssturm* and ordered to go to the Prebichl to register weapons. At first he heard shots, then discovered bodies lying along the road. He claimed to have distinctly heard one of the men say to another, "There lie some more, kill them!" He then watched as this guardsman poured shots "at close range into the bodies." Another witness also saw the man who had given the order firing his machine pistol. He also saw the guardsmen who had just fired and yet another man beating Jews with their weapons. Still another *Volkssturm* man claimed to have refused an order to participate in the beatings for which he was called a "cowardly dog, who deserves to be killed with the Jews." He

claimed to have declared: "I do not lay violent hands on an old, defenseless person. Why don't you do it yourself?" To this the one who had
threatened him was said to have replied, "Because I have no more
cartridges."[55] Significantly, despite being threatened, the man who in
this instance resisted following an order to kill was not harmed for his
refusal.

Also striking was evidence indicating that this massacre may have
taken place without the guidance or approval of the SS. It was as if local
men were taking advantage of a breakdown of order to participate in the
killing they had previously been denied. The Carinthian *Volkssturm* man,
on arriving at the scene, noticed two SS men accompanying the squad
leader. He heard one of them, an SS sergeant, proclaim: "I am supposed
to bring the transport full and complete to Mauthausen, and here you
shoot to pieces all my people!"[56] Another *Volkssturm* man reiterated that
the "SS people gave the order to halt firing on the transport."[57] Also
arriving on the scene were the police captain from Eisenerz "who also
held the rank of an SS captain," and the commandant of the Eisenerz
Volkssturm. At the foot of the Präbichl he found the squad leader reporting to the commandant, "Everything in Order!" The commandant
said he replied, "One can certainly not call that which has occurred
order!" When the police captain asked the squad leader "why was there
shooting?," he reportedly "turned away without a word, as if this did not
concern him." The police captain then demanded he come along to the
guard post, whereupon the squad leader finally stated, "well, the Jews
wanted to escape; for that reason there was shooting!"[58] Taken into their
custody, he was led to the office of the chief of the Eisenerz Gestapo.
Half an hour later, he emerged, stating triumphantly, "I have been
released!"[59]

Even in the final week of the war the SS did not relent in their
determination to kill those Jews still left in the remaining pocket of their
control. In the town of Persenbeug within the district of Melk, on the
night of 2-3 May 1945 between midnight and four o'clock in the morning
at least 214 Jews then being held in nearby barracks were murdered.[60]
The victims had been divided into four groups, three of which were led
from the barracks and shot inside ditches and afterwards doused with
gasoline and set afire. Two of the ditches were located some 160 and 220
yards from the home of a town resident.[61] Yet another group, consisting
mainly of women, children, and the elderly were fallen upon in their
barrack and shot down where they slept; their bodies were left on the
spot.[62]

According to the police, "it was established without question that a small SS detachment of at the most 8–10 men carried out the deed."[63] Testimony given in 1948, however, left unanswered the question concerning whether any members of the local party or security forces; the Wehrmacht, 2,000 of whose soldiers were quartered in Persenbeug on the night of the attack, some in homes in the vicinity; or local citizens knew in advance of the massacre or assisted in its execution. Did no one hear the shots, or see the flames that followed the deed? The police referred to two factors that might have led to the failure of persons in the area from reacting. In the first instance, SS men had told persons living in the vicinity they were going to be conducting night shooting exercises nearby.[64] The police believed this also succeeded in keeping the soldiers, whom the SS similarly informed, from becoming alarmed. Moreover, the police pointed out that "the night in which the Jews were murdered was stormy and it rained very hard."[65]

Even allowing for possible deception and the inclemency of the weather, it is understandable that persons who might discover shooting taking place outside their homes after midnight would not venture out into the darkness. A carpenter, Karl Brandstetter, and his wife were witnesses to the deed. Around midnight, Herr Brandstetter was aroused by the sound of vehicles. He looked out through the peephole in his door. For some time the headlights of what he termed a pair of "luxury vehicles" cast a glow enabling him to make out the assembly of "a large number of people." He watched and listened. "After that I heard how someone said, 'Fritz, turn out the light!' and then heard a salvo as from a machine gun, followed by individual shots. I saw how the people collapsed into the ditches. I heard no screams, but my wife, Maria Brandstetter [did]. In the early morning I went out of the house once and saw the burned corpses. . . . In the morning I then learned that also in another ditch in the vicinity of my house, by the Haus 'Lahnhof,' a larger number of Jews were shot."[66]

By 8 A.M. the police, led by inspector Franz Winkler, finally arrived to examine the scene. There they found the remains of "three groups of murdered Jews, partly next to one another, partly lying in heaps. Individual heaps of bodies, as well as bodies lying individually were also still burning. The Jews murdered in the barracks were discovered shot where they slept."[67] Accompanying a gendarme to the scene was the *Landrat* of Melk, Dr. Leopold Convall, who said he set out as soon as he heard of the massacre. He ordered the bodies to be identified as best as possible and buried individually.[68] While Convall went to the scene upon learning of the massacre, other local party officials "refused participation" in the inspection of the site, citing their unwillingness to look, or offering excuses: the *Ortsgruppenleiter* "based his refusal on momentary illness."[69]

Although party officials suddenly claimed to have found the sight of such a thing unbearable, they could not deny the deed had been committed: evidence of the crime was open to the light of day. In their haste the executioners moved on, leaving the bodies of their victims smoldering; items of identification were still available for the authorities to find. Even in the last days of a lost war, the murderers continued to strike. To be sure, by now the dead at least could hope to receive from the outside world the respect that was their due. Their bodies were at last properly identified and sorted, each was given an individual place of rest, members of a family buried beside one another. Yet this is poor solace for the persons who were killed in an area surrounded by civilians and soldiers. The massacre took place in their midst.

The world of these towns and villages was no longer safely cut off from that of killing. Where once the killing had been confined to the vicinity of Mauthausen and its many satellite camps, the routes of march cut swaths in excess of a hundred miles in length leading inward from the Austrian border to Mauthausen and its nearest outposts in Gusen, Gunskirchen, and Ebensee. The killing was now coextensive with the landscape. In the process, more and more bystanders became direct witnesses to the killings. What is more, this final period marked a broadening not only of knowledge, but for some a widening of the opportunity to participate in the crimes.

As ever, there were those who remained indifferent, those who hid in their homes, many who later took refuge behind the argument of helplessness, or who gave in to threat; many also who may have looked out of curiosity, or out of interest in the spectacle of death. The concerned bystander who wished to express his solidarity with the victims, however, did have one option. He or she could leave something to eat or drink by the roadside or between the lattices of the garden gate; and, if he or she dared, could hand or toss potatoes or fruit to the passing columns of victims. The guards threatened, on occasion they shoved or struck a civilian who behaved in this way, but in spite of their rude threats, the guards on the death marches did not force the citizenry into the ranks of the marchers, nor did they kill civilians who acted humanely.

In marching the inmate remnant across the countryside, in killing indiscriminately, and enacting their work of human destruction in the open, the SS had at last cut the wire that otherwise neatly separated the world of death from the world of life. This version of killing was but an extension of the killing that went on in the camps by other means, including that most perfected means that entailed concentration, enclosure, and concealment: the rock quarry and the gas chamber. In the end the killing was broad and open and mobile. It claimed the outer landscape as its domain, offering to everyone in the path of destruction a repeated glimpse of the horror. In the case of the escaped prisoners of war in February, the killing was, in a sense "democratized," albeit in an appeal to the citizenry to organize themselves as allies of the executioners. In the final weeks of the war in numerous instances the citizenry themselves took the initiative and organized massacres, as in Eisenerz. As the killing came out into the open it emphasized a spontaneity altogether lacking in the SS ideal of cold, rational, technological, unemotional, and scientific destruction.[70] To be sure, physical brutality and sadism were as much a part of the scheme of destruction as the cold and rational and "distanced" murders embodied in the gas devices. But now the bullet, the rifle butt, the club were the readiest instruments to hand, and it was not the SS alone who wielded these instruments.

One of the purposes of the gas chambers was to isolate the killing. It sought to define limits: killing centered between walls and beneath a ceiling; the prey concentrated, cut off, isolated from the outside. So too the camp embodied outer limits, perimeters delimiting the outskirts of the city of death. In fact, these limits were never absolute, even in the period of the camp's greatest efficiency in destruction. It was even less true as the war progressed and in the final phase of the war. Limits were surpassed: the killing could not be confined; nor could it be kept the special preserve of a trained elite of executioners. The concentration camp, embodiment of the society in which it developed and prospered, ultimately did its work in view of the citizenry and, sooner or later, called upon the citizenry to be accomplices, whether silently ignoring its presence in their midst, or joining in its work.

Very few dared the ultimate gesture of recognition and care: touching, lifting, if necessary dragging a straggler to safety. Others raised a finger to offer a bit of food or drink; most did not dare even this, preferring to withdraw indoors, on occasion first stepping over those who lay prostrate beneath their feet. As for those who glided past, eyes sunken and dark, with skin thinly stretched over the bones, they indeed disappeared into the woods, across the next meadow, behind the divide, beyond some wall unseen and seemingly far away.

Chapter 8

The Vanishing Traces

───────────

In the spring of 1945 outsiders from the world of the living entered the concentration camp universe. It was a world of stench and disease and death. Those who dared enter the camps in those first days after the liberation found themselves overwhelmed by the dust, the wretched perspiration, the foul air and bacteria that clung to the bodies of the survivors. Visitors soon found themselves befouled by this mess. Even as one sought to show one's sympathy and to help where possible, one longed to join the familiar universe of the living, and bathe oneself free of the odors and impurities of the camp.

Franz Loidl, a priest from the town of Ebensee who entered the camp shortly after the liberation, listened to the tales of horror the survivors related as they crowded about him. Each had his story to tell. Already in those first days the repetition of such accounts produced that numbness of feeling we all experience in the recounting of horror upon horror. Though from time to time he was indeed moved to express his own genuine revulsion and shock, Father Loidl remained at a distance. Yet, patiently, he listened: "In the confusion of questions and stories that now fall upon us my head truly buzzes. I know still that I often shook my head and beat my hands together with the exclamation: 'horrifying!' We listen to most of them sympathetically and shaken, because we see how speaking out does them good. Sometimes in somewhat strong words I give vent to my emotions out of honest indignation over especially striking occurrences."[1]

As he listens to the stories, which they illustrate by pointing to their wounds, the priest notes the filth in which he finds himself. Has he then become one of the mass of the suffering? Or does he remain an outsider, longing to wash away the horror and filth of a world still alien to him? "Not a few stories consist of solitary words, signs, and the showing of bodily wounds. In this babel of speech, in the reigning heat, the burdensome dust and the many-odored stench of perspiration clings to my brow. But the loathsome exhalations from the unwashed bodies and the shabbiest clothing of these poor people meant a true sacrifice for me. I do not know which of us was sickest."[2] Having finally left the barrack for the sick and infectious, he continues to think of the close contact he has had with the suffering:

> I am happy that I have again escaped the thick air inside there which in the midday heat in the wooden barracks had become yet more unbearable. My hands have become sticky from the shaking of many hands. Hopefully I have not drawn an infection somehow. Danger is amply present. Even speaking with the people is not without danger, since with many the lungs have been attacked. There is much and painful coughing. A couple of times I was on the verge of throwing up. One indeed comes from civilization. And here inside? . . . What a sad achievement of our arrogant century, this hideousness, this sinking into an unprecedented lack of civilization, and on top of that, in the heart of Europe![3]

Once again the odors intensify. "The nearer we approach the crematorium, the stronger the sweetish smell of corpses makes itself noticeable. Individuals have to take handkerchiefs to their noses, so unbearable it is. For days I could not get rid of it. Especially through the many burnings the air in the vicinity was poisoned, as the people complained. As long as I live I will never forget the view of the 140–150 corpses stacked upon one another in the storage room."[4] One of the sharpest senses touched by this horror was smell. It was not so easy to shield oneself from the odors, whereas one could always look away when the sight of the dead became too much to bear. "It is a view into the inferno," Father Loidl relates. "One does not tolerate the horrid all at once, and must first go away, and again look in, in order to catch a glimpse of the details." Then one noticed the skeletons, the "bluish-black skin" and the open eyes of the corpses awaiting burning.[5]

Afterwards, once outside the camp, the thoughts of Father Loidl and his companions turn to a coming meal. Having experienced this horror of exposure to the camp, having seen and smelled all this, how could one sit down to "receive something proper to eat?" How could one so rapidly reenter the civilized space of a dining room and a dinner table? In part, Father Loidl notes, the transition was eased by conceiving of his visit to the inferno as one of priestly compassion.

> Today we were permitted and able to do a great and especially good work, indeed almost all corporal and spiritual work of mercy in all manner of instances, an opportunity of a type that seldom arises. This gladsome awareness softens in memory the still too-fresh horrid impressions and their aftereffect. Although we had also braced ourselves for much, we were certainly not prepared for such awful things as our eyes and ears have witnessed.[6]

Father Loidl saw himself as having emerged from another world. He sensed that such things had only been thought to exist either in regions far away, or else in the dark imagining of works of art.[7]

Inmates too were sensitive to this stark confrontation of two worlds, and were at a loss to express their emotions in words. The inmate Eug. Thomé recalled the scene he witnessed when an American tank rolled into Mauthausen's sister camp in Gusen:

> The joy, the rejoicing of the thousands who suddenly slid out of their numbers into civilian rank can be rendered neither by human speech, nor human song, nor human music. Here the unbridgeable gap between the abstract and the concrete manifested itself. That has to be experienced. Even the frontiers between the immense joy of self and community lack all separation, all polarization, all estimation. Dream and reality yield to an inextricable whole whose apotheosis is situated between silence and scream.[8]

Yet this mood of indescribable exaltation soon gave way to an explosion of angry emotion culminating in spontaneous assaults on the overseers. "Human dignity suppressed to the utmost led in explosive fashion to a reckoning with the capos, block elders, criminals," several of whom were "taken from their hiding places and mercilessly delivered up to an inglorious death."[9]

The liberators stared in astonishment as the inmates rushed toward them expressing in frenzied agitation their otherworldly, half-mad ecstasy or joy. Approaching Mauthausen, an International Red Cross agent, and the American liberators were overwhelmed with the strange sights, sounds, and odors of the wild inhabitants of a death-like world gone mad:

> By the thousands they came streaming toward them, staggering toward them, crawling toward them to kiss and embrace them, to lift them upon weak, skeleton-thin shoulders, only to touch them like miracle-working holy men. Hollow, pallid ghosts from graves and tombs, terrifying, rot-colored figures of misery marked by disease, deeply ingrained filth, inner decay, incurable burn and frost damage to the soul, many of them become aged under the experience . . . lasting an eternity. All voices from out of the strange Ur-underground of human existence unite to a chorus, and a fugue upon the theme of horror and desperation. There are those who scream and rave in wild ecstasy, others are only able to whimper, to weep, suffocated, to stammer, to babble like children. . . . One of them throws himself across the hood of the white Opel, kisses it and strokes it, worships it, clings tightly to it, cannot be removed from his fetish . . . and the swelling heat of musty want develops in the open air to a flame, and rises, ignites rapidly forward and covers everything consumable.
>
> Commandant's building, kitchen, and warehouse are stormed. Whatever is not edible or momentarily utilizable is destroyed. The recoil of an immense relaxation transforms itself into an explosive heat, and this into a blasting of the core of consciousness. Images from out of the portfolios of a Hogarth, a Brueghel; studies from a madhouse. There squat skeletons in rags and crazy grins and drag themselves. . . . There people without strength, trembling from weakness, wrestle for sacks of flour and with shaking hands pour the Godly possession by the fistful down their throats. A quantity of precious, at first irreplaceable provisions becomes lost in the tumult, or else is sinfully and damagingly misused. Captured meat is devoured raw. Canned foods opened in feverish haste with beatings of stone fall victim to raging impatience. Heaps of wild creatures clustered from all nations of the sacred old world scuffle and strangle themselves on the ground for crumbs of bread, cigarette butts, potatoes, peas. Even the women furiously participate. The chaos howls toward heaven.[10]

A United States soldier with a photographic reconnaissance unit of the 11th Armored Division of the Third Army, who entered the Gusen concentration camp during the first days of the liberation, similarly described the shock of this otherworldly confrontation with an outpost of death. He too spoke in terms of spook-like figures, living skeletons, dark dreams, and an overwhelming odor of filth and decay:

> We didn't have any trouble finding the place for the road leading to the camp was choked with prisoners. They looked like ghosts in a night-

mare. . . . As soon as we parked the jeep all of these ghostly figures came crowding around us. They wanted food, water, cigarettes, etc. I believe if any one of them had a good meal, he'd kick the bucket. I took a few pictures of them for which they were more than glad to pose. It was a warm day and the awful stink from these supposedly human beings made it unbearable to stick around too long.

Next we went to the crematorium. Here is where the Nazis burned around 300 bodies a day. There were four big ovens in which were still bones, and skulls. By the way it smelled something awful. We were then taken to the gas chamber where there lay a countless number of dead. All were naked. Their bones protruded and the skin was tightly stretched over them. I couldn't stand that for long either. . . . There was much more to see. As I came out of the crematorium I saw a few fellows pushing a cart full of (starved to death) bodies. These too were marked and of course stunk to high heaven. Like most of the other dead these were slowly starved which resulted in death.

Near the crematorium was a yard where the SS would shoot their victims. God only knows how many fell before the guns of these maniacs. The last place I visited was the hospital which was run by the prisoners. Here they tried to hold onto life a few more days; but lack of medicine, food, and sanitation soon let death take the upper hand. As one of our fellows walked in, all of the patients rose up in bed and cheered, "Bravo Americano." My friend said that was the first time anyone wept with joy upon seeing him. The Americans took most of these patients to hospitals, thank God.

The whole camp was covered with filth. The barracks were very much overcrowded and reeked with the odor of dirty bodies. As many as five men slept on the same bunk. More likely than not the one on the bottom died of suffocation. . . .

This camp had 35,000 prisoners. As some of them would die or be killed, new ones came in. Some men had been there for five years. How they managed to live I'll never know. Those that were alive were walking skeletons.[11]

In the spring of 1945 the dead and their memory continued to lie like a discomforting weight upon the living. Remembrance of what was done to them acted as an unpleasant reminder of the deeds which were committed in the midst of the citizenry. The sites of death, though no longer active, lay scattered across the landscape. The question arose: what was to be done with the camps with their barracks, wires, quarries, death chambers, and crematoria? What was to be done with the graves of those who lay buried inconveniently close to the roads and byways traveled by residents and tourists? The discomfort of the citizenry found expression in the pages of local newspapers and in appeals to provincial officials. In time even the dead, proving themselves less easy to dispose of than the living, had to be confronted. Insofar as they had not already vanished with the hot ash and dust spewed from the chimneys, now the dead had to be removed from sight, collected from graves round about, and settled in a common memorial ground. A place was found for them to congregate, away from the beaten track of the living. They were to be denied the right to rest where they had fallen, for often they lay too close to the spaces favored by those among whom the killing had been committed.

A primary concern facing the citizenry was the fate of the grounds and structures of the concentration camps themselves. By 1949 voices were raised in open opposition to the proposal of preserving the main camp at Mauthausen as a memorial and warning for present and future generations. Arguments against the proposal were expressed in terms of financial as well as cultural considerations. The costs of renovating the camp for this purpose, amounting to an estimated 790,000 Austrian shillings in addition to a projected 50,000 shillings per year for upkeep, was argued to be excessive. [12] Were there not other projects in greater need of funds, it was asked, than "these works of renovation little serving the peace and understanding of peoples and especially by no means the prestige of Austria?" The living had pressing needs for which the money could better be spent: "that in a time of strangling housing shortage . . . of all things chambers for shooting people in the neck have to be restored, demonstrates such a high degree of cynicism towards the privations of the day and of the people that nothing more need be said." [13]

It was not only the claims of the living with which the dead and their remembrance had to contend. According to some, art, local tradition, indeed the "the heritage of our fathers" was deemed at stake in the controversial allocation of funds for the restoration of the concentration camp. When it was discovered that money was not yet forthcoming for the preservation of a local religious-artistic relic, polemicists chose to blame this neglect upon the decision to lay out such a large sum for the creation of a concentration camp memorial. Culture was brought forward to stake its claim against the remembrance of horror. The matter at hand involved a water-damaged fresco in a building constructed next to the church of the Karner in Mauthausen in the year 1260. Rediscovered in 1907, it was deemed "the oldest fresco in Upper Austria," portraying "Christ as judge of the world, the lamb of God, [and] bigger than life-size images of the apostles adorn its walls—a unique work of art, originating more than 700 years ago, known and praised by all European art historians." The newspapers underscored the fact that the now-despised Nazis had at least thought enough of this treasured art work to have undertaken to preserve it from the damage of dampness. "The same regime that left behind so few laudable traces of its rulership in the Mauthausen rock quarries was the same one that through the removal of the earthen mound provided for the drying of the already strongly endangered painting, and did so in the middle of wartime." In contrast, though it had been known since 1947 that the roof was leaking and that minor repairs were needed, the funds were not forthcoming. "It concerns only a work of art, however, and not a concentration camp," a report from Linz concluded with sarcasm.[14] Cultural considerations aside, the *Kleine Zeitung* in Graz went so far as to openly question the appropriateness of preserving the instruments and sites of terror as a warning to future generations or a place of pilgrimage for the families whose loved ones died in Mauthausen:

> Aside from everything else, does one really believe that the *relatives* of the unfortunate victims will have the inner need to look at the improved staircase of death, the gas chambers and the restored gallows in the renovated cell for shooting in the neck? No, precisely those who . . . 'will come here as to a cemetery in order to commemorate their murdered relatives' will *not* want to see everything. Precisely those who carry their *suffering* here will not have the need to wander through the chambers of terror only in order to receive a quite realistic idea of how it happened."[15]

The claims of the living and those of the dead, or those who chose to speak for them, were in conflict. Repeatedly, the contrasting attitudes of reverent respect or disregard for the former sites of mass murder surfaced to create tensions. Lying behind all this was the clash between those whose primary relation to the landscape of this region was wholly shaped by memory of the horrors of the Nazi era, and those who saw this area as their home. For the former, Upper Austria would have had little significance were it not the region where Mauthausen and so many of its satellite camps were located. Behind the other sentiment lay an attitude common to many residents of the communities bordering on the centers of death for whom the concentration camps held, at best, a local and temporary significance. It was difficult for many of them to see that the region to which their lives were still attached by reason of personal experience and family ties had been transformed by recent events into a landscape scarred with a universal moral significance far transcending the local world of their experience.

From time to time residents behaved in ways certain to arouse the indignation of foreigners who, contrary to the expectations of the *Kleine Zeitung,* did come to view the sites of terror and to pay their respects to the martyrs. On 20 August, 1949, a group of 60 visitors from France, "mostly petty state officials, lawyers, doctors, and the like, in great measure women and older persons," came to Castle Hartheim "in order to remain in the courtyard of the castle for some minutes of silent remembrance."[16] The visitors were informed before they entered that the castle was to be used that same day for a wedding party, but still they were unprepared for what followed. "Certainly the French visitors had expected that at the least a few moments of peace for a quiet commemoration would be rendered possible. In sharp contrast to that was the wedding mood that had reached a certain high point, and was evidenced by the ethnic Germans present in the castle, of whom the majority were men of youthful age. It is only understandable that out of these contradictory moods a conflict arose."[17]

Even as people criticized public expenditures for the preservation of the main camp at Mauthausen as a memorial, efforts were under way to convert the grounds of its other camps into new housing estates. In August 1949 came the announcement that funds were being assembled for the creation of a housing development comprising two hundred homes to be built on the grounds of the former concentration camp in Ebensee. Although at first the money was still in short supply and construction was limited, by August the first eight houses were being built.[18]

The dead, however, still had to be reckoned with. During the 1940s one of their most disturbing functions had been to serve, through their unmistakable presence in marked graves by the roadsides, as reminders of the deeds that had robbed them of life. By 1950 enough time had passed to permit local officials to remove some of these visible reminders, by agreeing to transfer the remains of hundreds of concentration camp victims who had the misfortune to have been buried in locations that were too public. As early as 2 December 1949, following a local inspection, a commission from the Landeshauptamt in Upper Austria decided to create a collective grave on the site of the former concentration camp of Ebensee. The new grave was to be built around a large cross erected on this site in memory of a Dr. Lepetit from Milan. This, it was decided, would be the centerpiece of a collective memorial incorporating the dead who would be brought there from scattered burial sites in the vicinity.[19]

According to the chairman of the district association of inmates in Gmunden, Albrecht Gaiswinkler, initiative for the removal of the bodies came from the former *Ortsbauernführerin,* a Nazi rural official. It was on a portion of her property, confiscated at war's end, that the victims had been buried. In addition to seeking their removal she appealed for the return of her property. A further ground cited as requiring the exhumation and transfer of the bodies was the need to widen the highway to accommodate "tourist traffic."[20]

On 7 June 1952 a commission of the District Association of Former Inmates and the Politically Persecuted in Bad Ischl, accompanied by a patrol leader of the gendarmerie post in Ebensee, went to inspect what they unexpectedly discovered was the scene of a recent exhumation. They were shocked to find the bodies rudely disturbed. Carelessly, remains had been left scattered about and coffins crudely broken open, then left behind:

> But what did this commission have to see? The formerly neat cemetery resembled a wild place of battle or a wartime field position struck by bombs.
>
> As we could immediately convince ourselves, the bones of our comrades lay about in the hundreds. In the exposed, abandoned pits lay pieces of skull bones, ribs, finger bones, and bits of vertebrae in wild and more than irreverent fashion.[21]

While the successful efforts to remove the inmates from their original resting place, and the careless manner in which the exhumation was carried out, offended this group of former inmates, it should not be overlooked that the eventual establishment of the collective grave near the Lepetit memorial was tastefully conducted. On 5 November 1952, representatives of inmate associations, including engineer Simon Wiesenthal of the Central Committee of Liberated Jews in Upper Austria, joined local government officials as well as Catholic, Protestant, and Jewish religious leaders in commemorating the new cemetery. "The pain-filled content of the hour of consecration grippingly resounded in the thousands-of-years-old song of lament of Cantor Roth," a government summary of the ceremony recorded.[22]

Following the war, returning Jews from Austria who had either succeeded in surviving by remaining in hiding, or who miraculously outlived the camps in the East, were forced to look on as residents continued to occupy their formerly confiscated apartments. In February 1946 members of Wiesenthal's Central Committee in Linz reported to a British-American committee of inquiry on the plight of Jews in Upper Austria. At that time only 80 Austrian Jews remained in the province among a total of some 4,000 Jewish survivors in the entire country.[23] The central committee members pointed out that Jewish survivors had met feelings of intolerance and lack of understanding from local authorities and the citizenry. As Wiesenthal noted,

> The majority of the very small group of Austrian Jews who find themselves here consist of old women who were Aryan-related and were disguised by their Aryan families. All sense the same hatred of the populace as do the foreign Jews. When an Austrian Jew returns he has to excuse himself, so to speak, and say 'pardon me for living' and has the greatest difficulties in receiving back what is his, or at least a small part of it. . . . Jews who have come back from the K.Z. [concentration camp] look today from the street into the windows of their former apartments in which the Nazis or their families have spread themselves out. In order to achieve something one has to engage in a true war of paper, and requests upon requests pile up in the bureaus. But very often it can be mastered through the intervention of an American authority.[24]

An attorney working with the Jewish committee in Linz cited one characteristic instance of a returning Jewish inmate who had been frustrated in his attempt to regain his confiscated apartment:

> A Linz Jew, who during the Hitler period was carried off to Auschwitz and returned four months ago with his wife and small child, turned to our committee and asked for help, since he has lost all his relatives as well as all his worldly possessions. Since he is an Austrian and Linz is the competent authority, I referred him to the housing office here, in order first of all that he be given back his apartment that he had lost in barbaric fashion. With the words 'Unfortunately we can do nothing' the housing office sent him back to the Jewish committee. We were therefore forced to send the man with his wife and child into the Bindermichl [displaced persons] camp where today he vainly awaits an apartment allotment. So this man who during the Hitler period lost everyone and everything and fortunately came away with his life pleads to no purpose for the allotment of an apartment; while on the contrary in his old apartment an Austrian family is living undisturbed. The assets of the Austrian Jews are still in the hands of those who drew advantage from the persecution of the Jews. Up until now almost nothing has been undertaken on the part of the Austrian authorities to protect the rights of the previous Jewish owners.[25]

Adding to the dissatisfaction of the surviving Jews in Austria was this very sensation of injustice while known or suspected criminals continued to be in positions of authority. Wiesenthal noted one instance

when he "was in Vienna with an acquaintance who had a matter to
complete at the State Police. There he recognized nine persons who were
members of an annihilation brigade of the S.P. [Security Police][26] in
Poland [who] destroyed 12,000 Jews in the city of Boryslav. These people
are now in service. We move among people, we meet them on the bus,
in the coffee house, we extend to them our hands, and think to ourselves: perhaps we have just spoken with the murderers of our families."
Under the circumstances, Jews were decidedly uncomfortable when
among the Austrian populace. "This condition impresses upon us an
abhorrence of the native population which is also co-responsible for our
tragedy in the East. Under these circumstances our stay here is a
torture."[27] It is not surprising that of the 4,418 Jews registered in February 1946 with the Jewish community in Vienna, only 1390, or less
than one-third, expressed a desire to remain in Austria.[28]

Nor is this unexpected in the light of numerous petty insults and
indignities that contributed to a climate of hatred against the reappearing
Jews. There occurred unfortunate anti-semitic outbursts such as the one
that took place at an Austrian sporting event involving Jewish athletes
in the spring of 1946. "During a football match between the Sport Club
Hakoah and the police sport club, a wild fist fight broke out among the
spectators that began with a spectator shouting an insult at the Jewish
team," it was reported. "Among a portion of the spectators a tumult
broke out, and one heard cries such as: 'Into the gas with them! Into the
gas!' "[29] In another reported incident, three Jewish displaced persons
were arrested when a "tumult" arose after they accused a civilian of
stealing food packets. When they arrived at the police station a number
of other displaced persons were already there staging a protest "against
another incident." Apparently using the commotion as a chance to break
free, two of the recently arrested Jews tried to flee. As they did so,

> a scuffle ensued and Moritz Gottesmann, a 16-year-old Polish Jew was shot
> and another punched down so that he lay unconscious. The police main-
> tain the shot at Gottesmann had been fired out of the window of the
> apartment lying above the police station, but an investigation revealed
> that in the corresponding apartment no one possessed any kind of
> weapon."[30]

Individual Jews daily faced related insults and indignities against
which they complained in vain to the Austrian authorities. For example,
on 1 July 1946 a Jewish laborer residing in Pichl stated that he and his
wife had been taunted by a Ukrainian who, along with others, were

agitating against Jews. Though he reported this to the town authorities and the police, because "in this case no actual mistreatment" had occurred the police were unable to intervene. Specifically, the Ukranian had cursed him, stating "Hitler will come and cut open your throat." Only two weeks earlier this Ukrainian had called his wife a "stinking Jew, accursed Jew," and other names. "The Ukrainians living there often come together in meetings, carry on politics, and without cease agitate against Jews so that my existence there is endangered," he pleaded.[31]

The words were all the more threatening for having been uttered on the soil of a country where the traces of the concentration camps littered the landscape. If any persons on the outside had first-hand knowledge of what was going on in or around these camps, surely they were to be found among those who were their neighbors. The residents of the concentration camp communities were in a unique position to witness numerous details of the mistreatment of the inmates. They saw the movement of prisoners to and from the transportation points, they saw them at their work sites, they viewed the general condition of the prisoners, and often witnessed atrocities.

Every man, woman, and child knew that at a minimum the SS demanded silent and passive acquiescence. The glances of the residents may have been averted, their attitude one of prudent non-concern, yet the chieftains of the enterprise were by no means indifferent to these reluctant onlookers. The administrators of the camp took an interest in their attitudes and responses. Their reactions were of some importance, for the nearby residents represented the front line of popular opinion. If the neighborhood was silent and acquiescent, the executioners could rest assured that their actions would meet with toleration in society at large.

The regime and the public were party to an unwritten understanding. The camp administrators would do all within their power to spare the residents direct knowledge of atrocities occurring inside the camp. In turn, the residents would make no effort to learn. Blindness was willed: "that which they were not supposed to see, they did not see; no, that which they were not supposed to feel, they did not feel."[32] Remaining ignorant, the residents would be spared the agony of worrying about whether what was happening inside the camp constituted a violation of humane behavior against which their consciences might demand they object.

To avoid discomforting moral questions it is best to be uninformed. The regime helped people remain so by warning them against being too curious. The public was told to keep back and not to stare. Those halting to look, the public was admonished, would be met with force. Of course, anything so forbidden was bound to arouse curiosity, but there were few who dared take the risk. The consequences of knowing too much were severe, and people learned that the prudent thing to do was to look away and not ask questions.

In spite of their wish to remain neutral, none of the residents were spared the choice of assisting the killing project in ways large or small. Many turned away, acting under the false illusion that by not choosing they would remain untouched. They failed to see that in turning their backs on the events occurring in their midst they quietly acquiesced in the killing.

Throughout the period of the camp's existence, citizens were faced with choices, at first seemingly minor, later of greater consequence, forcing them into a stance of siding with or opposing the killing. Their preferred stance of neutrality and noninvolvement became ever more precarious as the war progressed and evidence of what was going on in and around the camps increasingly came to spill out into the surrounding landscape.

If they were left in their homes undisturbed, the reason lies in their usefulness to the camp. From the beginning, the citizenry were encouraged to pitch in, in small ways. They were retained to fulfill numerous tasks in support of the camp's operations.

Like any new enterprise, a concentration camp draws on the material resources and skills of the surrounding community. The camp needed suppliers, drivers, carpenters, typists, foremen, and laborers, and these they recruited among the neighboring civilian population. This did not make these persons murderers, but it did succeed in drawing them into a minor, if vitally supporting role in the daily affairs of the camp. For some, their commercial contacts with the camp proved profitable. In exchange for services rendered they benefited from the steady contracts and the ready, cheap labor available for their own enterprises.

The SS saw their task as a professional one, and as far as possible they endeavored to spare the outside population direct sight of the killing. But in the end, as the system began to collapse with the decline of Germany's fortunes in the war, the killing went on in a less controlled fashion. The professionals did not hesitate to call in amateur killers from among the surrounding population. The killing spilled out ever more into the surrounding terrain, and the citizens were invited to participate directly in the bloodletting. Responsibility was diffused, the blood smeared far and wide. Exposed at last was the unacknowledged secret of society's complicity in the project of mass slaughter. Many citizens who previously had but indirect involvement thoughtlessly waded in.

Evil manifests itself not only through deeds, but through inaction and omission. The failure to act, the failure to inquire, the failure to remember, each represent a contribution to the killing project. Complicity is only partly a result of criminal acts. Inaction represents the first step in an ongoing process of bystander involvement.

In the period after the war, Germans and Austrians rejected the charge of collective responsibility. They saw in it only a euphemism for criminal liability. Regardless of whether the criminal accepts guilt for his crime, he at least knows that his action led to the death of another. There is a weapon and a corpse. Because they had not pulled a trigger, nor swung a rope over anyone's head, nor released deadly pellets into a chamber sealed with human beings, they felt free of wrongdoing.[33] If the SS could protect themselves from a sense of guilt by withdrawing behind the blanket of professional duty, it was unlikely that the average citizen who merely heard about or even watched the crimes would feel remorse.[34]

The citizen, who lived next to a concentration camp who dared express solidarity with the inmates through word or through deed faced the risk of arrest. The presence of the camp was a constant reminder that they too could share the fate of the outcasts in their midst. Those who did not face this prospect day by day, as did the citizens of these towns, cannot blame them for failing to offer their lives on behalf of others. However, as Karl Jaspers has pointed out, "passivity knows itself morally guilty of every failure, every neglect to act whenever possible, to shield the imperiled, to relieve wrong, to countervail. Impotent submission always left a margin of activity which, though not without risk could still be cautiously effective." When individuals in these circumstances recognize no dilemma and feel no anguish, we touch upon a profound moral failure. Averting one's gaze, imagining that through silence and inaction one could retreat to a neutral zone where life went on "as if nothing had happened" were the very illusions that made of these citizens allies to the crime. "Blindness for the misfortune of others, lack of imagination of the heart, inner indifference toward the witnessed evil—that is moral guilt."[35]

There was indeed such a "margin of activity" within which average citizens could act, abandoning neutrality and assisting the inmates. Few were those who dared the heroic act of hiding escaped inmates in their homes or barns, but the Langthaler family, to name a striking example, proved that under extreme circumstances citizens could save lives. On a lesser scale, one could leave food or water by the wayside for passing inmates to retrieve. It is impossible to know whether all those who decades later claimed to have left food for the inmates in fact did so, but their accounts as well as those of inmate survivors underscore that this was done and that such assistance was possible. The risk of offering food was undoubtedly greatest for someone who did so in a sensitive location. This appears to have been the case with Franz Winklehner, who until his arrest ran the agricultural cooperative near the railway station in Maut-hausen. He died at Dachau in 1941. The way one chose to look at the inmates—whether one rushed to catch a glimpse of those passing, stared, smiled, laughed, or turned away—was an expression of one's attitude toward the victims. It is improbable that any individual glance, whether of hostility, indifference, or sympathy materially affected the fate of a victim in the way that, say, a blow to the head most certainly did. But as the recollections of survivors make clear, inmates passing through the towns did search for eyes that might be watching them. Almost always in vain, they surveyed the landscape, they peered into windows, hoping for a look that signalled concern, a sign that the outside world had not abandoned them. A sympathetic look was never as consequential as the act of sheltering an escaped inmate or even offering nourishment to one who was being hunted or starved, but it was the least the onlooker could offer without serious danger. Even in instances where persons were bold enough to stop and watch the inmates passing by, the SS issued threats they did not carry out. "You can come right along," they remember the SS shouting to them, but none spoke of anyone taken into custody for having looked or come too close.

The events that took place inside the camps did not disturb the later lives of most bystanders. If anything, the passage of time has served to dampen whatever feelings of wrongdoing they might have sensed. The concentration camps left no lasting impression upon their view of them-selves and the world through which they moved in safety and prosperity. They never sought to inform themselves of what had happened. One encounters not a flat denial of the existence of the camps, only an indifference to their presence so long ago. In some instances one may not speak of forgetfulness, for one cannot forget what one has never at-tempted to know.

When, some forty years later, former inmates attempted to have a memorial erected outside the brewery in Redl-Zipf, a former guard com-mander and later deputy director of the firm stated why, in considering the matter, he did not wish to speak about the fate of the concentration camp inmates:

because, honestly said, I've got no grounds to do so. . . . I am in fact a beer salesman; even if I am already in retirement I have to think always of the protection of my beer label, because, under circumstances—things are not always understood the way they are said, you know—if that is falsely understood, among other things, I can cause much harm to my beer label.[36]

For many years the residents maintained a general silence concerning the camp. "In the Zipf area one did not want to speak of these things at all," noted the mayor of the nearby town of Neukirchen an der Vockla.[37] People expressed surprise upon learning of the heavy mortality in the camps. When, decades afterward, Meinhard H., the Zipf test site photographer, was informed of the many deaths, he exclaimed: "My God! I didn't know that."[38] Then too it was easiest to allow the traces of the camps to vanish from the landscape, as well as from memory, when one denied that they had been such terrible places after all. Conceding that "the working conditions were naturally very difficult here because one worked under time pressure," and insisting that the inmates received "something to eat," the deputy director refused to acknowledge that any of them perished in Zipf: "Mind you, in Zipf it cannot be determined how many and where which ones died. Scientifically, at least from the outside, in Zipf it is not discernible that a concentration camp inmate was ever killed."[39]

An 83-year-old resident of Ebensee expressed his doubts about the severity of the concentration camp in his town in these terms: "The opponents—and above all, those of them who were first—the Jews, for example, have shown interest. Naturally, they have now made propaganda against the National Socialists. And from this side, then, persecution has proceeded against former National Socialists."

"But you know that many Jews were killed in the concentration camp Ebensee?" he was asked.
"Actually not, because I was in the war."
"But you know now."
"Now, well. Who can tell me the truth?"
"So, you do not believe that."
"I have not made inquiries, and if it happened it was an evil deed."[40]

In any event, such matters did not lie close to his heart. The desire to inquire into the events of this period was not strong. If he had ever viewed the site of the former concentration camp in his town, then it was only once, and then most likely he viewed it from afar. For in fact his thoughts passed beyond the camps toward the mountains and a beloved clearing in the woods:

> "Have you visited the grounds and seen the memorial?"
> "Actually not, no."
> "In all these years you have never gone there?"
> "I was once up there. But I do not remember what is up there now, how it looks."
> "So, at some time after the war you *did* go there."
> "Yes, certainly I looked once, for I have traveled much. I was a great mountain climber. Scaled and climbed all the peaks up to the Swiss border. [Those] are my most beautiful experiences. And to this I attribute that in the eighty-third year of life I am in full health, now make small mountain tours and do other things. And I have my garden, my big garden in Unterach [on the *Attersee*], to tend. And I take an interest in the raising of beautiful trees like the sequoia."

At last, he speaks of a favorite spring: "And there everyone can drink, and there are many horses who do not pass [before] slaking their thirst."[41]

The dead have no voice of their own. The survivors, aware of the terrible divide separating themselves from both the victims and the world, find speech inadequate to describe the depths of their suffering and despair. The silence of the bystanders is not the silence of respect and awe before the unspeakable. Their eyes were not gouged, their tongues were not severed, their ears not sealed shut. Muteness is the sign of their complicity. Through continued silence the complicity continues to this day.

Not all remembrance is truth. Memory may distort, and when it confronts something unpleasant, the temptation to distort is very great indeed. Faced with memories of Nazism, people may fall back upon the same ramparts of mind that more than forty years ago shielded them from acknowledgment of crimes committed in their midst. In protecting one from discomforting truths, the mind has proved to be a versatile instrument. Sins of omission or complicity, to say nothing of acts of commission, can be explained away. The awareness of killing can be as purified in memory as once the burning flesh of the victims was turned to ashes. Winds have blown those ashes for over forty years. By now, many who killed or stood idly by while others did so lie buried, their hands incapable of any deed, their eyes closed forever. Those who remain among the living turn inward unto themselves, their families, their homes, they laugh and make love, listen to music, and continue to enjoy the fruits of the earth. The past rarely intrudes. It is forgotten, neutralized, explained away, if not enjoyed for its happier recollections.

To be sure, memory is notoriously unreliable. Even as skillful and probing a figure as Heinrich Böll, the German novelist, was wary of the accuracy of his own recollections. Confronting the task of recalling the details of his own life during the early years of Nazism, he spoke of a "justifiable mistrust of my memory," for, as he said, "all this happened forty-eight to forty-four years ago, and I have no notes or jottings to resort to." Böll was especially attuned to one of the trickiest aspects of memory: the attainment of correct synchronization, or the ability to reconstruct events in accurate sequence. While he can recall, for instance, the execution of a group of seven communists in Cologne, he was at first certain that the event happened in the autumn of 1934, when in fact, as he later discovered, it actually had occurred a year before.[42]

Loss of memory is often willful, as Theodor Adorno well knew: "The effacement of memory is more the achievement of an all-too-wakeful consciousness than it is the result of its weakness in the face of the superiority of unconscious processes."[43] The post-war era brought with it an awareness that pro-Nazi attitudes once held can no longer find expression without raising scorn or suspicion. Under these circumstances, participants or witnesses of the Nazi past are likely to erase any mention of deeds perpetrated or viewed that would place them now in a bad light. Over many years, people have succeeded in casting aside upsetting memories to the point of convincing themselves that they never happened at all. The playwright and novelist, Rolf Hochhuth, knew this, and in describing the persons he interviewed for *Eine Liebe in Deutschland*, stated: "Their reports are triumphs of the will over memory: you know the *aperçu*—I did that, says our memory; I *cannot* have done that, says our pride; you ought not to have done that, say the laws following the death of Hitler which declared Hitler's laws invalid: hence, memory yielded."[44]

Sadly, time works against the victim and in favor of both the perpetrator and the onlooker. Time creates an illusion of distance. The deeds, however monstrous, seem to lose their force the farther they recede into the past. The act of distancing and separation is crucial to the individual's ability to live, and eventually to die in peace despite his having committed unworthy acts or remained neutral.

Günther Anders employs a metaphor that captures the image of unconcern that best characterizes the attitude of the uncaring bystander. He tells the fable of a woman who from a tower views the death of her own child. "Down below I would have been driven to desperation," she cries, revealing that the distance permitted her to retain her composure beside the most terrifying event imaginable.[45] What occurs before one's eyes, no matter how compelling, is of increasingly less concern the further away one places oneself in relation to it. The real goal of the bystander then as now is to avoid confrontation with the past and the injury it may cause the soul. This is how onlookers viewed the murder of the concentration camp inmates. Like the woman in the tower, "they resisted going down into the street and looking the deed in the face."[46]

Anders is writing about the Germans, but what he says is certainly applicable to the Austrians as well. As evasive as has been the confrontation of Germans with National Socialism and the Final Solution, the Austrian approach to the past has been even more problematic. Austrians have long attempted to deny their nation's active involvement in the killing that was initiated under the license and supervision of their German neighbors. They have been able to take advantage of the ambiguity of Austria's relationship to Nazi Germany in triumph and defeat. On the one hand a constituent territorial element of the Third Reich, Austria was also an annexed country, and hence viewed in 1943 by Allied statesmen as a nation awaiting liberation from Germany.[47] Given the choice of identifying with Hitler or with the victorious powers, Austrians quite understandably have preferred to portray themselves as victims of fascism while conveniently overlooking the extent of Austrian participation in the Third Reich and the Final Solution. Yet Austrians undeniably played a major role in both. It is estimated that "although the Austrians accounted for only eight per cent of the population of the Third Reich, *about one third of all people working for the SS extermination machinery were Austrians. Almost half of the six million Jewish victims were killed by Austrians.*" A listing of leading functionaries of the killing project would include thousands of Austrians. Among the most involved: Adolf Hitler, the Reich Chancellor; Adolf Eichmann, deportation expert, and his assistant for logistics, Franz Novak, and Alois Brunner, an experienced coordinator of deportations in Austria, Greece, and France; Ernst Kaltenbrunner, successor to Reinhard Heydrich as head of the Gestapo; and Odilo Globocnik, director of the death camps of Sobibor, Treblinka, and Majdanek. Globocnik had numerous countrymen working for him in top positions. Among them were Hermann Höfle, chief of staff of Aktion Reinhard, code name for the killing operations in the Generalgouvernement, for whom some 90 Austrians worked either on the staff or in the camps. Among them was Franz Stangl, who became commandant of Treblinka following duty in the Hartheim "euthanasia" center, where mental patients and concentration camp inmates from Mauthausen and

Dachau were gassed. In Holland the High Commissioner, Arthur Seyss-Inquart, and Hanns Albin Rauter, the Higher SS and Police Leader, were responsible for the "expulsion and annihilation of 110,000 Dutch Jews." Adding to the list are the names of Franz Murer, the deputy commandant of the Vilna ghetto, and Eduard Roschmann, active in Riga. Moreover, one notes that "of the five thousand names on the list of war criminals active in Yugoslavia, where two million people were killed, 2,499 were Austrians." "More than one thousand Austrian policemen" served in the Schützpolizei (Schüpo) [urban police] and mobile execution units of the Einsatzkommandos.[48] A report on the round-up and execution of more than 100,000 Jews in East Galicia notes that "in the years 1941–44 several thousand Viennese, or rather Austrians, were active in the Schützpolizei, SD, and Gestapo-service offices, criminal police (Kripo), gendarmerie, county administration, and administrators of Jewish property."[49] According to Erika Weinzierl, some 30 to 40 per cent of the approximately 13,000 Austrians convicted by Austrian courts of crimes under National Socialism had been found to have committed acts directed against Jews.[50]

Austrians have been especially sensitive to the need to maintain a comfortable distance between themselves and events associated with their nation's involvement in the Third Reich. To be sure, there remains a strong need to account for this troublesome period in the life of the nation, the local community, and the individual. The past has simply been reworked to remove elements that might serve to open what are delicately referred to as the "wounds" of the past. There exists a conscious strategy of retreat from a meaningful and open confrontation with deeds that today might look sordid if illuminated directly.

Common is the explanation that we are still too close to the events of the Nazi era to judge them fairly without causing harm to the living. Typically, many of the generation that lived through the war proclaim themselves incapable of speaking out. Pleading that not enough time has passed, they call for ever more distance between them and memory. Inevitably, only death will provide a secure divide between those who were present when the deeds were committed, and the acts themselves. The chronicler of one Austrian town, given the opportunity to continue his story into the period of the Second World War, falls silent. "The chronicler closes his file," he declares, and explains why he cannot go on: "He has been left to describe the events of the war period. The distance is still too short even if the younger generation still knows this period only from hearsay or experienced it unconsciously as children. It would be too difficult to describe all these things as they really were. Too great is the danger of tearing open old wounds, to charge one person with a mistake, or honor another too little."[51]

Avoidance and distance from the events are also achieved when the past is neatly enveloped in sentiment. In a manner reminiscent of the propaganda images of the Nazi era, a local town in the 1970s recollects its infamous native son, Adolf Hitler, with a contemporary picture of the inconspicuous Hitler family home in the Linz suburb of Leonding, photographed in color to reveal a clear blue sky overhead and a trio of grade-school children, with bright yellow and green rucksacks, walking past the entryway. The juxtaposition of the youngsters and their youthful purity with the structure that symbolizes the weight of Hitlerian imagery, contrasting the destructive career of Adolf Hitler and the adventurous boyhood Nazi hagiographers liked to recall, is in accordance with a pattern of kitsch reminiscence that stretches back toward the Nazi past. One might have imagined it sufficient to photograph the home without the addition of the school children. But the superimposition of the children onto the scene of Hitler's youth, more than thirty years later, is central to the effort to render interesting, as well as harmless, an episode in the town's past that one seeks to integrate and overcome.[52] The text accompanying the photo underscores the impression, rendering the image of Hitler's presence as a local curiosity told in the story-book manner of an event of long ago:

> Here we mention a circumstance very meaningful in its day, namely, that the customs official, Alois Hitler, settled in Leonding in house number 61 with his family, including as well son Adolf, who for several years attended the Leonding primary school. Hitler's father died here and the family later moved away. When the son rose to become Führer of the "Third Reich" and after the "Anschluss" he also visited Leonding and his parental home; the modest village of Leonding won fame for several years as the "home village of the Führer" and became a site of pilgrimage for enthusiastic National Socialists. A considerable measure of the notoriety of our town is traceable to that time.[53]

The past is approachable in so far as it is coated in an aesthetic, however mundane, that draws its force from the proximity of innocence and horror.[54] The image disarms the horror of Nazism, recalling the saccharine shots of the Führer touching the cheeks of blond-haired children. These youngsters on their way to or from school in Leonding in 1976 have been made figuratively, if not literally, their descendants.

For the Austrian who voluntarily looks back on the National Socialist period with some unexpressed or overt sense of unease, the like-lihood is strong that he will attempt to make of this period something as "normal" as possible. He will deny anything specifically or uniquely terrible about it. He might refer to the era as one marked by prosperity and hope; or alternately, as his thoughts shift from the period immediately before the war to the harsh era—perhaps commencing in 1942 or 1943—when defeat seemed likely and the population succumbed to the direct effects of a lost war, he is likely to speak of the suffering he, or his family, or his nation faced in defeat.[55] He will perhaps speak of youthful enthusiasm falsely exploited, or describe the injustices committed by the enemy in wartime, but on the whole there will be little admission that he participated, whether as an agent, however small or great, or as an observer, however near or remote, of a uniquely horrid enterprise whose goal was the physical destruction of innocent people.

Austrians, trying to create a bond of normality between past and present, wish to believe that a continuity exists between their youthful and now aged selves. Slowly, they have succeeded in convincing themselves that nothing of any great consequence—aside from the tragic death and suffering of wartime—occurred during the Hitler period. In other words, their version of events has undergone alteration. In the process, memory has "yielded" to the conventions of the postwar era. The past is viewed according to the criteria of what is acceptable today.

When a participant or bystander voluntarily opens his memory to view, what emerges is often a stylized and highly selective version of the past. Memories are grouped in such a way as to emphasize one's own hardships, but they are often buttressed with warm sentiments associated with the primary experiences of childhood. Something of this nature was at work in the selective efforts of Dr. Kurt Waldheim, former United Nations General Secretary and later president of the Republic of Austria, to portray his past.

In Waldheim's selective account of his "Coming of Age," as he termed this chapter in his life up to 1945, the richness of anecdotes concerning his personal suffering contrasts with the silence that falls over his activities with German army intelligence. Readers who follow his brief account of the war will fail to learn that his wounding in Russia led to assignments with military intelligence in the Balkans, and contact with units deporting prisoners of war and Greek Jews; instead, they are offered only an image of a young family man suffering the hardships of a lost war. The cattle cars he describes are not crowded with Jews on their way to the extermination centers, but with Austrians inconvenienced by the occupation forces as they make their way to their new homes.[56]

When, as happened to Waldheim and his followers in the 1986 Austrian presidential electoral campaign, there surface annoyingly insistent questions about unspoken aspects of the wartime past, witnesses and participants may abandon favored images of innocence and victimization to fall back upon the ramparts of duty and defiance. In that campaign, Dr. Waldheim became a spokesman for the generation of Austrians who had served under the Hitler regime. With his wartime record under the spotlight of world attention, he accused his detractors from the World Jewish Congress—the organization that repeatedly raised the issue of his former intelligence activities—of "damaging our esteem abroad." Speaking before an audience "of mostly elderly and middle-aged people" in Carinthia on a drizzly morning in late April, 1986, he proclaimed: "What really troubles me is that this congress tries to ruin the reputation of a whole generation and make all these people bad people. But we will not allow it!" And he continued, "We were not doing anything but our duty as decent soldiers. We were not criminals but decent men who faced a terrible fate."[57]

Survivors who took upon themselves the task of bearing witness to the crimes of which they and their loved ones had been victim knew and valued the sanctity of memory. They feared the loss of memory as the necessary accompaniment of the disappearance of the suffering that underlay it, and instinctively knew that to erase its memory was tantamount to erasing the deeds. With the loss of memory, the world exonerated the killers, freed them of their burden of guilt, and simultaneously banished their victims to oblivion.

In part, this story has drawn upon the recollections of bystanders. This collection of memories is a desperate gathering of straws blowing in the last gusts of a storm that erupted more than four decades ago. Regrettably, such efforts to resurrect the past in the fallible expressions of memory of the respondents, even when prodded, represent only a small force against a deep trend toward forgetting. The efforts are minimal compared to the enormity of the deliberate silences, evasions, and distortions of a generation that slowly, mutely fades into the grave.

Lest this be the final word, let it be noted that a sensitive bystander could see how an otherwise peaceful locale had been transformed into a site of evil. In the immediate aftermath of the opening of the camps, Father Loidl looked with a caring eye upon the setting of the concentration camp in Ebensee. He saw that the concentration camp had despoiled forever a once-idyllic patch of beauty and stillness. This locale had absorbed into itself a vision of cruelty. What had once been a scene of refuge, a common ground for the collection of wood, a place for the ill or the idle to relax, or for bird watchers and nature lovers to tarry, had been ruined. Before the war he had often come here to enjoy its beauty. As he viewed it again in the spring of 1945 he thought of how this paradise had been destroyed. He saw before him a scathing of the physical and moral landscape. The spoilage of nature accompanied the destruction of human life.

> Here were once two land measures of large forest pasture with the little feed barn in the middle where, in the hours of dusk, one could listen to the bucks and deer. What a pleasant idyll that was each time. And how refreshing the rest for everyone who fled here from the noise and strife of human beings. Here I was often a solitary guest and epicure of untouched nature. Now the soil is tamped down; no timid buck will ever scurry over the carpet of meadow and moss, and no majestic deer will stir between the trees. Past is also the mood-filled harmony of the little bells of the grazing cattle that moved away into the magic of an alpine pasture. . . . Not fifty years ago my father had felled building wood for the expansion of his dilapidated parental home.—But only memories![58]

If, as Maurice Halbwachs argued, collective memory attaches to space,[59] then the site of a former concentration camp atop this "once-paradisiacal patch of earth," as Father Loidl termed it, posed a disturbing challenge to the residents' lasting perception of their world. In digging up the graves, tearing down the remains of the camp, constructing villas upon the soil of the former camps, local residents and officials contributed to the destruction of the memory of all that transpired. It was as if, like the aged resident and his garden by the lake, they wished to recall only the beauty of this space as it existed before the whirlwind. It took the informed awareness of one such as this priest, whose memory of this locale stretched backward to the time when his father collected wood there for the family home, and where "the level forest paths permitted a tranquil stroll," to balance this remembrance against that of the electrically charged barbed wire and the guard towers behind which thousands perished in agony.

All this posed not only a violent assault on nature, but a horrible tearing of the fabric of remembrance. Once again, an observer finds two worlds, the one of beauty and peace, the other of ugliness and uprooting: "this screaming contradiction!" Round about still lay a setting of constant beauty. Here Father Loidl yet saw the mountaintops and blue skies, but on the site of what had once been beloved woods and meadows, he found the traces of a world dedicated to death. The village too partook of this horrifying contrast between God-given nature and the man-made inferno: "In the valley the colorful spring meadows, and inserted into the midst of this display of nature like a jewel [lie] the church and locale of Ebensee. But here below, precisely where we linger, a place of torture comparable only to hell."[60] Comparable to hell, indeed, but only that: in truth the camp was indivisbly of *this* world and none other, its landscape darkened by a shadow of human creation.

Notes

The following are abbreviations for some major reference sources as they appear in the Notes:

AMM — Archiv Mauthausen Museum

Befragungsergebnisse — *Befragungsergebnisse*, Zipf, 28 July–1 August 1983, conducted by Christian Limbeck-Lilienau and Siegwald Ganglmair

DÖW — Dokumentationsarchiv des Österreichischen Widerstandes

KZ-Verband — Österreichische Lagergemeinschaft Mauthausen und Niederösterreichischer Landesverband der Widerstandkämpfer und Opfer des Faschismus

LLPA — Limbeck-Lilienau Private Archive

Maršálek — Hans Maršálek, *Die Geschichte der Konzenstrationslager Mauthausen: Dokumentation*

OÖLA — Oberösterreichische Landesarchiv Politische Akten

WVOÖ 2 — Dokumentationsarchiv des Österreichischen Widerstandes, ed. *Widerstand und Verfolgung in Oberösterreich 1934–1945: Eine Dokumentation Band 2*

WVNÖ 3   Dokumentationsarchiv des Österreichischen
                               Widerstandes, ed. *Widerstand und Verfolgung in
                               Niederösterreich; 1934–1945: Eine Dokumenta-
                               tion Band 3*
Y.V.   Yad Vashem Central Archives

Prologue

1. *The Seventy-First Came . . . to Gunskirchen Lager* Witness to the Holocaust Publication Series #1, 2d. printing (Atlanta: Emory University, January 1983), p. 5: account of Capt. J. D. Pletcher.

2. Ibid., pp. 23–4: account of Cpl. Jerry Tax.

3. On the survivor's expression of a need to relate his experience, *see* Terrence Des
Pres, *The Survivor: An Anatomy of Life in the Death Camps* (New York: Oxford University
Press, 1976), pp. 27–50.

4. *See* the discussion entitled "Total Domination" in Hannah Arendt, *The Origins
of Totalitarianism* (New York: World Publishing Company, 1972), pp. 437–59, especially
442, 445, and 451.

5. Remarks of Leon Zelman in Kurt Langbein and Elizabeth T. Spira, "Der Archipel
Mauthausen: Eine Dokumentation," *Österreichische Rundfunk*, Teleobjektiv, broadcast 1
November 1983.

6. Jean Majerus, "Vom R.A.D. ins K.Z.," in L'amicale de Mauthausen, *Letzeburger
zu Mauthausen* (Luxemburg, 1970), pp. 188–89. Archiv Mauthausen Museums (AMM)
A 6/I/4: Ein manuscript eines unbekannten Journalisten nach Angaben von Otto Wahl
. . . in den Märztagen 1946 anlässlich des ersten Mauthausener Prozesses in Dachau
verfasst. Lisa Scheuer, *Vom Tode der nicht stattfand: Theresienstadt, Auschwitz, Freiberg,
Mauthausen Eine Frau Überlebt* (Hamburg: Rowohlt Taschenbuch Verlag, 1983), p. 91.
Scheuer recalls that the incident at the fountain occurred in March 1945.

7. Elie Wiesel, *The Town Beyond the Wall*, cited in Robert McAfee Brown, *Elie
Wiesel: Messenger to All Humanity* (Notre Dame: University of Notre Dame Press, 1983),
pp. 71–72.

8. *See* Martin Gilbert, *Auschwitz and the Allies* (New York: Holt, Rinehart and
Winston, 1981); Walter Laqueur, *The Terrible Secret: Suppression of the Truth about
Hitler's Final Solution* (Boston, Little, Brown, and Company, 1980); Deborah E. Lipstadt,
Beyond Belief: The American Press and the Coming of the Holocaust, 1933–1945 (New York:
Free Press, 1986); Bernard Wasserstein, *Britain and the Jews of Europe, 1939–1945* (Ox-
ford: Clarendon Press, 1979); David S. Wyman, *The Abandonment of the Jews: America
and the Holocaust 1941–1945* (New York: Pantheon Books, 1984).

9. *See* Herwart Vorländer, ed. *Nationalsozialistische Konzentrationsläger im Dienst der
totalen Kriegsfürung: Sieben Würtembergische Aussenläger des Konzentrationslager Natzweiler/
Elsass* (Stuttgart, 1978); Elmer Luchterhand, "Knowing and Not Knowing: Involvement
in Nazi Genocide," in Paul Thompson, ed. *Our Common History: The Transformation of
Europe* (Atlantic Highlands, N.J.: Humanities Press, 1982), pp. 251–72; and Claude
Lanzmann, *Shoah: An Oral History of the Holocaust* (New York, Pantheon Books, 1985).

10. Ian Kershaw, *Popular Opinion and Political Dissent in the Third Reich: Bavaria
1933–1945* (Oxford: Clarendon Press, 1983), p. 364.

11. Ibid., p. 368.

12. Laqueur, pp. 4–5.

13. Ruth Andreas-Friedrich, quoted in Marlis Steinert, *Hitler's War and the Germans: Public Mood and Attitude During the Second World War,* ed. and trans. Thomas E. J. de Witt (Athens: Ohio University Press, 1977), p. 146.

14. Louis de Jong, "The Netherlands and Auschwitz," in Yisrael Gutmann and Livia Rothkirchen, ed. *The Catastrophe of European Jewry: Antecedents—History—Relfections* (New York–Jerusalem, 1976), p. 316. For additional discussion of the challenges of study of the Holocaust to the historical and related academic disciplines *see also* Yehuda Bauer, *The Holocaust in Historical Perspective* (Seattle: University of Washington Press, 1979), pp. 30–50; Lucy Dawidowicz, *The Holocaust and the Historians* (Cambridge, Mass.: Harvard University Press, 1981); Eduard Alexander, "The Attack on Holocaust Studies," in Sanford Pinsker and Jack Fischel, ed. *Holocaust Studies Annual* 1 (1983), pp. 2–6; and Saul Friedländer, "Introduction," in Gerald Fleming, *Hitler and the Final Solution* (Berkeley: University of California Press, 1982).

15. David Rousset, *L'univers concentrationnaire* (Paris, 1946), pp. 182–83.

16. Michel de Bouard, "Mauthausen," *Revue d'histoire de la deuxième guerre mondiale,* no. 15–16 (July–September 1954), pp. 41–80, quoted in Pierre Vidal-Naquet, "Paper Eichmann?," *Democracy* 1 (April 1981), p. 73.

17. Raul Hilberg, cited in Michael R. Marrus, *The Holocaust in History* (Hanover, N.H.: University Press of New England, 1987), p. 7.

Chapter 1: Mauthausen and the Concentration Camp System

1. As Primo Levi noted, the camps "constituted an extensive and complex system which profoundly compen[e]trated the daily life of the country; one has with good reason spoken of the *univers concentrationnaire*, but it was not a closed universe." Primo Levi, *The Drowned and the Saved* tr. Raymond Rosenthal (New York: Summit Books, 1988), p. 15.

2. Falk Pingel, *Häftline unter SS-Herrschaft: Widerstand, Selbstbehauptung und Vernichtung in Konzentrationslager* (Hamburg: Hoffmann and Compe, 1978), p. 92.

3. Martin Gilbert, *The Holocaust: A History of the Jews of Europe During the Second World War* (New York: Holt, Rinehart and Winston, 1985), p. 69; Martin Gilbert, *The Macmillan Atlas of the Holocaust* (New York: Da Capo Press, 1982), p. 28.

4. Enno George, *Die wirtschaftliche Unternehmungen der SS Schriftenreihe der Vierteljahrshefte für Zeitgeschichte* (Stuttgart: Deutsche Verlags-Anstalt, 1963), pp. 42–46.

5. Falk Pingel, "The Concentration Camps as Part of the Nazi System," in *The Nazi Concentration Camps* Proceedings of the Fourth Yad Vashem International Historical Conference (Jerusalem: Yad Vashem, 1984), p. 10. By the outbreak of war there were 6 concentration camps: Dachau, Sachsenhausen, Buchenwald, Mauthausen, Flossenbürg, and Ravensbruck.

6. "From the beginning of the war, the largest influx was from Poland. In 1940, some 8,000 Polish prisoners were sent to Mauthausen alone. This was the result of the policy of resettlement (*Aussiedlung*), of racial ideology, and of the battle against a relatively fast-developing resistance. As a rule, the only prisoners taken from the occupied countries of the West, including Czechoslovakia, were those who had been arrested during operations against acts of resistance. Here it was not a question of undifferentiated mass intake, as it had been in Poland." Pingel, "The Concentration Camps," pp. 10–11.

7. Pingel, "The Concentration Camps," p. 11.

8. Heydrich's scheme divided existing camps into three categories of ascending severity. In category I were Dachau, Sachsenhausen, and the Auschwitz main camp (Auschwitz I). Into these camps were to be placed those inmates deemed capable of being reformed; a sub-category, Ia, was to hold a select group of prisoners such as well-known politicians or clergy or the aged with whom the SS chose to take special care. These inmates were to be assigned to work at an herbal garden at Dachau. Category II prisoners, those seriously charged for their offenses yet still deemed "improvable," were to be assigned to Buchenwald, Flossenbürg, Neuengamme, Auschwitz II (Birkenau), Gross-Rosen, Natzweiler, and Stutthof. In a category by itself, category III, stood Mauthausen and its subsidiary camp of Gusen. Mauthausen and Gusen were camps to which inmates who were deemed the most dangerous and threatening were to be assigned. Particularly singled out were those inmates described as "severely charged, unreformable, and at the same time previously convicted criminals and asocials" deemed "scarcely trainable." Hans Maršálek, *Die Geschichte des Konzentrationslagers Mauthausen: Dokumentation* 2. Auflage (Wien: Österreichische Lagergemeinschaft Mauthausen, 1980), pp. 38–39.

9. Benjamin Eckstein, "Jews in the Mauthausen Concentration Camp," in *The Nazi Concentration Camps*. Proceedings of the Fourth Yad Vashem International Historical Conference (Jerusalem: Yad Vashem, 1984), p. 258.

10. Falk Pingel, *Häftlinge unter SS-Herrschaft*, pp. 81, note 73: 259–60 (note 73).

11. Pingel, "The Concentration Camps," pp. 5–6; Maršálek, pp. 21–22.

12. Death estimates are drawn from Raul Hilberg, *The Destruction of the European Jews* (New York: Holmes & Meir, 1985) Student Edition, p. 338, Table B–1. Here, total Jewish deaths as a result of the Final Solution are estimated to be 5,100,000, of whom 2,700,000 were killed in the six death camps of Auschwitz, Treblinka, Belzec, Sobibor, Kulmhof (Chelmno), and Lublin; 800,000 Jews died in the course of "Ghettoization and general privation"; more than 1,300,000 by shooting; 150,000 in the principal concentration camps, "Bergen-Belsen, Buchenwald, Mauthausen, Dachau, Stutthof, and others," including "Camps with killing operations (Poniatova, Trawniki, Semlin)" and "Labor and transit camps"; an additional 150,000 Jews were killed in camps inside Romania, Croatia, and elsewhere.

13. Yehuda Bauer, "The Death-Marches, January–May 1945," *Modern Judaism* 3 (1983), pp. 7, 9.

14. Bauer, pp. 1–4.

15. Maršálek, p. 26.

16. Maršálek, pp. 119–20.

17. Eckstein, "Jews in the Mauthausen Concentration Camp," p. 260; Maršálek, pp. 156, 218.

18. Maršálek, pp. 120–21. Gisela Rabitsch, "Das KL Mauthausen," in Hans Rothfels and Theodor Eschenburg, ed., *Studien zur Geschichte der Konzentrationslager* Schriftenreihe der Vierteljahrshefte für Zeitgeschichte Nr. 21 (Stuttgart: Deutsche Verlags-Anstalt, 1970), pp. 61–62.

19. Maršálek, pp. 281–82.

20. Maršálek, p. 77; Evelyn Le Chêne, *Mauthausen: The History of a Death Camp* (London: Methuen & Co., 1971), pp. 39–40.

21. Eckstein, pp. 260–61.

22. Maršálek, pp. 22–23, 228.

23. Maršálek, pp. 209–10; Betriebsleitung Städische Unternehmungen Steyr, O–Ö

An die Österreichische Lagergemeinschaft Mauthausen, p.A Herrn Hans Maršálek, 5 Nov. 1974.

24. Maršálek, pp. 72–73.

25. Nearly all the structures of the camp, including the 24 main inmate barracks of *Lager I* and *II* and the bunker, were completed by 1942. Rounding out the enclosure, the 6 additional barracks of *Lager III*, added in the spring of 1944, made for a circumference of 1,668 meters. As noted, additions to the camp included the *Krankenlager*, or so-called hospital camp, also referred to as the *Russenlager*, or Russian camp, consisting of buildings and a kitchen that were erected below the main wall of the camp in the Fall of 1941. A *Zeltlager*, or tent camp, was constructed in December 1944. Maršálek, pp. 72–73.

26. Maršálek, p. 248.

27. Maršálek, p. 73.

28. Approximately 30,000 square yards of this total comprised the main compound, that is, Lagers I, II, and III; the hospital and tent camps, situated beyond the walls, added 18,000 and 19,000 square yards respectively to the total area of the prisoner complex. Maršálek, p. 74.

29. Maršálek, p. 74.

30. "Es war eine Stadt von 95 Baracken, Zelten, und Steingebäuden." Maršálek, p. 74.

31. Edith Wyschogrod, "Concentration Camps and the End of the Life-World," in Alan Rosenberg and Gerald E. Myers, eds. *Echoes from the Holocaust: Philosophical Reflections on a Dark Time* (Philadelphia: Temple University Press, 1988), pp. 327–40. The phrase, "death-world" first appears on page 327.

32. The figure is for June 1943: Maršálek, p. 103.

33. Dokumentationsarchiv des Österreichischen Widerstandes (DÖW) Library: Vaclav Vaclavik, untitled ms., n.d., p. 11.

34. Vaclavik, p. 16.

35. Maršálek, pp. 210–11.

36. Maršálek, p. 228.

37. Maršálek, p. 252.

38. Komitee der Antifaschistischen Widerstandskämpfer der Deutschen Demokratischen Republik, *Aktenvermerk R.u.* (Berlin: Militärverlag der Deutschen Demokratischen Republik, 1979), p. 92.

39. *See* Chapter 3.

40. Maršálek, pp. 212, 226.

41. Choumoff, *Les Chambres a gaz de Mauthausen*, diagram following p. 28.

42. Choumoff, p. 20. Another estimate places the chamber's capacity at "about 120 victims." Le Chêne, *Mauthausen*, p. 84.

43. Maršálek, p. 211; Choumoff, p. 61.

44. The gas van, an order for which from Mauthausen was recorded in a memo by SS-Obersturmführer Walter Rauff on 26 March 1942. Camp Commandant Franz Ziereis admitted to having driven the truck knowing that inmates were being gassed during the trip. Estimates of the number of such journeys range from 15 to 20, with one estimate as high as 47. Eugen Kogon, Hermann Langbein, Adalbert Rückerl, et al., *Nationalsozialistische Massentötungen durch Giftgas* (Frankfurt am Main; S. Fischer Verlag, 1983), pp. 251–53; Choumoff, pp. 33–35; Le Chêne, pp. 80–82. Hans Maršálek, *Die Vergasung-*

saktionen im Konzentrationslager Mauthausen: Gaskammer Gaswagen Vergasungsanstalt Hartheim Tarnnamen. (Vienna, 1988), pp. 16–19.

45. Maršálek, pp. 21–22.

46. Maršálek, p. 22.

47. Maršálek, p. 23.

48. Eckstein, p. 261.

49. Maršálek, pp. 26, 133–34. Gisela Rabitsch, "Das KL Mauthausen," in Hans Rothfels and Theodor Eschenburg, eds., *Studien zur Geschichte der Konzentrationsläger* Schriftenreihe der Vierteljahrshefte für Zeitgeschichte Nr. 21 (Stuttgart: Deutsche Verlags-anstalt, 1970), p. 74.

50. Rabitsch, p. 75. Maršálek, pp. 79–89.

51. Harry Slapnicka, *Oberösterreich als es "Oberdonau" hiess: 1938–1945* (Linz: Oberösterreichischer Landesverlag, 1978), p. 304.

52. Slapnicka, p. 313.

53. Maršálek, p. 25.

54. Eckstein, p. 266.

55. Maršálek, p. 210.

56. Eckstein, p. 267.

57. See map reproduced in Thomas Albrich, *Exodus durch Österreich: Die jüdischen Flüchtlinge 1945–1948* (Innsbruck: Haymon Verlag, 1987), opposite p. 16.

58. Eckstein, pp. 267–71. *See also* Chapter 7, below.

59. Nelly Sachs, "This chain of enigmas" tr. Ruth and Matthew Mead, in *O the Chimneys* tr. Michael Hamburger, Christopher Holme, Ruth and Matthew Mead, and Michael Roloff (New York: Farrar, Strauss & Giroux, 1967), p. 239.

Chapter 2: In the Shadow of the Camp

1. Rudolf Köttstorfer, "Granit" in *Frohe Kinderzeit* 4. Schuljahr, 2. Heft (Vienna [?], November, 1945); Lehrmittelzentral des Amts für Berufserziehung und Betriebs-führung des Deutschen Arbeitsfront, *Der Steinmetz und Steinbildhauer* (Berlin: Verlag der Deutschen Arbeitsfront, 1937), p. 9.

2. Bruno Brehm, "Im Steinbruch," *Tages-Post* 74: 24 December 1938, pp. 15–16.

3. Hugo Rabitsch, *Jugend-Erinnerungen eines Zeitgenössischen Linzer Realschülers: Aus Adolf Hitlers Jugendzeit* (Munich: Deutscher Volksverlag, 1938), p. 13.

4. NSDAP Kreisleitung Perg, *20 Jahre Ortsgruppe Mauthausen der Nationalsozialis-tischen Deutschen Arbeiterpartei* (Linz: Jof. Feichtingers Erben, 1943).

5. Anton Poschacher, *100 Jahre Granitwerk Anton Poschacher* (Mauthausen, 1939), pp. 20–21, 24–26.

6. Albert Speer, *Inside the Third Reich* tr. Richard and Clara Winston (New York: Macmillan Company, 1970), p. 99.

7. "And nothing was more direct and autonomous in the completeness of its strength, nothing more noble or more awe-inspiring, than a majestic rock, or a boldly-standing block of granite. Above all, stone *is*. It always remains itself, and exists of itself; and, more important still, it *strikes*. Before he even takes it up to strike, man finds in it an obstacle—if not to his body, at least to his gaze—and ascertains its hardness, its roughness, its power. Rock shows him something that transcends the precariousness of his humanity: an absolute mode of being. Its strength, its motionlessness, its size and its strange outlines are none of them human; they indicate the presence of something that

fascinates, terrifies, attracts and threatens, all at once. In its grandeur, its hardness, its shape and its color, man is faced with a reality and a force that belong to some world other than the profane world of which he is himself a part." Mircea Eliade, *Patterns in Comparative Religion* tr. Rosemary Sheed (New York: World Publishing Company, 1966), p. 216.

8. Ludwig Commenda, *Neuer illustrierter Führer von Grein und Umgebung sowie das Machland Bahnstrecke Mauthausen-Grein mit einem Anhange Die Donautalbahn Grein-Krems: Eine geschichtliche, topographische und Landschaftliche Schilderung* (Grein: J. M. Hiebel, 1910), pp. 160–61.

9. Peter Schubert, *Schauplatz Österreich: Topographische Lexikon zur Zeitgeschichte in drei Bänden* Band 2 (Wien: Verlag Brüder Hollinek, 1980), pp. 46–47.

10. 4,389 of them were engaged in agriculture and forestry, 5,683 in industry and handicrafts, 1,524 in trade and transport, 24 in credit and insurance, 166 in public service, 262 in free professions, 74 in domestic service; 2,083 were without any profession and 156 provided no information regarding their profession. Bundesamt für Statistik, *Die Ergebnisse der Österreichischen Volkszählung vom 22. März 1934* (Wien: Verlag der Österreichischen Staatsdruckerei, 1935), pp. 10–11.

11. The entire county listed 43,618 persons with 20,382 in agriculture and forestry, 12,624 in industry and handicrafts, 3,301 in trade and transport, 56 in credit and insurance; 586 were public servants, 693 in the free professions, 180 in domestic service, 5,069 without a profession and 727 registered no profession at all. Ibid.

12. Ibid.

13. Fourteen were Protestants, 6 were *Altkatholisch*, one was recorded as other, perhaps Greek-Orthodox, with 15 listed as having no religion. Ibid., pp. 10–11.

14. Ibid., pp. 2–3, 6–7.

15. *Times* (London, 30 March 1938). [Excerpt in DÖW and Archiv Mauthausen Museum (AMM)].

16. Reichspostdirektion Linz, *Amtliches Fernsprechbuch für den Bezirk der Reichspostdirektion Linz* (1942), p. 76.

17. Maršálek, 2. Auflage, p. 18. AMM A/4/1,2.

18. Author's interview with Phillip M., Mauthausen, 18 February 1983. He noted that he arrived in Mauthausen in August or September 1938.

19. AMM A/3/3: "Bericht, Franz Jany, 3.9.1944. Also cited in Maršálek, p. 31.

20. Maršálek, p. 19.

21. AMM Q/4/1: Aktenvermerk, Landwirt K., 18 März 1965.

22. Ibid.

23. AMM A/6/I/2: Angaben des wirkl. Hofrates Dr. Gustav Brachmann, 16 März 1965.

24. AMM P/10/1: Lagerkommandant K.L.M., SS-Sturmbannführer Sauer an die Bezirkshauptmannschaft Perg: Beschwerde über die Gendarmeriestation Mauthausen, 18 Januar 1939. Also cited in Dokumentationsarchiv des Österreichischen Widerstandes, ed. *Widerstand und Verfolgung in Oberösterreich 1934–1945: Eine Dokumentation* Band 2 (WVOÖ) 2: 587.

25. AMM P/10/2: Stationsführer Fleischmann an die Bezirkshauptmannschaft in Perg, 26 Januar 1939.

26. AMM P/10/6; AMM A/6/I/2: Angaben des wirkl. Hofrates Dr. Gustav Brachmann, 16 März 1965. Commandant Albert Sauer, the first commandant, whom District Governor Brachmann recalls having charged with responsibility for this incident,

left Mauthausen by 17 February 1939. The incident would have taken place before that date.

27. AMM P/10/3: Gendarmerieposten Mauthausen, Landkreis Perg, Oberdonau, an den Landrat des Kreises in Perg, 7 November 1939. Report of the Gendarmeriepostenführer. The tavern owner, citing "certain reasons [aus gewissen Grunden] declined to press for damages. Three truck drivers involved in the fight against the SS men similarly refused to ask redress for bodily injuries because they had often driven for the concentration camp and wanted to protect their employer from possible disadvantageous consequences."

28. AMM P/10/6; AMM A/6I/2: Angaben des wirkl. Hofrates Dr. Gustav Brachmann, 16 März 1965.

29. AMM P/10/7: Gendarmerieposten Mauthausen, Kreis Perg, Oberdonau an den Kommandeur der Gendarmerie des Reichsgauses Oberdonau in Linz, 22 Dezember 1939.

30. Apparently, no relation to the famed German author of Indian stories.

31. WVOÖ 2: 587–89. DÖW E 17.845. Schreiben der Staatsanwaltschaft beim OLG Wien an den Reichsjustizminister betreffend Vorfälle im KZ Mauthausen, 3. 2. 1939.

32. Ibid.

33. Ibid.

34. Ibid.

35. Ibid.

36. Ibid.

37. Aus: Schreiben des Gendarmeriepostens Mauthausen an den Landrat in Perg betreffend Anzeige von Eleonore Gusenbauer wegen unmenschlicher Behandlung der KZ-Häftlinge, 27.9.1941; AMM Q/2/1; DÖW E 18.080: cited in WVOÖ 2: 591. See also: Rabitsch, Konzentrationslager, p. 361; Maršálek, p. 207, note 16.

38. WVOÖ 2: 591.

39. For descriptions of conditions in the Mauthausen quarries, see Maršálek, p. 94; and Evelyn Le Chêne, Mauthausen: The History of a Death Camp (London: Methuen & Co., 1971), pp. 64–71; Enno George, Die Wirtschaftlichen Unternehmungen der SS, Schriftenreihe der Vierteljahrshefte für Zietgeschichte Nummer 7 (Stuttgart: Deutsche Verlags-Anstalt, 1963), pp. 44–45.

40. Author's interview with Herr and Frau Juan S., and Manuel G., Mauthausen, 9 February 1983. National Archives (NA) RG 153-5-31-vol. 1-Exhibits. EX D-28, 5/8/46.

41. Interview with Herr and Frau Juan S. and Herr Manuel G., Mauthausen, 9 February 1983.

42. Maršálek, p. 94. By 1942, long after most of the main camp had been completed, the number of civilian employees diminished somewhat. In May 1942, there were a "daily average of 3,844 inmates, 29 SS members, 29 civilian employees, 60 civilian laborers, 22 apprentices and 5 foreigners" employed in the 4 principal quarries of the Mauthausen/Gusen complex.

43. Statistisches Amt für die Reichsgau der Ostmark, Gemeindeverzeichnis für die Reichsgaue der Ostmark auf Grund der Volkszählung vom 17. Mai 1939 nach dem Gebietsstand vom 1. Jänner 1941 Ausgabe 2 (Wien, 1940), p. 55.

44. DÖW 13.502. Lg Linz KMs 29/40. Urteil des SG beim LG Linz gegen Johann Steinmüller aus Gusen wegen Vergehens gegen das Heimtückegesetz, 21.3.1940.

45. DÖW 13.502. Lg Linz JS 67/39, 8.7.1939. Vernehmungsniederschrift, Johann Steinmüller, Geheime Staatspolizei Linz an die Staatsanwaltschaft beim Lg Linz.

46. DÖW 13.502. Urteil, Lg Linz als SG KMs 29/40, 21.3.1940. In his testimony

before the Gestapo on 1 August 1939 Steinmüller referred to the presence of the sawmill owner, and the unidentified man. The judgment mentions specifically only the waitress and the laborer, while making reference to "several guests" besides them.

47. DÖW 13.502: Statement of Franziska Pree, LG Linz Js 67/39, 19 September 1939.

48. DÖW 13.502: Urteil, 21.3.1940.

49. Maršálek, p. 165.

50. AMM A 6/I/4: reported statements of Otto Wahl, March 1946. *See also* similar testimony in AMM V/3/II/2: statements of Otto Wahl.

51. AMM A 6/I/4.

52. AMM P/20/1: Aktenvermerk concerning Johann B., Tischlermeister in Mauthausen; n.d.

53. Ibid.

54. AMM A 11/1. KL Mauthausen Leiter der Verwaltung: Tätigkeitsbericht Nr. 2 ab 1.10.1941. From Nurenberg Document PS-2176. *See also* Le Chêne, pp. 42–46.

55. Anna Strasser, *Tatsachenbericht* (St. Valentin, 1983), p. 6.

56. Interview with Phillip M. and wife, 18 February 1983.

57. Eugen Kogon, Hermann Langbein, Adalbert Rückerl, et al., *Nationalsozialistische Massentötungen durch Giftgas* (Frankfurt am Main: S. Fischer Verlag, 1983), p. 248.

58. L'amicale de Mauthausen, *Letzeburger zu Mauthausen* (Luxemburg, 1970), p. 112.

59. National Archives (NA), Record Group (RG) 338/00-50-5-22, United States vs. Peter Bärens, et al., direct and cross-examination of Ernst Kirschbichler, 21 October 1947, pp. 486–92.

60. NA RG 338/000-50-5-22: Sworn statements of Roman Weilguny, 17 January 1948; Johann Leitner, 19 January, 1948; Johann Feyrer, 19 January 1948; Georg Aichinger, 9 December 1948; Josef Quast, 17 November 1947.

61. NA RG 338/000-50-5-22: Sworn statements of Rosa Kirschbichler, 13 November 1947; Georg Aichinger, 9 December 1947; Maria Steinhuber, 28 November 1947; Maria Kogler, 9 December 1947; Karl von Dorp, 15 April 1948.

62. NA RG 338/000-50-5-22: War Crimes Review Board No. 1, report of 21 May 1948.

63. NA RG 338/000-50-5-22: Re–cross-examination of Ernst Kirschbichler, 21 October 1947, pp. 499–500; sworn statement of Paul Wolfram, 18 February 1948.

64. Leiter der Städtische Unternehmungen.

65. See Prologue.

66. "Er wünschte recht viele Leichen aus Mauthausen: Der Leiter des Steyrer Krematoriums vor dem Linzer Volksgericht," in *Tagblatt* 23 April 1947. [Available in AMM P/13] He denied having a personal financial stake in raising the quota of bodies shipped from Mauthausen. However, the article noted that the director was sentenced to a year's imprisonment after having been found guilty by a local court under a statute covering Crimes against Human Dignity.

67. AMM V/3/20: Ausführlicher Bericht des ehemaligen Kriminalkommissars des Polizeipräsidium in Berlin, [G.] Kanthack, der als Häftling mehrere Jahre in der Politischen Abteilung gearbeitet hat. Each camp administration included a Political Department "staffed by SS police officers . . . who were assigned to the camps to compile the dossiers of the prisoners and to investigate escapes and conspiracies. They took their orders from both the commandant and the Gestapo." Henry Frieddländer, "The Nazi

Camps," in Alex Grobman and Daniel Landes, eds. *Genocide: Critical Issues of the Holocaust* (Los Angeles: Simon Wiesenthal Center, 1983), pp. 223–24.

68. Ibid.

69. AMM V/3/22: Angaben des Josef Herzler. The gold circulated via the external work details. The camp commandant strove to put a halt to this activity. When in the spring of 1943 word of this trade reached him, and "the SS felt themselves betrayed," two of the capos involved were ",immediately sent to a punishment company. For the Jews this had the advantage that constant beatings in part let up, and they lived longer—that is, until hunger and exhaustion killed them."

70. *Front und Heimat: Briefwechsel mit den Soldaten des Kreises Perg* 3 (March/April 1942): 12.

71. *Front und Heimat* 4 (July/August 1943): 13.

72. *Front und Heimat* (November/December 1943): 15, 16.

73. Bruno Bettelheim, *The Informed Heart: Autonomy in a Mass Age* (New York: Free Press, 1960), p. 286.

74. *Front und Heimat* 4 (November/December 1943): 16.

75. *Front und Heimat* 4 (May/June 1943): 13; *Front und Heimat* 4 (July/August 1943): 13.

76. AMM S/4/2: Chronik Gendarmerie Post Schwertberg, 1945.

77. Ibid.

78. Ibid.

79. AMM V/3/20: *Bericht* Kanthack; DÖW 16.536: Betr.: SS-Obersturmführer Karl Schulz, geb. 9.9. 1902.

80. AMM V/3/20: *Bericht* Kanthack.

81. Ibid. This specific incident is reported to have occurred in the fall of 1944: *See* DÖW 16.536. The incident is also reported in Vincenzo e Luigi Pappalèttera, *La paròla agli aguzzini Le SS e i Kapo di Mauthausen svelano le leggi del Lager* 3d ed. (Arnoldo Mondadori Editore, 1970), p. 62.

82. Anna Strasser, *Tatsachenbericht: März 1938–Mai 1945* (St. Valentin, 1982).

83. *Tatsachenbericht*.

84. Interview with Anna Strasser, Vienna, 31 February 1982.

85. Ibid.

86. Ibid.

87. *Tatsachenbericht*, p. 5.

88. Ibid.

89. Ibid., p. 6.

90. Ibid.

91. Ibid.

92. Ibid., p. 7.

93. Ibid.

94. She worked with Anna S. in the agricultural cooperative bureau.

95. *Tatsachenbericht*, p. 8.

96. Ibid. Herr Franz Winklehner, who turned 58 years old in August 1940, died in the Dachau concentration camp on 26 February 1941: Staatskommissariat für Russisch, Religiös und Politisch Verfolgte in Bayern, ed., *Die Toten von Dachau Deutsche und Österreicher: Ein Gedenkbuch und Nachschlagwerk* (München: Graphische Kunstanstalten, 1947), p. 78.

97. *Tatsachenbericht*, p. 8.

98. Ibid., p. 9.

99. Ibid., pp. 10–11.

100. Ibid.

101. Ibid.

102. *Tatsachenbericht*, p. 11.

103. Author's interview with Frau Strasser, 31 March 1982.

104. Ibid.; *Tatsachenbericht*, p. 11.

105. Maršálek, pp. 132, 156.

106. AMM A/6/I Nr. 2: Angaben Brachmann, 16 März 1965.

107. Some 20 arrived on 12 May 1941; 348 followed on the transport from Buchenwald on 17 June 1941; and 291 "directly from Amsterdam" on 25 June 1941. The Jews seized in the wake of the Amsterdam demonstrations and subsequently shipped to Buchenwald and Mauthausen, where they died, were young men "between 20 and 35 years of age." Maršálek, pp. 40, 121. Of some 900 Jews from Holland [Maršálek, p. 122, places the figure closer to 850] sent to Mauthausen in the course of the entire year 1941, only 9 were alive at year's end, but they too perished in the course of the war. Benjamin Eckstein, "Jews in the Mauthausen Concentration Camp," in *The Nazi Concentration Camps* Proceedings of the Fourth Yad Vashem International Historical Conference (Jerusalem: Yad Vashem, 1984), p. 264.

108. Eugen Kogon, *The Theory and Practice of Hell* tr. Heinz Norden (New York: Berkeley Publishing Corporation, 1960), pp. 179–80. Kogon refers to the "148 steps" of the *Totesstiege*, or "staircase of death," which the inmates were forced to negotiate; in fact there were 186 steps. Kogon refers to a total of 340 arrivals from Buchenwald; there were 348.

109. Cited in Evelyn Le Chêne, *Mauthausen: The History of a Death Camp* (London: Methuen & Co., 1971), pp. 69–70, in turn citing Olga Wormser and Henri Michel, *La tragédie de la déportation 1940–1945* (Paris, 1955), p. 398: testimony of Paul Tillard.

110. Kogon, p. 180.

111. Author's interview with Phillip M., Mauthausen, 18 February 1983.

112. AMM A/6/I/2: Angaben, Dr. Gustav Brachmann, 16 Marz 1965.

113. Author's interview with Anna P., Mauthausen, 9 February 1983.

114. Pierre Weydert, cited in Christian Bernadac, *Les 186 marches: Mauthausen* (Paris: Éditions France-Empire, 1974), p. 67.

115. AMM P/10/6; AMM A/6/I/4: reported statements of Otto Wahl, March 1946.

Chapter 3. The Castle

1. For background on the development and operation of the euthanasia program of which the events described below were an integral part, *see* Eugen Kogon, Hermann Langbein, Adalbert Rückerl, et al., *Nationalsozialistische Massentötungen durch Giftgas: Eine Dokumentation* (Frankfurt am Main, 1983), pp. 27–78; Ernst Klee, *"Euthanasie" im NS-Staat: Die "Vernichtung lebensunwerten Lebens"* (Frankfurt am Main: S. Fischer Verlag, 1983); and Robert Jay Lifton, *The Nazi Doctors: Medical Killing and the Psychology of Genocide* (New York: Basic Books, 1986), Part I.

2. The so-called euthanasia program was ordered into full operation in October 1939 when Adolf Hitler signed a secret order permitting the killing. In so doing, Hitler authorized Bouhler and Brandt "to widen the authority of individual doctors with a view to enabling them, after the most critical examination in the realm of human knowledge,

to administer to incurably sick persons a mercy death." Cited in Raul Hilberg, *The Destruction of the European Jews* 3 vols. Rev. ed. (New York: Holmes & Meier, 1985); 3, p. 872. The order was back-dated to 1 September 1939. In fact, during the first half of that year killings were carried out on children whom the medical commission determined to be suffering from a number of physical ailments. With the signing of the Hitler order in the autumn, the operation came to include the killing of adults. Florian Zehethofer, "Hartheim und Euthanasie," in *WVOÖ* 2, pp. 509–510.

3. Vinzenz Nohel, Aussage, 4.9.1945 LG Linz, Vg 11 Vr2407/46 DÖW 14.900, cited in *WVOÖ* 2, p. 521. Nohel stated that "Some 6 weeks after 2 April 1940 [the day he began work in Hartheim] the preparations and construction were complete and operations were begun." Hans Maršálek states that the first gassing in Hartheim took place "immediately after Easter 1940," Maršálek, p. 212.

4. After August 1941, the killing of patients continued on a reduced scale, through the lethal administration of injections and drugs.

5. The implications of the program were far-reaching. The technical capacities perfected in the euthanasia program became the model for use in concentration and extermination camps. The operations demonstrated the effectiveness of assembly-line procedures for mass murder, and established the technical feasibility of the gas chamber as an instrument of mass killing. The integrated killing unit containing gas chamber, corpse-storage area, and crematorium first was used in the euthanasia centers. By 1942 the experience of the euthanasia killing centers had been applied on a monumental scale in the extermination centers: Treblinka, Sobibor, Belzec, Lublin-Maidanek, Auschwitz. In that year, too, Mauthausen established its own gas chamber.

6. Zehethofer, im *WVOÖ* 2, p. 511.

7. Maršálek, p. 212.

8. The figure of a minimum of 4,608 inmates from the two camps is from Serge Choumoff, *Les chambres a gaz de Mauthausen* (Paris, Amicale des Déportes et familles de disparus du camp de concentration de Mauthausen, 1972), pp. 56, 61. Choumoff estimates that, of these, 1,380 inmates from Mauthausen and Gusen were killed in Hartheim in 1941 and 1942, and 3,228 in 1944. It is also estimated that at least 3,000 inmates from Dachau were also killed at Hartheim, 2,524 of whom were killed from 15 January to 14 October 1942: DÖW E18.370/1. 15 Vr 363/64. KS 1/69 (GstA). Strafsache gegen Hans-Joachim Becker, Friedrich Wilhelm Siegmund Robert Lorent (judgment on 27 May 1970), report section entitled "Die Häftlings-Euthanasie," pp. 73–74.

9. Florian Zehethofer, "Das Euthanasieproblem im Dritten Reich am Beispiel Schloss Hartheim (1938–1945)," *Oberösterreichische Heimatblätter* 32 (1978): 46; AMM B/15/54: "Euthanasie- und Vergasungsanstalt Hartheim."

10. Cited in Zehethofer, pp. 51–52.

11. "Linzer Volksblatt," 18 October 1945, cited in Zehethofer, p. 53.

12. Author's interview with Herr Karl S., Grieskirchen, 28 June 1983.

13. Ibid.

14. S. Karl an den Herrn Vorsitzenden des Euthanasie-Prozesses in Frankfurt/Main, 16 October 1969. Copy in author's possession.

15. Interview with Karl S., 28 June 1983.

16. Zehethofer, p. 53.

17. DÖW E. 18.370/1: Lg Linz 15vr 363/64. Zeugenvernehmung, Maria Meindl, 6 August 1971.

18. Karl S., letter of 16 October 1969.

19. DÖW E 18.370/1: Lg Linz 15 Vr 363/64. Statements of Stefan Achleitner, 19 February 1964; Aloisa Ehrengruber, 24 February 1964; Juliane Königsdorfer, 8 November 1968; Wladyslaw Tubiarz, 23 December 1969; Aleksandra Zeimlewska, 23 December 1969; Janina Kowalik, 29 April 1970; Josef Jungwirth, 6 August 1971; Maria Meindl, 6 August, 1971.

20. "verschlug ihnen formlich die Sprache." Literally: nailed shut, or boarded-up speech.

21. AMM B/15/41: Authentischer Bericht über die Menschenvernichtung in Schloss Hartheim. Also cited in Zehethofer, p. 55.

22. DÖW E 18.370/1. Lg Linz 15 Vr 363/64. Jungwirth statement, 6 August 1971.

23. AMM B/15/41.

24. Karl S., letter of 16 October 1969.

25. "Linzer Volksblatt," 18 October 1945, cited in Zehethofer, p. 53.

26. DÖW E 18.370/1. Lg Linz 15 Vr 363/64. Statement of Wladislaw Tubiarz, 23 December 1969.

27. DÖW E 18.370/1. Lg Linz 15 Vr 363/64. Statements of Stefan Achleitner, 19 February 1964 (Bericht); Maria Meindl, 6 August 1971; Josef Jungwirth, 6 August 1971; Rudolf Ritzberger, 6 August 1971; Schumann letter, 16 October 1969; AMM B/15/54. Stefan Achleitner referred to the man as "the speaker, dressed in a captain's uniform. Karl S. remembered him as "an SS officer with the rank of major, yet not in black, but in field-gray uniform." Farmer Rudolf Ritzberger, though, identified him as "a German officer by the name of Wirth." Herr Achleitner noted that whereas all the residents were requested to attend the meeting, only a small number appeared.

28. DÖW E 18.370/1. Lg Linz 15 Vr 363/64. Statement of Maria Meindl, 6 August 1971.

29. DÖW E 18.370/1. Lg Linz 15 Vr 363/64. Statements of Josef Jungwirth, 6 August 1971, and Rudolf Ritzberger, 6 August, 1971.

30. Letter of Karl S., 16 October 1969.

31. Ibid. See also report on statement of Stefan Achleitner, 19 February 1964: DÖW E 18.370/1. Lg Linz 15 Vr 363/64.

32. DÖW E 18.370/1. Lg Linz 15 Vr 363/64. Statement of Maria Meindl, 6 August 1971.

33. According to a 1964 Austrian Ministry of the Interior survey, at least 71 Austrians served in the castle on the Hartheim staff. DÖW E 18.370/1. Lg Linz 15 Vr 363/64, Verzeichnis jener Personen, die auf Grund der vom Landgericht Frankfurt/Main zur Verfügung gestellten Namensliste als Österreichische Staatsangehörige mit der Euthanasieanstalt Hartheim in Beziehung zu bringen sind, 15.12.1964. According to Vinzenz Nohel, one of the castle's crematory attendants, "some 70 persons were employed in the whole facility." DÖW E 18.370/2. Lg Linz Vg 8Vr 2407/46, Vernehmung des Beschuldigten, 4.9.1945.

34. DÖW E 18.370/1. Renno Karton, Lg Linz 15 Vr 363/64.

35. Ibid.

36. Quoted in Klee, p. 353.

37. DÖW E 18.370/1. Renno Karton, Lg Linz 15 Vr 363/64.

38. Ibid.

39. Cited in Klee, p. 148.

40. Klee, p. 355.

41. Maršálek, p. 215, n. 19. DÖW E 18.370/1. Lg Linz 15 Vr 363/64: List of

Austrian citizens connected with the Hartheim euthanasia institution, 15 December 1964. Klee, pp. 352–53.

42. Maršálek, p. 212.

43. Klee, p. 352.

44. DÖW E 18.370/1. Lg Linz, 15 Vr 363/64, statements of Stefan Schachermayr 17.12.1964 and 11.3.1964. Schachermayr noted that on May 1, 1941 he was transferred to military service.

45. DÖW E 18.370/2: Lg Linz, Vg 8Vr 2407/46: statements of Margit Troller, 25 June 1946 and Helene Hintersteiner, 18 August 1945; DÖW 14.900: Lg Linz, Vg 6 Vr 6741/47, statements of Gertraud Dirnberger and Margit Troller, 25–26 November 1947.

46. DÖW 14.900: Lg Linz, Vg 6 Vr 6741/47, statements of Elisabeth Lego and Karoline Burner, 25–26 November 1947.

47. Cited in Gitta Sereny, *Into that Darkness: An Examination of Conscience* (New York: Vintage Books, 1983), pp. 79–80.

48. Ibid., p. 80.

49. See Nohel's statement of 4 September 1945, cited in Klee, p. 167, and WVOÖ 2, pp. 520–23. Nohel also received a 50-mark separation allowance.

50. WVOÖ 2, pp. 521–22.

51. Nohel noted that there were two 2-man teams operating in the crematory; however, on a list of Austrian citizens associated with Hartheim, compiled in 1964, there were 8 men who served as crematory attendants. DÖW E 18.370/1. Lg Linz 15 Vr 363/64 Verzeichnis jener Personen, die auf Grund der vom Landgericht Frankfurt/Main zur Verfügung gestellten Namensliste als Österreichische Staatsangehörige mit der Euthanasieanstalt Hartheim in Beziehung zu bringen sind, 15.12.1964.

52. Statement of Vinzenz Nohel before the Kriminalpolizei Linz, LG Linz Vg 11 Vr 2407/46, 4 September 1945, cited in WVOÖ 2, pp. 520–23.

53. Ibid. Nohel noted that "once 150 persons were gassed all at once. The gas chamber was so full that those inside were hardly able to fall over, and as a result were so cramped together that we could hardly pull the bodies apart. Since earlier gassings had already taken place, the body room was so full that the corpses on the bottom were already decaying by the time we got started burning."

54. DÖW E 18.370/1. Lg Linz 14 Vr 363/64, statement of Elisabeth Lego [attached to Zeugenvernehmungen, Bruckner 5 October 1964, and Buchberger, 24 February 1964].

55. Ibid.

56. DÖW E 18.370/1. Lg Linz, Vg 15 Vr 363/64, Report of 17 February 1964 on statement of Bruno Bruckner, 24 May 1962; LG Linz 15 Vr 363/64, statement of Matthias Buchberger, 24 February 1964.

57. DÖW E 18.370/1. Lg Linz, Vg 15 Vr 363/64, statements of Matthias Buchberger, 24 February 1964, and Heinrich Barbl, 5 October 1964.

58. DÖW E 18.370/1. Lg Linz, Vg 15 Vr 363/64, statement of Heinrich Barbl, 5 October 1964.

59. Ibid.

60. DÖW E 18.370/1. Lg Linz, Vg 15 Vr 363/64, statement of Matthias Buchberger, 24 February 1964.

61. Ibid.

62. Under National Socialist rule Austria was incorporated into the Reich and renamed the "*Ostmark.*"

63. Statement of Vinzenz Nohel before Kriminalpolizei Linz, 4 September 1945, cited in WVOÖ 2, pp. 520–23; and Klee, p. 167.

64. DÖW E 18.370/1. Lg Linz, Vg 15 Vr 363/64, statement of Matthias Buchberger, 24 February 1964.

65. Ibid.

66. Ibid.

67. Hartheim lies within Alkoven, Upper Austria.

68. DÖW 14.900: Lg Linz, Vg 8Vr 6062/46, statement of Franz Hödl, 13 March 1947, excerpt also available in WVOÖ 2, p. 525; DÖW E 18.370/1: Lg Linz 15 Vr 363/64, statement of Franz Hödl before Bezirksgericht, 18 November 1964; Aus: Aussage des Georg Renno vor dem Untersuchungsrichter des Landgerichtes Frankfurt am Main betreffend ärztliche Tätigkeit in Hartheim, 5.2.1965, from Generalstaatsanwalt Frankfurt am Main, Js 18/61, DÖW E 18.214: cited in WVOÖ 2, 1.532.

69. Hödl statement, 13 March 1947.

70. DÖW E 18.370/1. Lg Linz Vg 15 Vr 363/64, statement of Franz Mayrhuber, 19 November 1964.

71. DÖW E 18.370/1. Lg Linz Vg 15 Vr 363/64, statement of Johann Lothaller, 19 November 1964.

72. DÖW E 18.370/1: Lg Linz 15 Vr 363/64, statements of Rudolf Loidl, 11 and 20 November 1964.

73. AMM B/15/54: "Euthanasie- und Vergasungsanstalt Hartheim."'

74. Helene Hintersteiner worked in the office and stated that she was in charge of "around 14 office girls." DÖW 18370/2: Lg Linz, Vg 8Vr 2407/46, 18 August 1945.

75. DÖW E 18.370/1. Lg Linz, 15 Vr 363/64, statement of Elisabeth Lego [attached to statements of Matthias Buchberger, 24 February 1964 and of Bruno Bruckner, 5 October 1964].

76. Ibid.

77. DÖW E 18.370/1. Lg Linz, 15 Vr 363/64, statement of Margit Troller [attached to statements of Buchberger and Bruckner]. Similarly, in 1946 she maintained that whereas she filled out correspondence informing the relatives of the death of loved ones in Hartheim, and gradually discovered that the mentally ill were brought to Hartheim to be gassed, "I never saw anything that happened." DÖW E 18.370/2: Lg Linz, Vg 8vr 2407/46, statement of Margit Troller, 25 June 1946.

78. DÖW 18.370/2: Lg Linz, Vg 8Vr 2407/46, statement of Helene Hintersteiner, 18 August 1945.

79. Yet, she noted that "in the period from June 1941 until December 1942 I was on leave because of pregnancy."

80. DÖW E 18.370/1: Lg Linz, 15 Vr 363/64, statement of Karoline Burner, 16 November 1964.

81. DÖW E 18.370/1: Lg Linz, 15 Vr 363/64, statement of Gertraud Dirnberger, 17 November 1964. "Concerning the further course of events I can say nothing with certainty, because I never saw what happened once the arrivals had disappeared behind the boarded wall," she stated.

82. Ibid.

83. Ibid.

84. Aus: Aussage der Anna Griessenberger . . . in der Hauptverhandlung vor dem Lg Linz als Volksgericht, 25 und 26. 11. 1947, from Lg Linz, Vg 6 Vr 6741/47, DÖW 14.900, cited in WVOÖ 2: 525–27.

85. Ibid., p. 526.

86. Ibid.; DÖW E 18.370/1. Lg Linz 15 Vr 363/64, statement of Maria Hammelsböck, 22 May 1964. "If I am further asked, if I was present 10, 50, or 100 times, I can at least say that it was not 50 or 100 times. I do not want to pin myself down numerically," she noted.

87. DÖW E 18.370/1: Lg Linz 15 Vr 363/64, statement of Maria Hammelsböck, 22 May 1964. "I did not observe the patients carrying out any kind of resistance. The undressing always went along without friction."

88. Ibid.

89. DÖW E 18.370/1: Lg Linz 15 Vr 363/64, statement of Hermine Pimpl, 14 September 1964.

90. DÖW E 18.370/1: Lg Linz 15 Vr 363/64, statement of Maria Hammelsböck, 22 May 1964.

91. Ibid.

92. Aus: Aussage der Anna Griessenberger . . . vor dem Lg Linz als Volksgericht, 25. und 26.11.1947, DÖW 14.900: Lg Linz, Vg 6 Vr 6741/47: cited in WVOÖ 2, p. 526.

93. DÖW 14.900: Lg Linz Vg 6 Vr 6741/47, statement of Elisabeth Lego, 25–26 November 1947.

94. Ibid.

95. DÖW 18.370/1: Generalstaatsanwalt Frankfurt am Main Js 18/61, statement of Dr. Georg Renno, 31 October 1961.

96. Ibid. DÖW E 18.370/1: Bericht, Angaben des Bruno Bruckner, Bundesministerium für Inneres, Abteiliung 2C, Zahl: I–P 91.133–2C/1/64, 17 February 1964. Bruckner joined the National Socialist Party and became a member of the SA in March 1934, eventually achieving the rank of SA Obersturmbannführer. He is said to have distinguished himself through enthusiasm displayed at Nurnberg party rallies. On 30 June 1934 he was dismissed from his post as a school janitor, and was unemployed until 28 August 1938, when he took up a position as porter at the Linz slaughter house. He was sent to Hartheim on 1 July 1940 and remained there until 10 October 1942, after which, beginning on 31 August 1943, he served in the army. DÖW E 18.370/2: Lg Linz. Bericht, Kriminalbeamter Postl, 16 April 1947.

97. DÖW E 18.370/2: Lg Linz, Bericht, Kriminalbeamter Postl, 16 April 1947. DÖW E 182701/1: Untitled report of the Dokumentationszentrum des Bundes Jüdischer Verfolgter des Naziregimes, 13 February 1964, p. 13.

98. Bericht, Angaben des Bruno Bruckner, 17 February 1964.

99. Klee, p. 173.

100. Klee, pp. 173–74.

101. DÖW 14.900: Lg Linz Vg 6 Vr 6741/47, statement of Gertraud Dirnberger, 25–26 November 1947.

102. Statement of Vinzenz Nohel before the Kriminalpolizei, 4 September 1945, Lg Linz Vg 11 Vr 2407/46, cited in WVOÖ 2, pp. 520–23.

103. Raul Hilberg's work on bureaucracy and mass murder is most instructive and helped to inform my understanding of the workings of the euthanasia facility at Hartheim, and the behavior of its employees. See again his essay, "German Railroads/Jewish Souls," in Society 14 (November/December 1976): 60–72, in addition to Raul Hilberg, The Destruction of the European Jews 3 vols. Rev. ed. (New York: Holmes & Meier, 1985). See also: Hermann Langbein, Menschen in Auschwitz (Frankfurt/M: Ullstein, 1972), p. 37.

Chapter 4. Into the Valley of Redl-Zipf

1. *See,* for example, "Die erste Rakete zum Mond," *Linzer Wochenblatt* 13 (6 January 1938).

2. Speer, *Inside the Third Reich,* pp. 367–68.

3. From a memo recorded by Albert Speer we learn that on 8 July 1943 "the Führer once again stresses that the AIV [V-2 rocket] is to be promoted with all emphasis. He considers this a measure capable of being carried out with relatively limited means, and one that is decisive for the war effort." Mappe: Zipf (in the possession of Dr. Siegwald Ganglmair, DÖW). Included in Dieter Matzka and Wilma Kiener: "Schlier" (Bisherige Recherchen). Christian Limbeck-Lilienau Private Archive (LLPA). Much of the material from the "Mappe: Zipf" coincides with the Limbeck-Lilienau collection.

4. Speer, *Inside the Third Reich,* p. 369.

5. Mappe: Zipf, "Führerbesprechung vom 19–22 August 1943" The document is signed Speer, and dated 23 August 1943: Abschrift.

6. Oberösterreichische Landesarchiv Politische Akten/Schachtel 79 [OÖLA] PA/ Sch. 79): Geheimwaffen-Teilfertigung "Schlier" in Limbeck-Lilienau Private Archive (LLPA).

7. Ibid.

8. Limbeck-Lilienau, "Geschichte . . ." Writing to its board of directors on 5 October 1943, the management of the Zipf Brewery Co. took note of the previous discussion, informing the board that the cellars were required for a project of "vital" importance. Consequently, "attempts of the management to defend against this were without success." The project "will be carried out, and the start of the operation soon is to be furthered to the best of one's ability." Matzka and Kiener, "Schlier" (Bisherige Recherchen).

9. Interview with Christian Limbeck-Lilienau and Frau Theresia S., Zipf, 4 July 1984. Matzka and Kiener, "Schlier" (Bisherige Recherchen).

10. OÖLA PA/Sch. 79: Geheimwaffen . . . "Schlier." Author's interview with Limbeck-Lilienau, and Theresia S. Matzka and Kiener add that the transformer weighed 80 tons, and that the walls and ceiling of the transformer station were some 13 feet (4 meters) thick.

11. Matzka and Kiener, "Schlier" (Bisherige Recherchen).

12. OÖLA /Sch. 79: Geheimwaffen . . . "Schlier."

13. Ibid. Mappe: Zipf.

14. DÖW Library: Vaclav Vaclavik, untitled ms., n.d., p. 33.

15. Quoted by Matzka and Kiener, "Schlier" (Bisherige Recherchen).

16. Elias Canetti has remarked, "Every secret is explosive, expanding with its own inner heat." In Redl-Zipf, where the secrecy of military operations was intensified by the secrecy of a forced labor camp, the explosiveness was great indeed. The testing was highly dangerous. Carelessly executed controls and inadequate materials twice in 1944 resulted in explosions which together killed nearly 50 civilian personnel. Elias Canetti, *Crowds and Power* tr. Carol Stewart (Harmondsworth, Middlesex, England: Penguin Books, 1981) rev. ed., p. 344. OÖLA C 17/Sch. 79 Geheimwaffen . . . "Schlier", Mappe Zipf: Fernschreiben *Gauleiter* Eigruber to Albert Speer, 30.8.1944; Matzka and Kiener, interview with Ing. Meinhard H., 20 January 1984.

17. Vaclavik, pp. 26–27.

18. Ibid., p. 26.

19. Ibid.
20. Ibid.
21. Ibid., p. 27.
22. DÖW Library: Zivan Bezić, *Im Schatten des Krematoriums: Erinnerungen eines Lagerhäftlings* unpublished tr., 1976, pp. 93–94.
23. Ibid., pp. 93, 102.
24. Ibid., p. 96.
25. Ibid., p. 104.
26. Ibid., p. 96.
27. Ibid., p. 110.
28. Ibid., pp. 100, 103, 109.
29. "*Befragungsergebnisse*, Zipf, 28 July–1 August 1983, conducted by Christian Limbeck-Lilienau and Siegwald Ganglmaier (drafter of the protocol)," deposited in DÖW. Hereafter: *Befragunsergebnisse*.
30. Ibid.
31. Ibid.
32. Matzka and Kiener, interview with Frau K., 18 March 1984.
33. *Befragunsergebnisse*. Author's interview with Frau Theresia S., 4 July 1984.
34. Ibid.
35. Author's interview with Frau Theresia S., 4 July 1984.
36. Ibid.
37. Ibid.
38. Ibid.
39. *Befragunsergebnisse*. Author's interview with Herr Be., Zipf, 4 July 1984.
40. *Befragunsergebnisse*.
41. Ibid.
42. Ibid.
43. Ibid.
44. Ibid.
45. Matzka and Kiener, interview with Dorothea H., 21 January 1984.
46. Ibid.
47. Ibid.
48. Ibid.
49. *Befragunsergebnisse*.
50. Ibid.
51. Ibid.
52. Ibid.
53. Matzka and Kiener, interview with Meinhard H., 20 January 1984.
54. Ibid.
55. Ibid.
56. Ibid.
57. Letter of Mitzi G., Zipf, to Siegwald Ganglmair, February 1984.
58. Matzka and Kiener, interview with Franz E., Zipf, 18 March 1984.
59. Letter of Mitzi G., Zipf, to Siegwald Ganglmair, February 1984.
60. *Befragunsergebnisse*.
61. Matzka and Kiener, interview with Franz E., Zipf, 18 March 1984.

Chapter 5. Outside the Monastery

1. The monastery, originally the site of a Babenberg castle, grew over the centuries. The present structure largely bears the stamp of its eighteenth-century, baroque design, the handiwork of Jakob Prandtauer, architect to Abbot Berthold Dietmayr who reigned from 1700–1733. "The complex must have looked magnificent even in the Middle Ages. The Gothic church, consecrated in 1429, was itself ambitious. The Margraves, and later the Emperors, made important contributions to its decoration." Wolfgang Braunfels, *Monasteries of Western Europe: The Architecture of the Orders* (Princeton: Princeton University Press, 1972), pp. 183–84.

2. Paul Lewis, "An Abbey's Grandeur Restored in Austria," *New York Times*, January 12, 1986. Travel Section, p. 19.

3. Abbot Burkhard Ellegast, *Stift Melk* (English Edition) tr. Father Roger Klassen, 2nd ed. (St. Pölten: Niederösterreichisches Pressehaus Druck- und Verlagsgesellschaft), p. 13.

4. Taking ingenious advantage of the strikingly vertical aspect of the design, which is no less dramatic than its horizontal features, the dining hall is warmed by an "early central-heating system that funnels hot air up into the banqueting hall from the kitchens underneath" through "a big brass grille set in the middle of the floor." Lewis, "An Abbey's Grandeur Restored."

5. Elegast, pp. 12–15.

6. Ibid., p. 14; Lewis.

7. Braunfels, p. 183.

8. Franz Würml, *Melk: Stadt und Stift Geschichte und Geschichten* (Wiener Dom-Verlag), pp. 98–99.

9. "Triumphale Fahrt des Führers nach Wien," *Tages-Post* 62 (15 March 1938), p. 2.

10. Author's interview with Frau G. S., Melk, 13 May 1983.

11. Undated family chronicle, in possession of Helmut K., Baden bei Wien.

12. Author's interview with Johannes K., Melk, 20 April 1984.

13. Ibid.

14. Author's interview with Father R., Melk, 18 July 1984.

15. Christian Bernadac, *Le Neuvième Cercle: Mauthausen* vol. II (Paris: Presses Pocket, 1977), pp. 285, 403.

16. Benjamin Eckstein, "Jews in the Mauthausen Concentration Camp," in *The Nazi Concentration Camps* Proceedings of the Fourth Yad Vashem International Historical Conference (Jerusalem: Yad Vashem, 1984), p. 265; Maršálek, p. 126.

17. Österreichische Lagergemeinschaft Mauthausen und Niederösterreichischer Landesverband der Widerstandskämpfer und Opfer des Faschismus (henceforth, KZ-Verband), ed., Hans Maršálek, Verfasser, *KZ-Melk: ein Nebenlager des KZ Mauthausen*. *See also:* Anton Harrer, "Unternehmen 'Quarz'—Konzentrationslager Melk," *Melker Kulturbeiträge* (June, 1983), p. 22.

18. AMM B 30/II/8; Evelyn Le Chêne, *Mauthausen: The History of a Death Camp*, p. 245.

19. Author's interview with Dr. Johann (Hans) E., Vienna, 3 February 1984. AMM B 30/II/8.

20. Direct Examination of Hermann Hofstadt, NA RG 153–5–31-vol. 1., p. 968. Trial Record Part 4, Altfuldisch et. al. Also cited in Vincenzo e Luigi Pappalèttera, *La*

Paròla agli Aguzzini: Le SS e i Kapo di Mauthausen svelano le leggi del Lager (Arnoldo Mondadori Editóre, 1970) 3 ed., p. 182.

21. KZ-Verband.

22. KZ-Verband; Harrer, "Unternehmen 'Quarz.' "

23. KZ-Verband; The 1934 population figure is from Alfred Hoffmann, *Österreichisches Städtebuch: Niederösterreich* (Vienna, 1968), p. 260.

24. René Gille, cited in Bernadac, *Le neuvième cercle*, pp. 286–88.

25. Ibid., pp. 288–89.

26. Ibid., p. 289.

27. Ibid., p. 290.

28. Ibid.

29. Ibid., pp. 289–90.

30. Ibid., p. 290.

31. Ibid., p. 290.

32. Ibid., pp. 296–97.

33. Ibid., p. 298.

34. René Gille, cited in Bernadac, *Le neuvième cercle*, p. 298.

35. Ibid., p. 403.

36. Pierre Pradales, cited in Bernadac, p. 392.

37. Gille, cited in Bernadac, p. 327. Gille added: "The winter has been very deadly. Of some one thousand five hundred Frenchmen that we were on the 23rd of April 1944, we are perhaps three hundred by then." Some 700 others who came to Melk in September 1944 fared even worse. By the end of the winter "no more than 150" are still alive, and of these only some 65 are eventually liberated. "Of 500 Greeks [who] arrived in July, only about 10" survived to the end of the war. Ibid., p. 403.

38. Dr. E., a Viennese lawyer born in Linz in 1906, was sent to Auschwitz, and arrived there on 13 December 1943. With the dissolution of the Auschwitz camp in the face of the approaching Red Army, he was among those forced to evacuate by foot and by train to Mauthausen, where he was enrolled on 25 January 1945. Held for three days in quarantine in Mauthausen, he was then shipped, again by rail, to Melk. Here he worked first in the tunnels in Loosdorf, and then in a shoe-making detail until Melk was dissolved in April. Sent to Ebensee, he was liberated there in May 1945. Author's interview with Dr. Johann (Hans) E., Vienna, 3 February 1984. Yad Vashem Central Archives (Y.V.): Häftlings-Personal-Karte, Inmate number: 116673 DR. Sch.

39. Ibid. "Because, indeed, four times every day the inmates were brought through the locale Melk to and from the railroad; that is, the inmates marched in two shifts of men at least four times through the locale," he noted.

40. Ibid.

41. Ibid.

42. Author's interview with Father R., Melk, 18 July 1984.

43. Ibid.

44. Author's interview with Frau Erika S., Melk, 20 April 1984.

45. Author's interview with Frau Maria R., Melk, 13 June 1984.

46. Ibid.

47. Author's interview with Frau Erika S.

48. Ibid.

49. Author's interview with Frau G. S.

50. A town about one and a quarter mile east of Melk.

51. Author's interview with Frau Maria R.

52. Author's interview with Frau Ri., 13 June 1984.

53. Author's interview with Father R.

54. Private Archive Anton Harrer: H. E., Diary. Entry 1698: 18.4/19.4/21.4.1944.

55. Ibid. 1717: 2.7.1944. 1726: 6.8.1944.

56. Ibid. Entry 1750: 6.11.1944.

57. Author's interview with Herr Gustav M., Melk, 16 June 1984.

58. Ibid.

59. Author's interview with Frau Ingeborg S., Melk, 27 June 1984.

60. Pierre Pradales, cited in Bernadac, p. 393.

61. René Gille, cited in Bernadac, p. 292.

62. Pradales, cited in Bernadac, p. 394.

63. Pradales, cited in Bernadac, pp. 394–95.

64. Pradales, cited in Bernadac, p. 396.

65. Manuscrit inédit Pierre Pradales (septembre 1973), cited in Bernadac, p. 399.

66. Author's interview with Frau G. S.

67. Ibid.

68. Author's interview with Frau Erika S.

69. Author's interview with Frau Maria R.

70. Author's interview with Frau Ri. Curiously, Father R. cannot recall having seen the smoke from the crematorium. Instead, he spoke only of rumors about its existence. "In any event, I did not see it. [Ich auf jedenfall habe nichts davon gesehen]".

71. Author's interview with Frau Maria R.

72. Ibid.

73. Ibid.

74. Author's interview with Frau Erika S.

75. Ibid.

76. Ibid.

77. Ibid.

78. Ibid.

79. Ibid.

80. Ibid.

81. Ibid.

82. Ibid.

83. Ibid.

84. Ibid.

85. Anton Harrer Private Archive: H. E., Diary. Entries 1717: 30.6/ 8.7.1944. 1721: 13.7.1944. 1723: 21.7.1944. 1750: 5.11.1944. 1731: 23.8.1944. 1763. Father R. also spoke of town residents gathering in the monastery shelter during the air raids.

86. Ibid. 1717: 8.7.1944.

87. Ibid.

88. Bernadac, pp. 320, 333.

89. NCOIC Reference Services Branch, Office of Air Force History: 450th Bombardment Group, Narrative Mission Report No. 100, 9 July 1944, Mission: 8 July 1944—

Markersdorf A/D, Austria. Two more B-24 aircraft of the 449th Bombardment Group reported having dropped 4 tons on oil storage tanks at Melk on the same morning: 449th Bombardment Group, Narrative Report No. 94, 8 July 1944.

90. Author's interview with Frau G. S. She also cites the swiftness of the air attack, and the watchfulness of the guards, as further reasons for the surviving inmates' failure to take advantage of the attack to try and escape.

91. Gille, cited in Bernadac, p. 333.

92. Author's interview with Frau G. S.

93. Author's interview with Frau Erika S.

94. Gille, cited in Bernadac, pp. 334–35.

95. Interview with Maria R.

96. *See* Saul Friedländer, "Historical Writing and the Memory of the Holocaust," in Berel Lang, ed., *Writing and the Holocaust* (New York: Holmes & Meier, 1988), pp. 72–73. [Entire article, pp. 66–80].

97. "Die Staatsoberschule mit Schülerheim in Melk," *Melker Kreisnachrichten* 24 Dezember 1938, Folge 12, p. 2.

98. Author's interview with Father R.

99. Ibid.

100. Ibid.

101. Ibid.

102. Ibid.

103. Ibid.

104. Ibid.

105. Ibid.

106. Ibid.

107. Ibid.

108. Ibid.

109. Ibid.

110. Ibid.

111. Ibid.

112. See below, chapter 8.

113. Ibid.

114. "And yet there are those who, faced by the crimes of others or their own, turn their backs so as not to see it and not feel touched by it. This is what the majority of Germans did during the twelve Hitlerian years, deluding themselves that not seeing was a way of not knowing, and that not knowing relieved them of their share of complicity or connivance." Primo Levi, *The Drowned and the Saved* tr. Raymond Rosenthal (New York: Summit Books, 1988), pp. 85–86.

115. Martin Buber, cited in Robert Alter, *Defenses of the Imagination: Jewish Writers and Modern Historical Crisis* (Philadelphia: Jewish Publication Society of America, 1977), p. 63.

116. He also saw one such woman in Melk. Gille, cited in Bernadac, pp. 326, 402. Amstetten lay "25 miles up-river from Melk." Gille was assigned to Amstetten from 5 June 1944 to 6 March 1945. Ibid., p. 298.

117. Robert Monin, cited in Bernadac, p. 307.

118. See George Steiner, *Martin Heidegger* (New York, Penguin Books, 1980), p. 139.

119. Quoted in Pappalèttera, p. 179.

120. Kurt Langbein and Elizabeth T. Spira, "Der Archipel Mauthausen," *Österreichische Rundfunk,* "Teleobjektiv," broadcast 1 November 1983.
121. Louis Deblé, cited in Bernadac, pp. 35–36.
122. Braunfels, *Monasteries of Western Europe,* pp. 232–33.

Chapter 6. Escape from Mauthausen

1. AMM S/4/2: Chronik des Gendarmeriepostens Schwertberg, 1945. "It was so bright on this night when they broke out," recalled Frau J. from Marbach. "It was a very moon-bright night, and it was strangely cold, there was snow," noted Frau F., also from Marbach. Peter Kammerstätter, *Der Ausbruch der Russischen Offiziere und Kommissäre aus dem Block 20 des Konzentrationslagers Mauthausen am 2. Februar 1945 (Die Mühlviertel Hasenjagd), Materialsammlung: Aussagen von Menschen, die an der Verfolgung beteiligt waren, oder zusehen müssten, und solchen, die Hilfe gaben* (unpublished ms., Linz, 1971), pp. 60, 65.
2. Kammerstätter, *Der Ausbruch* 5–6, 19–23; Maršálek, pp. 255–258; Bruno Baum, *Die Letzten Tage von Mauthausen* (Berlin: Deutscher Militärverlag, 1965), pp. 47–49.
3. Kammerstätter, *Der Ausbruch,* p. 30.
4. Originally planned for the night of 27–28 January, the escape had to be postponed until 2 February after some of the officers who planned the escape were taken away and executed by the SS. Maršálek, pp. 259–60; Baum, p. 51.
5. Kammerstätter, *Der Ausbruch,* p. 48.
6. Like the *Gestapo,* or Secret State Police, the *Kripo,* or Criminal Police, "competent in the handling of common crimes," comprised a division of the Security Police in the Reich Main Security Office. They should be distinguished from the *Ordnungspolizei,* or Order Police, which included both the urban and rural uniformed police. Raul Hilberg, *The Destruction of the European Jews* (New York: Holmes & Meir, 1985) Student Edition, pp. 71, 81.
7. Kammerstätter, *Der Ausbruch,* pp. 25–26.
8. Ibid., p. 49.
9. In the entire history of Mauthausen and its satellite camps, only 639 inmates actually managed to escape even temporarily, most of them escaping in 1944 and 1945. Prior to mid-1944 the attempts failed in nearly every instance. When captured, an escaped inmate was brought back to the camp and executed, commonly following grievous torture. Maršálek, pp. 247–253.
10. Kammerstätter, *Der Ausbruch,* p. 5–6.
11. Maršálek, pp. 262–263. Kammerstätter, *Der Ausbruch,* pp. 29, 100ff. Maršálek indicates that the SS actually claimed to have retaken all but 17 to 19 of the escaped captives. Of these only some 12 survivors have been accounted for. Among 3 of the 4 inmates who found refuge among the civil populace near Mauthausen, 2 of the men, Nikolaj Zemakalo and Michail Rjabtschinski, were rescued by Johann and Maria Langthaler; the other fortunate survivor found protection with the family of Theresia Mascherbauer and her family. Their stories are recounted below.
12. Kammerstätter, *Der Ausbruch,* p. 80.
13. AMM S/4/1: Chronik des Gendarmeriepostens Mauthausen, 1945; also cited in Kammerstätter, pp. 58–59.
14. Ibid.
15. AMM S/4/2: Chronik des Gendarmeriepostens Schwertberg, 1945.

16. Kammerstätter, *Der Ausbruch*, pp. 67–68.

17. Kammerstätter, *Der Ausbruch*, p. 63. Yet this same woman stated that the next day she rebuked some of the local men from the *Volkssturm* (home guard) for participating in the hunt of inmates who, she knew, were being shot nearby. Ibid., p. 64.

18. Ibid., p. 71.

19. Ibid., pp. 82–83.

20. Ibid., p. 70.

21. Ibid., p. 73.

22. Ibid., p. 86.

23. Ibid., p. 61.

24. Ibid., p. 89.

25. Ibid., p. 91.

26. Ibid., pp. 90–91.

27. Ibid., p. 108. According to the chronicle of the gendarmerie post in Schwertberg "an estimated 100 escapees were shot by the SS and Volkssturm in this duty area."

28. Ibid., p. 71.

29. Ibid., pp. 107–108.

30. Ibid., p. 65.

31. AMM S/4/2.

32. Ibid.

33. Kammerstätter, *Der Ausbruch*, p. 133.
Twelve inmates are known to have been killed by *Volkssturm* men from Schwertberg. After the war N. was tried for crimes associated with these killings, but acquitted because of "lack of conclusive proof of guilt [*Mangels schlüssiger Schuldbeweis freigesprochen*]". Witnesses had claimed "that the accused N. gave no direct order to shoot, rather only ordered his people to shoot at fleeing or insubordinate inmates." Ibid., pp. 136, 145, from *Linzer Volksblatt*, 13 August 1947 and *Tagblatt*, 20 December 1948.
Kohout indicated that camp commandant Ziereis telephoned the mayor of Schwertberg with an order to slay the inmates. He in turn is said to have then relayed it to N. Peter Kammerstätter concluded that ultimate responsibility for intiating and coordinating the wide hunt for the inmates lay with the Gauleiter, August Eigruber, "since only the Gauletier Reichstatthalter August Eigruber and not Ziereis could, on the basis of his position, deploy the Wehrmacht, gendarmerie, *Volkssturm*, and Hitler Youth. He assigned SS Standartenführer Gauinspektor Franz Peterseil to coordinate the operation, and put into action the *Gausturm* (a special unit for special tasks which was directly subordinate to the *Gauleitung*) with its leader, Dr. Adolf D." Kammerstätter, *Der Ausbruch*, p. 13.

34. Ibid., p. 131. This statement requires qualification. Not everyone accepted the official explanation. Langthaler himself knew otherwise, because his own parents were hiding one of the escapees. *See* below. In addition, the police were skeptical of this claim. As post commander Kohout indicated in his account, from the first announcement of the breakout, they were suspicious of the SS claim that the escapees were criminals: "Everyone who was in the concentration camp was always [referred to as a] 'hardened criminal,' even the most harmless Jehovah's Witness and innocent political opponent. That it was a matter of criminals was not believed from the very beginning." AMM S/4/2. Yet, this assessment was written after the war's end, but in any case only confirms that party officials were relying on public fears of hardened criminals to whip up support for the chase.

35. Kammerstätter, *Der Ausbruch*, p. 152.
36. Ibid., p. 134.
37. Ibid., p. 148.
38. Ibid., p. 188.
39. Ibid., pp. 62, 64. "In the tavern he boasted, I have blown the light out of one of them," the second resident recalled him saying, in words that were almost identical.
40. Ibid., pp. 183–84.
41. AMM S/4/2.
42. Ibid. It is noteworthy that afterwards "a portion of the population avoided B.'s shop." When Soviet forces entered Schwertberg in the spring they came searching for him. On 26 May 1945 he was found in the woods; he had committed suicide by slashing his arteries.
43. AMM S/4/2. See also: Kammerstätter, *Der Ausbruch*, pp. 63, 65, 188.
44. "Neue Zeit," Nr. 242, 18 October 1946 and Nr.102, 2 Mai 1947; *Oberöster-reichische Nachrichten*, Nr. 102, 2 Mai 1947, reproduced in Kammerstätter, *Der Ausbruch*, pp. 154–57. After the war he was given only a three-year sentence for attempted murder. Although the accused fired into the back of the victim from a distance of only 15 steps, the court could not determine if his shot was fatal. After being struck, the inmate had fallen to the ground, and was stepped on and kicked in the head by one of B.'s fellow militiamen.
45. "Neue Zeit," Nr. 271, 22 November 1946, reproduced in Kammerstätter, *Der Ausbruch*, p. 172. At their post-war trial the youths confessed to the deed, but were released for having acted "under coercion." "Neue Zeit," Nr. 281, 4 December 1946, cited in Kammerstätter, *Der Ausbruch*, p. 173.
46. AMM S/4/2.
47. Ibid.
48. Kammerstätter, *Der Ausbruch*, pp. 10, 150.
49. Ibid., p. 204.
50. Ibid., p. 92.
51. Ibid., p. 151.
52. Of the children "the youngest was 14, the oldest, who for reasons of illness was not drafted into the army, was 21 years old." Jelena Bruskowa, "Die Heldentat einer Mutter," *Sowjetunion Heute* Héft 11/12 (1975), p. 21. Copy from AMM S/6/5.
53. Ibid., pp. 21, 28.
54. Kammerstätter, *Der Ausbruch*, p. 114.
55. Ibid., p. 115.
56. Ibid., p. 116. The words are strikingly reminiscent of those of Magda Trocmé in Philip Hallie, *Lest Innocent Blood be Shed: The Story of the Village of Le Chambon and How Goodness Happened There* (New York: Harper Colophon, 1979), p. 284.
57. Kammerstätter, *Der Ausbruch*, pp. 116, 117.
58. Ibid., p. 116.
59. By then the second inmate, Nikolai Zemkalo, had joined the first.
60. Kammerstätter, *Der Ausbruch*, p. 119.
61. Ibid., p. 119.
62. Ibid., p. 120.
63. Ibid., p. 121.
64. Maršálek, p. 262; Kammerstätter, *Der Ausbruch*, p. 93.
65. Kammerstätter, *Der Ausbruch*, pp. 93–94, 98–100.

66. Ibid., p. 94.

67. Ibid., pp. 94, 100–101.

68. Ibid., p. 101.

69. Ibid., pp. 98, 101, 103.

70. Ibid., p. 95.

71. Ibid., pp. 95, 102.

72. One additional Austrian family, in Lanzenberg, Gemeinde Perg, has been identified as having harbored an escaped inmate. Maršálek, pp. 262–63.

73. Richard L. Rubenstein, *The Cunning of History: The Holocaust and the American
Future* (New York: Harper and Row, 1978) [Harper Colophon pb.], p. 34.

74. In Nazi logic, this was an intolerable event: the escape of a slave, especially a
slave belonging to races 'of inferior biological value,' seemed to be charged with symbolic
value, representing a victory by one who is defeated by definition, a shattering of the
myth. Also, more realistically, it was an objective damage since every prisoner had seen
things that the world must not know." Levi, *The Drowned and the Saved*, p. 154.

75. Ibid.

76. Raul Hilberg, comments in Berel Lang, ed., *Writing and the Holocaust* (New York
and London: Holmes & Meier, 1988), p. 274.

77. Ernst Bloch, *The Principle of Hope* tr. Neville Plaice, Stephen Plaice, and Paul
Knight (Cambridge, Massachusetts: MIT Press, 1986), p. 990.

78. On the calculated broadening of responsibility for the crimes of the Nazi regime,
see Hannah Arendt's essay of January 1945, "Organized Guilt and Universal Responsibility," in Ron H. Feldman, ed., *The Jew as Pariah: Jewish Identity and Politics in the
Modern Age* (New York: Grove Press, 1978) pb. ed., pp. 225–36.

Chapter 7. The Death Marches

1. At best, we have only estimates of the full number of Hungarian Jews sent to
Mauthausen at this time. Commandant Ziereis estimated their number as high as 60,000.
Maršálek, p. 128, estimates that some 20,000 had been set to work on fortifications of
this so-called "south-eastern wall" along the Austrio-Hungarian border. As many as
15,000 to 17,000 others, including women and children, are believed to have worked in
Viennese factories.

2. Maršálek, p. 144; Eckstein, "Jews in the Mauthausen Concentration Camps," in
The Nazi Concentration Camps. Proceedings of the Fourth Yad Vashem International
Historical Conference (Jerusalem: Yad Vashem, 1984), pp. 268–69.

3. Peter Kammerstätter, *Der Todesmarsch Ungarischer Juden von Mauthausen nach
Gunskirchen im April 1945: Eine Materialsammlung nach 25 Jahren*, (unpublished ms.,
Linz, 1971), p. 9; Eckstein, pp. 269–70.

4. Kammerstätter, *Der Todesmarsch*, p. 106.

5. Ibid., p. 38.

6. Ibid., pp. 40–41.

7. Ibid., p. 41.

8. Ibid., pp. 40–42. In 1965 the remains of 87 Jews were exhumed from the Lorch
cemetery and brought to the Jewish cemetery in Linz. "Oberösterreichische Nachrichten", 31 March 1965, cited in Kammerstätter, *Der Todesmarsch*, pp. 121–122.

9. Ibid., p. 54.

10. DÖW 14792.

11. Kammerstätter, *Der Todesmarsch*, Beilage 3: "Bericht über unhaltbare Zustände," Enns, 18.4.1945, addressed "an das hochwürdigste, bischöfliche Ordinariat" in Linz.

12. Kammerstätter, *Der Todesmarsch*, p. 113.

13. Ibid., p. 105.

14. Ibid., p. 108.

15. Ibid., p. 107.

16. Ibid., p. 107.

17. Ibid., pp. 107–108.

18. Ibid., p. 54.

19. Ibid., pp. 55–56.

20. Ibid., p. 77.

21. Ibid., p. 78.

22. Ibid., p. 83.

23. Ibid., p. 69.

24. Ibid., p. 102, also reproduced in Bauer, "The Death Marches", p. 13.

25. Kammerstätter, *Der Todesmarsch*, p. 56.

26. Ibid. p. 75.

27. Dr. Stephan Viranyi, "Von Bruck a.d.Leitha bis zur Gunskirchner Befreiung," cited in Kammerstätter, *Der Todesmarsch*, pp. 20–21.

28. Kammerstätter, *Der Todesmarsch*, p. 105.

29. Ibid., pp. 92–93.

30. Ibid., p. 93.

31. Ibid., p. 30.

32. Ibid., p. 87–88.

33. Ibid., p. 79.

34. Ibid., p. 37.

35. Ibid., pp. 108–9.

36. Cited in Maršálek, pp. 289–90.

37. Ibid., p. 289.

38. DÖW: E 20.164: *Niedershcrift*: Leopold Fisch, Georg Ujhelly, und Piroska Blau, 22 Mai 1945; also cited in *Widerstand und Verfolgung in Niederösterreich 1934–1945: Fine Dokumentation* (WVNÖ) 3, pp. 392–93; and *Bericht über die sanitären Verhältnisse im Judenlager in Gmünd im Zusammenhang mit dem Volksgerichtprozess gegen Hans Lukas*. Figures on deaths in the Gmünd labor camp are provided in the *Bericht*. Only figures for this period in January and February 1945 were available to the author of the report. Of those recorded as having died in these 46 days, 364 were men and 82 were women. The *Niederschrift* indicates that "the total number of cases of death after the inmates had been transported from the camp finally reached 600 . . . ," yet would have been higher were it not for the assistance offered by a local physician, Dr. Arthur Lanc, and Dr. Krisch, a veterinarian, both of whom managed to obtain some medicine for the Jews. These rescue efforts are described in greater detail in the *Niederschrift*.

39. *Niederschrift*.

40. *Bericht*.

41. Ibid.

42. Ibid.

43. Ibid.

44. Ibid.

45. Ibid.

46. Ibid.

47. Ibid.

48. Ominously, however, his report of 23 May 1945 concluded by noting "that of the Jewish transport on 18 April 1945 which departed Gmünd with the destination Theresienstadt no one is supposed to have arrived in Theresienstadt, as a Jewish refugee from Theresienstadt reported in Gmünd a few days ago." *Niederschrift.*

49. *Neue Zeit: Organ der Sozialistischen Partei Steiermarks,* 2 (2 April 1946): 1. One of the men who dug graves for the bodies counted 250 dead. *Neue Zeit* 2 (3 April 1946): 1. *See also:* Raul Hilberg, *The Destruction of the European Jews* v. 3 (New York: Holmes & Meier, 1985), p. 984.

50. *Neue Zeit* 2 (2 April 1946): 1.

51. Ibid.

52. *Neue Zeit* 2 (3 April 1946): 1.

53. Ibid.

54. *Neue Zeit* 2 (4 April 1946): 1.

55. Ibid.

56. Ibid.

57. Ibid.

58. *Neue Zeit* 2 (5 April 1946): 1.

59. Ibid. On 29 April 1946, 10 of 15 persons finally accused in connection with the massacre, including the *Kreisleiter,* the squad leader, and the guardsman who was described as having fired on and beaten Jews, were condemned to death by a British tribunal. *Neue Zeit* 2 (30 April 1946).

60. The number corresponds to the count of those victims whom the police afterwards were able to identify by name.

61. "My lodging lies some 20 minutes above, that is, north of the street Persenbeug-Grein passing along the north bank of the Danube. In my immediate vicinity is a deep ditch whose escarpments are steep and high," he noted. DÖW 9358: Bezirksgericht Persenbeug. Zeugenvernehmung Karl Brandstetter, 21 June 1948, in Strafsache gegen unbekannte Täter.

62. DÖW 9358: Lg Wien. Vg Vr 748/55, Bericht des Gendarmerieposten Kommandos. Persenbeug an das Bg Tbbs a.d. Donau Betreffend Massaker an Juden in Persenbeng in Mai, 6.8.1945. Also excerpted in *WVNÖ* 3, pp. 396–97.

63. Ibid.

64. Ibid.

65. Ibid.

66. DÖW 9358: Zeugenvernehmung Karl Brandstetter, 21 June 1948.

67. DÖW 9358: Bericht des Gendarmerieposten Kommandos Persenbeug, 6.8.1945.

68. Ibid. Zeugenvernehmung Dr. Leopold Convall, 14 April 1948. Five survivors were also found. They had been inside a small barrack and did not move when the others had been told they were to be transferred to a labor detail.

69. Ibid.

70. Yehuda Bauer, "The Death Marches, January–May 1945," *Modern Judaism* 3 (1983), p. 12.

Chapter 8. The Vanishing Traces

1. Franz Loidl, *Entweihte Heimat* (Linz, 1946), p. 17.
2. Ibid.
3. Ibid., p. 21.
4. Ibid., p. 24.
5. Ibid.
6. Ibid., p. 27.
7. Ibid., p. 18.
8. L'amicale de Mauthausen, *Letzeburger zu Mauthausen* (Luxemburg, 1970), p. 361.
9. Ibid.
10. Friedrich von Gagern, *Der Retter von Mauthausen* (Vienna, 1948), pp. 33–35.
11. DÖW: Letter of Louis Cernjar, Eleventh Armored Division, Third Army, dated 9 May 1945. For testimony of U.S. soldiers who liberated Mauthausen and its subsidiary camps, see Robert H. Abzug, *Inside the Vicious Heart: Americans and the Liberation of Nazi Concentration Camps* (New York: Oxford University Press, 1985), pp. 111, 118–22; *The Seventy-First Came . . . to Gunskirchen Lager* Witness to the Holocaust Publication Series #1 (Atlanta, 1983) 2d. printing.
12. "Zweimal Mauthausen," *Echo der Heimat* (Grieskirchen), 5 May 1949; "790.000 × 50.000?," *Kleine Zeitung* (Graz), 4 May 1949; "Denkmalpflege," *Freie Stimmen* (Linz), 7 May 1949. Copies available in DÖW III B/b.
13. *Echo der Heimat.*
14. *Freie Stimmen*, 7 May 1949. The latter remark also appeared in slightly altered form in the *Echo* article. The state had failed to find the money for preservation of the building housing the fresco "since it does not indeed concern a K.Z., but rather a cultural memorial of the first rank."
15. *Kleine Zeitung*, 4 May 1949.
16. "Zu den Vorgängen in Hartheim," *Linzer Volksblatt*, 26 August 1949.
17. Ibid.
18. *Salzkammergut-Zeitung* (4 August 1949).
19. AMM B/5/38/3: O. Ö Landesregierung, Abschrift der Niederschrift— aufgenommen om 2 Dezember 1949 aus Anlass der Besprechung auf dem ehemaligen K2-Gelände Ebensee.
20. AMM B/5/38/8: *Mahnruf, n.d.*, "Die Schande von Ebensee."
21. Ibid.
22. AMM B/5/38/4: "Weihe des neuen Opferfreidhofes in Ebensee, 5 November 1952."
23. Yad Vashem Archive: Y.V.–M–9/65; Zentral-Komitee der befr. Juden in Ober-Österreich: Rapport, Besprechung mit der britisch-amerikanishchen Untersuchungskommision für Palestina, 20 February 1946.

On 1 February 1946 the Israelitische Kultusgemeinde in Vienna registered 4,418 Jews in Austria. These included 1,700 who came back from concentration camps and 300 others who returned from abroad. This is to be contrasted with the prewar Austrian Jewish population of 185,000. Of these, 126,500 succeeded in emigrating between March 1938 and 1942. Of the remainder all but 2,000 were deported to their deaths in the East. "Die Juden in Österreich," *Die Presse* (30 March 1946).

Many of the Jews in Austria after the end of the war were survivors from other nations. Hence, the Jewish Central Committee noted the existence of 80 Austrian Jews in the province, but as many as 200 other Jews living outside the displaced persons camps. Y.V.–M–9/65.

24. Ibid.

25. Ibid.

26. The *Sicherheitspolizei*, or Security Police, included both the Gestapo and the Criminal Police, as well as the Security Service, the intelligence branch within the Reich Security Main Office (RSHA).

27. Y.V.–M–9/65; Zentral-Komitee der befr. Juden in Ober-Österreich: Rapport, February 1946. The report concludes by nothing that by then the men had been arrested.

28. *Die Presse*, 30 March 1946.

29. "Antisemitismus nicht verschwunden," *Die Tat*, 23 May 1946, reproducing an article in *Aufbau: Reconstruction*, nr. 16. A report is also available in the *National-Zeitung*, 6/7 July 1946, quoting in part an article in *Makkabi*, 1 June 1946, nr. 6. This report confirms that there were shouts of "Into the gas with them!", but notes that "it was only thanks to the intervention of several stouthearted men that no fight broke out."

30. *Die Tat*, 23 May 1946, quoting *Aufbau*.

31. Y.V. M–9/67.

32. Günther Anders, *Besuch im Hades: Auschwitz and Breslau 1966 Nach "Holocaust" 1979* (Munich, Verlag C.H. Beck, 1979), p. 186.

33. So too can it be said of those who shared unacknowledged responsibility for the crimes: "It must be kept in mind that most of the participants did not fire rifles at Jewish children or pour gas into gas chambers. A good many, of course, also had to perform these 'hard' tasks, but most of the administrators and most of the clerks did not see the final, drastic link in these measures of destruction." Hilberg, p. 1024.

34. See comments in Hannah Arendt, *The Jew as Pariah: Jewish Identity and Politics in the Modern Age*, ed. Ron H. Feldman (New York: Grove Press, 1978), p. 234; Anders, *Besuch im Hades*, pp. 186–193.

35. Karl Jaspers, *The Question of German Guilt* tr. E. B. Ashton (Westport: Greenwood Press, 1967), pp. 69–70, 73.

36. Kurt Langbein and Elizabeth T. Spira, *The Archipel Mauthausen*, Interview with Karl G.

37. Ibid. Interview with Josef H.

38. Matzka and Kiener, interview with Meinhard H., 20 January 1984.

39. Langbein and Spira, *Der Archipel Mauthausen*, interview with Karl G.

40. Author's interview with Engelbert K., Ebensee, 29 June 1983.

41. Ibid.

42. Heinrich Böll, *What's to Become of the Boy? or Something to Do with Books* tr. Leila Vennewitz (New York: Alfred A. Knopf, 1984), pp. 4–5.

43. Theodor W. Adorno, "What Does Coming to Terms with the Past Mean?," in Geoffrey Hartman, ed. *Bitburg in Moral and Political Perspective* (Bloomington: Indiana University Press, 1986), p. 117.

44. Rolf Hochhuth, *Eine Liebe in Deutschland* (Reinbek bei Hamburg, Rowohlt Taschenbuch Verlag, 1984), p. 61. *See* complete discussion, pp. 55–62.

45. Günther Anders, *Der Blick vom Turm* (Munich: Verlag C.H. Beck, 1968), p. 7.

46. *Günther Anders, Besuch im Hades*, pp. 201–2.

47. Gordon A. Craig, "The Waldheim File," *The New York Review of Books* v. 33 (October 9, 1986) n.15: 3.

48. Joseph Wechsberg, ed., *The Murderers Among Us: The Simon Wiesenthal Memoirs* (New York: McGraw-Hill Book Company, 1967), pp. 189–90. Radomir Luza, *Österreich und die grossdeutsche Idee in der NS-Zeit* (Vienna: Hermann Böhlaus Nachf, 1977), pp. 146–47. On the case of Franz Stangl, see Gitta Sereny, *Into that Darkness: An Examination of Conscience* (New York: Vintage Books, 1983).

49. T. Friedmann, *Schupo-Kriegsverbrecher von Stryj vor dem Wienern Volksgericht: Dokumentationssammlung* (Haifa, 1967), II.

50. Erika Weinzierl, *Zu Wenig Gerechte: Österreicher und Judenverfolgung 1938–1945,* 2d ed. (Graz: Verlag Styria, 1985), p. 89. *See also:* Dieter Stieffel, *Entnazifizierung in Österreich* (Vienna: Europaverlag, 1981), pp. 247–48, 257.

51. Leopold Ziller, *Vom Filcherdorf zum Fremdenverkehrsort: Geschichte von St. Gilgen am Aber-(Wolfgang-)See* 2.Teil (1800–1938) (N.p., 1973), p. 165.

52. On "the theme of purity" and the "striking contrast to the cruelty and injustice that has decreed death" see Saul Friedländer, *Reflections of Nazism: An Essay on Kitsch and Death* tr. Thomas Weyr (New York: Harper and Row, 1984), p. 32.

53. Walter Knoglinger (Redaktion und Zusammensetzung), Leopold Finster, Josef Hackl, Josef Andreas Kauer, et al. (Redaktionskomitee), *Stadt Leonding* (Selbstverlag der Stadt Leonding, 1976), p. 101.

54. Friedländer, *Reflections.*

55. Dan Diner, "Zwischen Aporie und Apologie: Über die Grenzen der Historïsierbarkeit des Nationalsozialismus," in Dan Diner, ed. *Histurikerstreit* (Frankfurt am Main: Fischer Taschenbuch Verlag, 1987), p. 67.

56. Kurt Waldheim, *The Challenge of Peace* (London: Weidenfeld and Nicolson, 1980), pp. 25–6. On Waldheim's hidden war record, see Gordon A. Craig, "The Waldheim File," *The New York Review of Books* v. XXXIII, no. 15 (October 9, 1986) pp. 3–4, 6.; Peter Lubin, "The Organization Man," *The New Republic* (April 7, 1986), pp. 16–19; Robert Edwin Herzstein, *Waldheim: The Missing Years* (New York: Arbor House/William Morrow, 1988).

57. James M. Markham, "Waldheim Campaigns to Memories in Borderland," *New York Times* (May 1, 1986), p. 2.

58. Loidl, *Entweihte Heimat,* p. 15.

59. Maurice Halbwachs, *The Collective Memory,* tr. Francis J. Ditter, Jr. and Vida Yazdi Ditter (New York, 1980), pp. 156–57.

60. Loidl, p. 16.

Select
Bibliography

Abzug, Robert H. *Inside the Vicious Heart: Americans and the Liberation of the Concentration Camps*. New York, 1985.

Allen, William S. *The Nazi Seizure of Power: The Experience of a Single German Town 1922–1945*. Rev. ed. New York, 1984.

Amery, Jean. *At the Mind's Limits*. Trans. Sidney Rosenfeld and Stella Rosenfeld. Bloomington, 1980.

Anatoli, A. *Babi Yar*. Trans. David Floyd. New York, 1971.

Anders, Günther. *Besuch im Hades: Auschwitz und Breslau 1966; Nach "Holocaust" 1979*. Munich, 1979.

Arad, Yitzhak, ed. *Holocaust and Rebirth: A Symposium*. Jerusalem, 1974.

Arendt, Hannah. *Eichmann in Jerusalem: A Report on the Banality of Evil*. New York, 1963.

———. *The Origins of Totalitarianism*. New York, 1951.

Arndt, Ino, and Scheffler, Wolfgang. "Massenmord an Juden in NS-Vernichtungslagern." *Vierteljahrshefte für Zeitgeschichte*. 24 (1976): 112–60.

Aycoberry, Pierre. Trans. Robert Hurley. *The Nazi Question*. New York, 1981.

Bassett, Richard. *Waldheim and Austria*. New York, 1989.

Bauer, Yehuda. "The Death Marches, January–May 1945," *Modern Judaism* 3 (1983), 1–21.

———. *A History of the Holocaust*. New York, 1982.

———. *The Holocaust in Historical Perspective*. Seattle, 1978.

———, and Rotenstreich, Nathan, eds. *The Holocaust as Historical Experience: Essays and Discussions*. New York, 1981.

Baum, Bruno. *Die Letzten Tage von Mauthausen*. Berlin, 1965.

Becker, Ernest. *Escape from Evil*. New York, 1975.

Bernadac, Christian. *Des jours sans fin: Mauthausen III*. Paris, 1976.

―――. *Le neuvième cercle*. Paris, 1977.

―――. *Les 186 marches: Mauthausen*. Paris, 1974.

Bettelheim, Bruno. *The Informed Heart: Autonomy in a Mass Age*. New York, 1960.

―――. *Surviving and Other Essays*. New York, 1979.

Botz, Gerhard. *Wohnungspolitik und Judendeportation in Wien 1938 bis 1945: Zur Funktion des Antisemitismus als Ersatz nationalsozialistischer Sozialpolitik*. Vienna-Salzburg, 1975.

Bracher, Karl Dietrich. *The German Dictatorship: The Origins, Structure and Effects of National Socialism*. Trans. Jean Steinberg. New York, 1970.

Braham, Randolf C., ed. *Perspectives on the Holocaust*. Boston, 1983.

Brook-Shepard, Gordon. *Der Anschluss*. Vienna, 1963.

Broszat, Martin. *Studien zur Geschichte der Konzentrationslager*. Stuttgart, 1970.

―――; and Frölich, Elke, eds. *Bayern in der NS-Zeit*. 6 vol. Munich, 1977–1983.

Brown, Robert McAfee. *Elie Wiesel: Messenger to All Humanity*. Notre Dame, 1983.

―――; Dawidowicz, Lucy S.; Rabinowitz, Dorothy; and Wiesel, Elie. *Dimensions of the Holocaust: Lectures at Northwestern University*. Evanston, 1977.

Browning, Christopher R., *Fateful Months: Essays on the Emergence of the Final Solution*. New York, 1985.

Buchheim, Hans; Broszat, Martin; Jacobsen, H.-A.; and Krausnick, Helmut. *The Anatomy of the SS State*. Trans. Richard Barry, Marian Jackson, and Dorothy Long. London and New York, 1968.

Bukey, Evan. *Hitler's Hometown: Linz Austria 1908–1945*. Bloomington, 1986.

Bullock, Alan. *Hitler: A Study in Tyranny*. New York, 1962.

Caleffi, Piero. *Si fa presto dire à fame*. Milan, 1954.

Choumoff, Pierre Serge. *Les chambres a gaz de Mauthausen*. Paris, 1972.

Cohen, Elie A. *Human Behavior in the Concentration Camp*. Trans. M. H. Braaksma. New York, 1953.

Conquest, Robert. *Kolyma: The Arctic Death Camps*. Oxford, 1979.

Dahrendorf, Ralf. *Society and Democracy in Germany*. New York, 1967.

Dawidowicz, Lucy. *The Holocaust and the Historians*. Cambridge, Mass., 1981.

―――. *The War against the Jews: 1933–1945*. New York, 1975.

De Bouard, Michel. "Le kommando de Gusen." *Revue d'Histoire de la Deuxième Guerre Mondiale*. 45 (January 1962): 45–70.

―――. "Mauthausen." *Revue d'Histoire de la Deuxième Guerre Mondiale*. 4 (July–September 1954): 39–80.

Des Pres, Terrence. *The Survivor: An Anatomy of Life in the Death Camps*. Oxford, 1976.

Diner, Dan. "The Historian's Controversy—Limits to the Historization of National Socialism." *Tikkun* 2 (1987): 74–78.

―――, ed. *Ist der Nationalsozialismus Geschichte?* Frankfurt am Main, 1987.

Dokumentationsarchiv des Österreichischen Widerstandes. *Widerstand und Verfolgung in Oberösterreich 1934–1945: Eine Dokumentation*. Vol. 2. Vienna, 1982.

Donat, Alexander, ed. *The Death Camp Treblinka*. New York, 1979.

Dreyfus, Hubert L., and Rabinow, Paul. *Michel Foucault: Beyond Structuralism and Hermeneutics*. Chicago, 1983.

Eliade, Mircea. *Patterns in Comparative Religion*. Trans. Rosemary Sheed. Cleveland and New York, 1966.

————. *The Sacred and the Profane: The Nature of Religion*. Trans. William L. Trask. New York, 1959.

Elkins, Stanley. *Slavery: A Problem in American Institutional and Intellectual Life*. Chicago, 1976.

Engelmann, Bernt. *In Hitler's Germany: Everyday Life in the Third Reich*. Trans. Krishna Winston. New York, 1986.

Evans, Richard J. *In Hitler's Shadow: West German Historians and the Attempt to Escape from the Nazi Past*. New York, 1989.

Feig, Konnilyn G. *Hitler's Death Camps: The Sanity of Madness*. New York, 1981.

Fein, Helen. *Accounting for Genocide: National Responses and Jewish Victimization during the Holocaust*. New York, 1979.

Fleming, Gerald. *Hitler and the Final Solution*. Berkeley, 1982.

Folke, Harald, and Reimer, Uwe. *Alltag unterm Hakenkreuz: Wie die Nazis das Leben der Deutschen Veränderten*. Reinbeck bei Hamburg, 1979.

Frankl, Viktor. *Man's Search for Meaning*. Trans. Ilse Lasch and Gordon W. Allport. New York, 1963.

Freund, Florion. *Arbeitslager Zement: Das Konzentrationslager Ebensee und die Raketenrüstung*. Vienna, 1989.

Friedländer, Saul. "From Anti-Semitism to Extermination: A Historiographical Study of Nazi Policies toward the Jews." *Yad Vashem Studies* 16 (1984): 1–50.

————. *Reflections of Nazism: An Essay on Kitsch and Death*. Trans. Thomas Weyr. New York, 1984.

Friedman, Philip. *Roads to Extinction: Essays on the Holocaust*. New York, 1980.

Fritz, Walter. *Die Österreichischen Spielfilme der Tonfilmzeit (1929–1938) mit dem Anhang die Spielfilmproduktion in den Jahren der Annexion (1938–1944)*. Vienna, 1968.

Ganglmair, Siegwald. " 'Ich bitte, aber, dass mein Name nicht genannt wird!' " *Landstrich*, 3 (May 1982): 6–32.

Georg, Enno. *Die Wirtschaftlichen Unternehmungen der SS*. Schriftenreihe der Vierteljahrshefte für Zeitgeschichte Nr. 7. Stuttgart, 1963.

Gilbert, Martin. *Atlas of the Holocaust*. New York, 1982.

————. *Auschwitz and the Allies*. New York, 1981.

————. *Final Journey: The Fate of the Jews in Nazi Europe*. London, 1979.

————. *The Holocaust: A History of the Jews of Europe During the Second World War*. New York, 1986.

Gold, Hugo. *Geschichte der Juden in Österreich*. Tel Aviv, 1971.

Goldhagen, Erich. "Weltanschauung und Endlösung: Zum Antisemitismus der nationalsozialistischen Führungsschicht." *Vierteljahrshefte für Zeitgeschichte* 24 (1976): 379–405.

Gordon, Sarah. *Hitler, Germans, and the "Jewish Question"*. Princeton, 1984.

Grobman, Alex, and Landes, Daniel, eds. *Genocide: Critical Issues of the Holocaust*. Los Angeles, 1983.

Gutman, Yisrael, and Rothkirchen, Livia, eds. *The Catastrophe of European Jewry: Antecedents—History—Reflection: Selected Papers*. New York-Jerusalem, 1977.

Haffner, Sebastian, *Anmerkungen zu Hitler*. Munich, 1978.

Halbwachs, Maurice. *The Collective Memory*. Trans. Francis J. Ditter, Jr., and Vida Yazdi Ditter. New York, 1980.

Hallie, Philip. *Lest Innocent Blood be Shed: The Story of the Village of Le Chambon and How Goodness Happened there*. New York, 1979.

Hamerow, Theodore S. "The Hidden Holocaust." *Commentary*, 79 (March 1985): 32–42.

Hartman, Geoffrey., ed. *Bitburg in Moral and Political Perspective.* Bloomington, 1986.

Häslinger, Josef. *Politik der Gefühle: Ein Essay über Österreich.* Darmstadt, 1987.

Henry, Frances. *Victims and Neighbors: A Small Town in Nazi Germany Remembered.* South Hadley, Mass., 1984.

Hilberg, Raul. *The Destruction of the European Jews.* Revised and Definitive Edition. 3 vols. New York, 1985.

———. "German Railways/Jewish Souls." *Society*, 14 (November/December 1976): 60–74.

Holzer, Willibald I. *Im Schatten des Faschismus: Der Österreichische Widerstand gegen den Nationalsozialismus 1938–1945.* Vienna, 1981.

Horwitz, Gordon John. *The Mauthausen Concentration Camp Complex and the Civil Populace, 1938–1945.* Diss., Cambridge, Mass., 1985.

Insdorf, Annette. *Indelible Shadows: Film and the Holocaust.* New York, 1983.

Jaspers, Karl. *The Question of German Guilt.* Trans. C. B. Ashton. New York, 1961.

Jaszi, Oscar. *The Dissolution of the Habsburg Monarchy.* Chicago, 1929.

Kempowski, Walter. *Haben Sie davon Gewusst?: Deutsche Antworten.* Hamburg, 1979.

Kern, Stephen. *The Culture of Time and Space.* Cambridge, Mass., 1983.

Kershaw, Ian. *The Nazi Dictatorship: Problems and Perspectives of Interpretation.* London, 1985.

———. "The Persecution of the Jews and German Popular Opinion in the Third Reich," *Leo Baeck Institute Year Book* 26 (1981): 261–89.

———. *Popular Opinion and Political Dissent in the Third Reich: Bavaria 1933–1945.* Oxford, 1983.

Kirchhoff, Rosel. *Am Lagertor.* Munich, 1972.

Klee, Ernst. *"Euthanasie" im NS-Staat: Die "Vernichtung lebensunwerten Lebens."* Frankfurt am Main, 1983.

Koestler, Arthur. *The Yogi and the Commissar.* New York, 1965.

Kogon, Eugen. *The Theory and Practice of Hell.* Trans. Heinz Norden. New York, 1950.

———; Langbein Hermann; and Rückerl, Adalbert, et al. *Nationalsozialistische Massentötungen durch Giftgas: Eine Dokumentation.* Frankfurt am Main, 1983.

Komitee der Antifaschistischen Widerstandskämpfer der Deutschen Demokratischen Republik. *Aktenvermerk R. u..* Berlin, 1979.

Krausnick, Helmut; Buchheim, Hans; Broszat, Martin; and Jacobsen, Hans-Adolf. *Anatomy of the SS State.* Trans. Richard Barry, Marian Jackson, and Dorothy Long. New York, 1968.

Kren, George M., and Rappoport, Leon. *The Holocaust and the Crisis of Human Behavior.* New York, 1980.

Kulka, O. D., and Rodrigue, Aron. "The German Population and the Jews in the Third Reich: Recent Publications and Trends in Research on German Society and the 'Jewish Question'. *Yad Vashem Studies* 16 (1984): 421–35.

Lafitte, Jean. *Ceux qui vivent.* Paris, 1958.

Lang, Berl, ed. *Writing and the Holocaust.* New York, 1988.

Langbein, Hermann. *Menschen in Auschwitz.* Vienna, 1972.

Langbein, Kurt, and Spira, Elizabeth T. "Der Archipel Mauthausen." *Österreichische Rundfunk.* Teleobjektiv series. (Broadcast 1 November 1983).

Langer, Lawrence L. *The Holocaust and the Literary Imagination.* New Haven, 1975.

Lanzmann, Claude. *Shoah: An Oral History of the Holocaust.* Trans. A. Whitelaw and W. Byron. New York, 1985.

———. "Shoah as counter-myth." Trans. Jonathan Davis. *The Jewish Quarterly* 33 (1986): 11–12.

Laqueur, Walter. *The Terrible Secret: Suppression of the Truth about the Final Solution.* Boston, 1981.

Le Chêne, Evelyn. *Mauthausen: The History of a Death Camp.* London, 1971.

Legters, Lyman, ed. *Western Society after the Holocaust.* Boulder, 1983.

Levi, Primo. *The Drowned and the Saved.* Trans. Raymond Rosenthal. New York, 1988.

Levin, Nora. *The Holocaust: The Destruction of European Jewry, 1939–1945.* New York, 1973.

Lewin, Kurt. "Kriegslandschaft." 5–6 *Zeitschrift fuer angewandte Psychologie:* 440–47.

Lewy, Gunther. *The Catholic Church and Nazi Germany.* New York, 1964.

Lifton, Robert J. *The Nazi Doctors: Medical Killing and the Psychology of Genocide.* New York, 1986.

Lipstadt, Deborah E. *Beyond Belief: The American Press and the Coming of the Holocaust.* New York, 1986.

Littell, Franklin H., and Shur, Irene G., eds. *Reflections on the Holocaust: Historical, Philosophical, and Educational Dimensions.* Annals of the American Academy of Political and Social Science. Philadelphia, 1980.

Luza, Radomir. *Österreich und die grossdeutsche Idee in der NS-Zeit.* Vienna, 1977.

Maier, Charles S. *The Unmasterable Past: History, Holocaust and German National Identity.* Cambridge, Mass., 1988.

Manvell, Roger, and Fraenkel Heinrich. *The Incomparable Crime: Mass Extermination in the Twentieth Century: the Legacy of Guilt.* New York, 1967.

Marrus, Michael R. *The Holocaust in History.* Hanover, 1987.

Maršálek, Hans. *Die Geschichte des Konzentrationslagers Mauthausen: Dokumentation.* Vienna, 1980.

———. *Die Vergasurgsaktionen im Konzentrationslager Mauthausen: Gaskammer Gaswagen Vergasungsanstelt Hartheim.* Vienna, 1988.

Marshall, Barbara, "German Reaction to Military Defeat, 1945–1947," in Berghahn, Volker R., and Kitchen, Martin, eds., *Germany and the Age of Total War.* London, 1981.

Mayer, Arno. *Dynamics of Counterrevolution in Europe.* New York, 1971.

———. *Why did the Heavens not Darken? The Final Solution in History.* New York, 1988.

Mayer, Milton. *They Thought They Were Free.* Chicago, 1955.

Merl, Edmund. *Besatzungszeit im Mühlviertel.* Linz, 1980.

Midgley, Mary. *Wickedness: A Philosophical Essay.* pb. ed. New York, 1986.

Mitscherlich, Alexander, and Mitscherlich, Margarete. *The Inability to Mourn: Principles of Collective Behavior.* Trans. Beverly R. Placzek. New York, 1975.

Mittendorfer, Johann. "Oberösterreichische Priester in Gefängnissen und Konzentrationslagern zur Zeit des Nationalsozialismus." *Jahresbericht des Bischöflichen Gymnasiums Kollegium Petrinum in Urfahr-Linz an der Donau.* 72–73 (1975/76): 77–102, 39–104.

Morse, Arthur. *While Six Million Died.* New York, 1968.

Moser, C. Gwyn. "Jewish U-Boote in Austria, 1938–1945," in *Wiesenthal Center Annual.* 2 (1985): 53–62.

Moser, Jonny. *Die Judenverfolgung in Österreich, 1938–1945.* Vienna, 1966.

Mosse, Georg L. *Nazi Culture: A Documentary History.* New York, 1981.

————. *Towards the Final Solution: A History of European Racism.* Madison, 1985.

————. "War and the Appropriation of Nature," in Berghahn, Volker R., and Kitchen, Martin, eds. *Germany in the Age of Total War.* London, 1981.

Oliner, Samuel P., and Oliner, Pearl M. *The Altruistic Personality: Rescuers of Jews in Nazi Europe.* New York, 1988.

Pappalèttera, Vincenzo. *La Parola agli Aguzzini.* Milan, 1970.

Pauley, Bruce F. "Fascism and the *Führerprinzip:* The Austrian Example." *Central European History* 22 (1979): 272–96.

————. *The Habsburg Legacy: 1867–1939.* Huntington, New York, 1977.

————. *Hitler and the Forgotten Nazis: A History of Austrian National Socialism.* Chapel Hill, 1981.

Pingel, Falk. *Häftlinge unter SS-Herrschaft: Widerstand Selbstbehauptung und Vernichtung im Konzentrationslager.* Hamburg, 1978.

Presser, Jacob. *The Destruction of the Dutch Jews.* Trans. Arnold Pomerans. New York, 1969.

Rabitsch, Gisela. *Konzentrationslager in Österreich 1939–1945.* Diss., Vienna, 1967.

Rabitsch, Hugo. *Jugend-Erinnerungen eines Zeitgenössischen Linzer Realschülers: Aus Adolf Hitlers Jugendzeit.* Munich, 1938.

Reitlinger, Gerald. *The Final Solution: The Attempt to Exterminate the Jews of Europe, 1939–1945.* New York, 1961.

Richardi, Hans-Günther. *Schule der Gewalt: Die Anfänge des Konzentrationslagers Dachau, 1933–1935.* Munich, 1983.

Rosenkranz, Herbert. *Das Gelbe Stern in Österreich.* Vienna, 1978.

————. *Reichskristallnacht: 9 November 1938 in Österreich.* Vienna, 1968.

Rousset, David. *L'univers concentrationnaire.* Paris, 1946.

Rubenstein, Richard L. *The Cunning of History.* New York, 1978.

Sarcinelli, Franco. *Vita e morte nei campi di concentramento di sterminio.* Milan, 1972.

Schausberger, Norbert. *Der Griff nach Österreich: Der Anschluss.* Vienna, 1978.

————. *Rüstung in Österreich: eine Studie über die Wechselwirkung von Wirtschaft, Politik, und Kriegsführung.* Vienna, 1970.

Schoenbaum, David. *Hitler's Social Revolution: Class and Status in Nazi Germany.* New York, 1967.

Schubert, Peter. *Schauplatz Österreich: Topographisches Lexicon zur Zeitgeschichte in drei Bänden.* Vienna, 1980.

Sereny, Gitta. *Into that Darkness.* London, 1974.

Slapnicka, Harry. *Oberösterreich als es "Oberdonau" hiess: 1938–1945.* Linz, 1978.

Smith, Marcus J. *The Harrowing of Hell: Dachau.* Albuquerque, 1972.

Sperber, Mannes. *Churban oder die Unfassbare Gewissheit.* Vienna, 1979.

Stadler, Karl. *Österreich 1938–1945 im Spiegel der NS-Akten.* Vienna, 1966.

Steiner, George. *In Bluebeard's Castle: Some Notes Toward A Redefinition of Culture.* New Haven, 1971.

————. *Language and Silence: Essays on Language, Literature, and the Inhuman.* New York, 1967.

Steinert, Marlis. *Hitler's War and the Germans.* Ed. and Trans. Thomas E. J. de Witt. Athens, Ohio, 1977.

Steinmetz, Selma. *Österreichs Zigeuner im NS-Staat.* Vienna, 1966.

Stern, J. P. *The Führer and the People.* Berkeley, 1975.

Stiefel, Dieter. *Entnazifizierung in Österreich.* Vienna, 1981.

Stokes, Lawrence. "The German People and the Destruction of the European Jews." *Central European History* 6 (1973): 167–91.

Strasser, Anna. *Tatsachenbericht: März 1938–Mai 1945.* St. Valentin, Lower Austria, 1982.

Syberberg, Hans-Juergen. *Hitler: A Film from Germany.* Trans. Joachim Neugroschel. New York, 1982.

Sydnor, Charles W. "The Selling of Adolf Hitler: David Irving's Hitler's War." *Central European History* 12 (1979): 169–99.

Tec, Nechama. *When Light Pierced the Darkness: Christian Rescue of Jews in Nazi-Occupied Poland.* New York, 1986.

Turner, Henry A., ed. *Nazism and the Third Reich.* New York, 1972.

Vidal-Naquet, Pierre. "History, Myth, and the Holocaust." *Democracy* 1 (April 1981): 70–95.

Von Staden, Wendelgard. *Darkness over the Valley.* Middlesex, 1982.

Vorländer, Herwart, ed. *Nationalsozialistische Konzentrationslager im Dienst der totalen Kriegsführung: Sieben würtembürgische Aussenkommandos des Konzentrationslagers Natweiler/Elsass.* Stuttgart, 1978.

Wasserstein, Bernard. *Britain and the Jews of Europe.* New York, 1979.

Weinzierl, Erika. *Zuwenig Gerechte.* Rev. ed. Graz, 1985.

Wiesel, Elie. *Night.* Trans. Stella Rodway. New York, 1960.

Woolf, S. J., ed. *Fascism in Europe.* London and New York, 1981.

Wyman, David. *The Abandonment of the Jews: America and the Holocaust.* New York, 1984.

Zehethofer, Florian. "Das Euthanasieproblem im Dritten Reich am Beispiel Schloss Hartheim (1938–1945)." *Oberösterreichische Heimatblätter.* 32 (1978): 46.

Zinnhobler, Rudolf, ed. *Das Bistum Linz im Dritten Reich.* Linz, 1979.

Zucotti, Susan. *The Italians and the Holocaust: Persecution, Rescue, and Survival.* New York, 1987.

Oral Testimony

I. Author's Interviews Cited in the Text:

Dr. Hans E., Vienna, 3 February 1984.

Manuel G., Mauthausen, 9 February 1983.

Johannes K., Melk, 20 April 1984.

Dr. Engelbert K., Ebensee, 29 June 1984.

Philip M., Mauthausen, 18 February 1983.

Gustav M., Melk, 26 June 1984.

Maria R., Melk, 13 June 1984.

Frau Ri., Melk, 13 June 1984.

Frau G. S., Melk, 13 May 1983.

Frau Juan S., Mauthausen, 9 February 1983.

Theresia S., Redl-Zipf, 4 July 1984.

Karl S., Grieskirchen, 28 June 1983.

Anna S., Vienna, 31 March 1982.

Erika S., Melk, 20 April 1984.

Father R. Melk, 18 July 1984.

II. Additional Collections of Oral Testimony:

Kammerstätter, Peter. *Der Ausbruch der Russischen Offfiziere und Kommissäre aus dem Block 20 des Konzentrationslagers Mauthausen am 2 Februar 1945 (Die Mühlviertel Hasenjagd), Materialsammlung: Aussagen von Menschen, die an der Verfolgung beteiligt waren, oder zusehen mussten, und solchen, die Hilfe gaben.* Linz, 1971.
————. *Der Todesmarsch Ungarischer Judgen von Mauthausen nach Gunskirchen im April 1945: Eine Materialsammlung nach 25 Jahren.* Linz, 1971.
Langbein, Kurt, and Spira, Elizabeth T. "Der Archipel Mauthausen." *Österreichische Rundfunk.* Teleobjektiv series. (Broadcast 1 November 1983).
Limbeck-Lilienau, Christian, and Ganglmair, Siegwald (Ausarbeiter der Protokolle). *Befragungsergebnisse.* Zipf, 28 July–1 August 1983.
Matzka, Dieter and Kiener, Wilma: Interviews with residents and former employees in Redl-Zipf for the film "Deckname Schlier."

Index